A YEAR OF
Living
Prayerfully

How a Curious Traveler Met the Pope,
Walked on Coals, Danced with Rabbis, and
REVIVED HIS PRAYER LIFE

JARED BROCK

Tyndale House Publishers, Inc.
Carol Stream, Illinois

Visit Tyndale online at www.tyndale.com.

TYNDALE and Tyndale's quill logo are registered trademarks of Tyndale House Publishers, Inc.

A Year of Living Prayerfully: How a Curious Traveler Met the Pope, Walked on Coals, Danced with Rabbis, and Revived His Prayer Life

Designed by Jennifer Ghionzoli

Edited by Jonathan Schindler

Published in association with the literary agency of Ann Spangler and Company, 1420 Pontiac Road, SE, Grand Rapids, MI 49506.

Library of Congress Cataloging-in-Publication Data

Brock, Jared.
    A year of living prayerfully : how a curious traveler met the pope, walked on coals, danced with rabbis, and revived his prayer life / Jared Brock.
        pages cm
    Includes bibliographical references.
    ISBN 978-1-4143-9213-4 (hc)
    1. Prayer—Christianity. 2. Christian pilgrims and pilgrimages. I. Title.
    BV210.3.B755 2015
    248.3'2—dc23   2014041094

Printed in the United States of America

21	20	19	18	17	16	15
7	6	5	4	3	2	1

For my grandfather Clarence Black. The sun has not risen a day in my life that didn't find you on your knees in prayer for me.

Contents

Foreword

I SAW THIS ON A BUMPER STICKER recently: "You're unique, just like everyone else."

It made me think of Jared Brock—or, as I know him, Jay. It made me think of him, not because the slogan fits him but because it doesn't.

Jay *is* unique, like *no one* else.

Indeed, I've never met anyone so gloriously, extravagantly, utterly himself. He is the original, and there are no copies. He inhabits his own skin without remainder and without apology, and brings to every thing he does—and he does a lot—childlike wonder and serpentlike shrewdness. And always he abounds with life. He laughs from the belly, lives from the heart, loves without caution, and thinks from a mind as rich and supple and generous as any I've ever met. And now he's written a book!

And not just any book. It's, well, unique, like no one else's. It's on prayer, as you can see, but look, look inside: this is not your standard manual of prayer, full of scoldings and techniques and pep talks and guilt trips. This is . . . something entirely different.

I'll try to describe it in just a moment.

But first a *caveat emptor*: once you start, you can't stop. You will be swept up in the sheer force of the storytelling, the beauty of the prose, the many comedies of error, the exotic cast of characters, and—above all—the drama of Jay's prayer life. He is pulled heels first from a life of rote and dutiful prayers and thrown headlong into an encounter with the living, listening, speaking God. You will be pulled and thrown likewise. Consider yourself warned.

Now about the book. It's like Jay himself, like his flesh became words. It is delightful and engaging company. It is a memoir, a history, a paean, a confession, a whodunit, a field guide, a travelogue. Jay, sometimes all alone and sometimes alongside his beautiful, long-suffering wife, Michelle, wends his way across the globe and finds himself, sometimes by sheer dint of human persistence and sometimes by seemingly divine intervention, in the thick of things: dancing with Hasidim, lunching with the pope, tripping across fire, forcing his wife to a *mikvah* bath in a near-frozen lake, hanging out with celebrities and celibates and communists and fundamentalists, and on and on.

But mostly it's about one man learning to pray. It's about one man having his world reordered as he, by turns, limps and leaps, crawls and runs, begs and storms his way to the throne of grace.

On the way, we cheer him on, worry for him, worry for Michelle, laugh at him, laugh with him, hope the best for him, wonder if he'll live to tell the story. We also fall in love with him (and even more, Michelle; sorry, Jay).

And strangely, wonderfully, we learn to pray with him.

But not to pray like him. His story frees us to live our own story, to find and enter our own fellowship with the Father through the Son by his Spirit.

My prediction is that this story of the revolution of one man's prayers will invite you to a revolution of your own, but it will be unique, like no one else's.

Consider yourself invited.

Mark Buchanan

Author's Note

MANY NAMES AND CERTAIN LOCATIONS have been changed in order to protect the identities of those involved. The sequence of events has been altered in order to facilitate a somewhat sane reading experience. For all you smart researcher types who want to figure out the actual order, you might as well put this book in a blender.[1] All I can promise is that everything in the following pages actually happened.

---

[1] Don't forget to add orange juice.

How My Journey Started

MICHELLE AND I MET IN the seventh grade. I was one of the cool kids, despite dozens of photographs to the contrary. Michelle, a missionary kid, was fresh off the boat from Africa by way of Finland. On the first day of class, she wore a hunter-green sweater with a loon on the front.

By the end of the school year, we had fallen in love. And by "love," I mean that we held hands and talked on the phone for a maximum of thirty minutes per day, three days per week. During those conversations, my bedroom door was always open so my parents could monitor what I was saying.

I kissed Michelle on the cheek at a Newsboys concert that summer, on "Christian Day" at a local theme park. We broke up twice but eventually got ourselves sorted. We've been married for over five years now, and 90 percent of it has been bliss. The other 10 percent has been commuting.

I was born and raised in the church. My parents grew their kids God's Way™, but that didn't keep me from getting permanently kicked out of Sunday school in the fifth grade. Michelle grew up in a Christian home, so she was also well versed in the clichés and quirks of the church.

Having spent the better part of our childhoods in church, by the time we were adults, we were familiar with the art of sermons, communion, worship, offerings, announcements, and more sermons. We knew that a "contemporary service" was anything but, and that gluten-free communion wafers were the next big business opportunity.

Above all else, we were well versed in the mechanics of prayer. Standing, sitting, or kneeling—we'd done it all. We'd even prostrated ourselves before the Lord, which is actually far more wholesome than it sounds. We'd mastered the expected tones and inflections, the buzzwords and key phrases, the proper timing and the perfect amount of brevity. We knew the amount of passion and conviction that would stir a crowd to emit a round of "mmhmms" and "amens."

There was a point when we were able to pray with deep faith, watching as God performed miracles and saved our friends who were far from Him. To the average church attendee, there was little doubt that we were prayer experts. But our experience of prayer weakened with time. I'm not sure why, exactly. Maybe we got too busy. Maybe we had more faith back in our youth group days.

By the time we hit our twenty-sixth birthdays, we both felt as if God were distant. We sensed a deep need to understand prayer and practice it more faithfully. In the last few years, we had been faced with some horrific realities in our world, including poverty, human trafficking, sexual exploitation, and corporate greed. These issues towered over us and exposed the gaping holes in our spiritual walk. They left us with a gnawing hunger for God's help. We wanted to be prayer warriors, but we felt like prayer wanderers.

We had also been reevaluating our lives. We were not as radically generous as we wanted to be. We weren't serving as we could or loving as we should. We didn't even know where to start. We needed wisdom, guidance, and understanding like never before. Where was God in all this? I don't really know.

Then we went to Amsterdam.

"If God wants us to pray without ceasing, it is because He wants to answer without ceasing." ARMIN GESSWEIN

Michelle and I were in the middle of shooting a documentary about sex trafficking, and we had the opportunity to do some interviews in the Netherlands. On our first night in Amsterdam, we visited De Wallen, the most famous of the city's three red-light districts. As we walked there, we could hear chanting from over a mile away. By the time we arrived, the scene was overwhelming. About three hundred men had congregated outside a bar. They were watching a soccer game, and most of them were drunk. The smell of vomit and urine hung in the air and clogged the canal. Police officers on horseback tried to steady their mounts. The women in the windows beckoned, tapping on the glass with their nails.

Michelle had a chance to visit some of the women with a friend who worked for an abolitionist group in the city. As soon as Michelle's friend approached, the prostituted women dropped their seductive act. They were tired, sick, and scared. One woman stared out the window at the mob. She whispered one word: "Dangerous." If the men's team won, they would come in and celebrate with the girls. If their team lost, they would take out their drunken aggression on the girls. Either way, the girls would lose.

The sex behind the closed doors of the red-light district is completely divorced from any conceptions we might have about romantic love. After a night in De Wallen, women are left tending to their bruises. It's the furthest thing I know from the Cinderella story.

In the middle of the red-light district stands the oldest building in Amsterdam—an eight-hundred-year-old church. In the shadow of the belfry, men rent bodies. Every hour on the hour, men abuse women to the sound track of church bells.

As I stood in the middle of this scene, I was completely

overwhelmed. "God," I cried out, "You need to end this! We need to end this. I need power in prayer."

I also knew that I had lost that power, somewhere along the way.

"Let not the wise boast of their wisdom."   JEREMIAH 9:23

What do you do when prayer becomes routine? What do you do when your prayers feel like they are hitting the ceiling and going nowhere? How do you keep your prayers from becoming boring? It's great to know about prayer, but what do you do when it becomes a rote tradition in your life? What if God is silent? What if God does *the exact opposite* of what you've just prayed?

On the verge of our five-year wedding anniversary, those were the questions that wouldn't leave Michelle and me alone. We had founded an advocacy charity called Hope for the Sold, dedicated to combating sex trafficking, and our work was expanding. But we were stuck. We needed more power. Not only did we want to see our prayers answered, but we also wanted to sense that God was listening. We wanted a deeper relationship with Jesus. We wanted to talk with God. We wanted to hear from God. We wanted to know what He was thinking. Because that's the point, isn't it? Man's desire is to know the mind of God.

At this point, my prayer life was pretty weak. Prayer was a routine for me, a habit I did out of guilt. It was mostly one-sentence prayers at meals and bedtimes. It wasn't the rich life of prayer I wanted. If I'm really honest, God was my Santa Claus.

And then there was all this baby talk. Everyone we knew was pregnant—the women, at least. Our whole community was settling into homes and family life, and children were popping up everywhere. While Michelle and I weren't rushing to start a family, having children had always been in the back of our minds. And it scared me.

I wasn't worried about changing diapers or losing sleep or accidentally launching a child down a flight of basement stairs. I worried that I wasn't good enough. I worried that I wouldn't be a "heavenly" father. I worried that I wouldn't pray like my father and grandfather did and that I wouldn't have the power I needed from God to guide my kids from birth to adulthood.

Michelle was also struggling with deep-seated insecurity. Despite being the most incredible woman I know, she often felt inadequate. She was looking for mentors and support, but very few strong women had stepped up to the plate.

And so we decided to embark on an adventure—a year of living prayerfully.

Pilgrimage was a common practice in the Middle Ages. It allowed Christians to refocus their entire lives on things above, taking a physical journey toward a spiritual goal. Some people visited the birthplace of Christ or the areas where the apostles ministered. Others traveled to the hometowns of saints or to far-off places in hopes of miraculous healing or special revelation.

Yet Christians have lost this practice somewhere along the way. I think I know why. In the late Middle Ages, a Christian could earn indulgences by going on a pilgrimage. Thus, a journey that started as a quest for a spiritual relationship turned into a legalistic ritual. When the sassy reformer Martin Luther tacked his complaints to the church door in Wittenberg, it was the beginning of the end for widespread pilgrimages.

For a long time I've wanted to resurrect the prayer pilgrimage and follow in the old pilgrims' footsteps. But more than that, I longed to be a deeply spiritual being, highly in tune with my Creator and His world.

For our year of living prayerfully, I compiled a list of Judeo-Christian faiths, sects, and denominations. The plan was to research their prayer methods, traditions, and beliefs. We'd travel the world to meet religious leaders, prayer experts, and everyday people who have made prayer a vital part of their lives. We wanted to learn new things. We hoped to spice up our prayer life.

But our year of living prayerfully was more than that. We wanted to do more than just add a little spice. This year wasn't about sprinkling pepper on an omelet; it was about learning how to cook. I knew we weren't alone in this pursuit. Almost every single one of us has prayed to someone or something at some point in our lives. I don't think prayer is merely a sociological phenomenon. I don't think it's something we do just to fit into a community or when we've exhausted all other options. I think it's hardwired into our spiritual DNA. God is the inevitability of humanity's search for true meaning.

I had no idea what an adventure this year would be. I hadn't planned to visit a nudist church or walk across a bed of hot coals. I couldn't picture myself having a two-hour debate with an elder at Westboro Baptist Church. I hadn't planned on defying the North Korean dictatorship. I didn't, in my wildest dreams, think I'd get to have lunch at the pope's house.

I knew I couldn't waste this year, sleepwalking through airports, because not everyone has the opportunity I'd been given. My friends were already consumed with school and work and raising kids. I was doing this prayer pilgrimage for me, but I was also doing it for them. I was doing it for lots of people—for my small group, for my church, for my family and friends around the world. This book is simply an old-school record of a prayer pilgrimage, for all those who, for whatever reason, can't go on one for themselves.

I wrote this for you.

CHAPTER 1

Hamilton, Ontario

MICHELLE AND I DECIDED TO live prayerfully for an entire year. It was a nice, shiny idea. But where should we start?

With For Dummies, obviously. I borrowed a copy of *Christian Prayer for Dummies* from the library. The cover was so enticing:

Find your own prayer style!
Explanations in plain English!
"Get in, get out" information!
Icons and other navigational aids!
Tear-out cheat sheet!

That last one was really important. I would hate to pray without cheating. I flipped to the cheat sheet.

The cheat sheet included items like "Incorporate Christian Prayer into Your Life in Three Weeks" and "How to Hear God's Voice during Christian Prayer," but I was skeptical. This book was published in 2003. A lot had changed since then. Would it still work today? I didn't have a landline anymore; surely the Almighty had updated His contact methods too. Was He an Apple or an Android guy?

I was also suspicious of the book's author. According to his For Dummies author page, the author had created fourteen For Dummies products, including *Christianity for Dummies, Christian Prayer for Dummies,* and *Yahoo! SiteBuilder for Dummies.* Which compelled me to ask, Did Yahoo still exist?

Page one. Right in the middle, boxed and bolded, I read this disclaimer:

The advice and strategies contained herein may not be suitable for your situation. You should consult with a professional where appropriate.

This left me with all sorts of questions, such as when, exactly, would be an appropriate time to consult a professional? Wasn't that why I was reading the book in the first place? Where did one find a prayer professional? What, precisely, *is* a prayer professional?

I grabbed a dictionary and found this definition for the word *professional*: "Following an occupation as a means of livelihood or for gain: *a professional builder.*"

Clearly, I needed to find someone who got paid to pray.

I googled "prayer professional," and it produced 44,300,000 results (in 0.2 seconds), but they all appeared pretty fruitless.

Well, not entirely. I found a prayer request from a consultant that read, "I request prayer for my trip to Denver July 9–20 to be safe and successful to achieve my goal of 32 net sales @ net volume of $222,500." So that was something.

I changed my web query to "prayer consultant," which produced much better results. Using LinkedIn, I connected with a prayer consultant named Don Pierson. Don's actual title is "Prayer Strategies Specialist," which sounded impressive. I scheduled a phone call with him for the next day.

"Prayer is like a greased pig at a county fair—often pursued but rarely grasped." CHRISTIAN PRAYER FOR DUMMIES

With Don's call a day away, I had plenty of time to consult *Christian Prayer for Dummies*. I skimmed through the table of contents, and I'll be honest—I skipped directly to Chapter 17: "Ask and It Shall Be Given—I'd Like a Porsche, Please."

I was disappointed to discover that you actually have to read the context of a Bible verse if you want your prayers to work. I also learned that Italian sports cars weren't around when the Bible's original manuscripts were written, so it might be better to ask for a chariot or a donkey (which gets better mileage anyway).

One thing caught my eye:

THE HEALTH BENEFITS OF PRAYER:

1. You double your chances of successful in vitro pregnancy if you're prayed for.

2. Heart attack survivors recover quicker if they're being prayed for by someone.

3. Getting people to pray for you gets you out of the hospital faster after you've had an angioplasty.

This was great news, to be sure, but maybe the author needed to add an unregistered surgeon's warning. Prayer isn't a strict cause-and-effect relationship. Candy junkies can't manipulate God into getting rid of their diabetes. Prayer is not a substitute for healthy eating and daily exercise.

I skimmed some more. My favorite line: "Hudson Taylor had a

lifelong passion to become a Christian missionary to inland China, and not just because he liked Kung Pao chicken."[1]

After the author called the Lord's Prayer "The Original Christian Prayer for Dummies," I called it quits, returning the book to the library, where I assumed it would remain until next year's Friends of the Library book sale.

"The LORD sustains him on his sickbed; in his illness you restore him to full health." PSALM 41:3, ESV

Prayer Strategies Specialist Don Pierson is the prayer point man for a denomination in Tennessee, a member of the staff who literally gets paid to pray. A former pastor, church planter, and missionary, he's been around the block.

Having been on the prayer job for thirteen years, he has no idea how one lands such a job. "I get asked that a lot," he told me. "All I know is, I have a calling based on Hosea 10:12: 'Sow righteousness for yourselves, reap the fruit of unfailing love, and break up your unplowed ground; for it is time to seek the LORD, until he comes and showers his righteousness on you.' I'm here to break up fallow ground." He informed me that one can get a master's degree in prayer but that no one has offered a doctorate yet. Probably so that no televangelist could start a show called *The Prayer Doctor*.

Don has 3,197 churches under his wing, and he spends his time leading retreats, revivals, classes, concerts of prayer, and assemblies. He helps pastors develop strategies to unify their churches for spiritual awakening, and he preaches almost every day. The guy is a spiritual mover and shaker; he gets stuff done. Don was heading out to a meeting as we spoke, and I could hear him driving while talking on his cell phone. I quickly prayed for his safety.

---

[1] I'm sure you realize the obvious untruth of this statement. Taylor arrived in China in 1854, but Kung Pao chicken didn't arrive until 1866.

Don told me there are three types of prayer. Crisis prayer is the most popular of the three. Such prayers are urgent, earthly, and temporal. The help-me-pass-this-test, please-heal-my-neighbor, fix-my-marriage kind of prayers that we all pray.

Then there are calling prayers. The prayers of Paul were dominated by calling, especially in Colossians 4. Paul had received a word from God—a very clear direction and purpose—and it trumped every circumstance. Paul was in prison, but he prayed for boldness instead of rescue or escape. His calling was greater than his crisis. When he prayed for others, he prayed for their character in spite of present circumstances.

Then there are Kingdom prayers. Don doesn't believe that we create these prayers, but that "Kingdom prayers come from the King." These are prayers like Jesus' prayer to "send out workers into [the] harvest field." Kingdom prayers are bigger than any one person, denomination, or time in history.

Don believes his job is to help people move from crisis prayer to calling and Kingdom prayer. "Crisis prayer has consumed our churches," he said. "The number of lost people is increasing, but all we're praying about is colds and cancer."

He continued, "I want to see transformation. I pray that people will return to God and begin to pray the way He wants us to pray. Most new believers pray calling and Kingdom prayers, but I've noticed a disturbing trend in older believers. They pray mostly crisis prayers." I gave him a loud "hmmm" and hoped he didn't realize I was one of those people.

"So how do we reverse the trend, Don?"

"If your heart is consumed with Kingdom and calling, you pray differently. When you seek first the Kingdom, the other things don't concern you."

He asked me if was married, and I said yes. "If you don't talk to your wife, your relationship will get sick. You'll never know each other's hearts and wills, and it's the same way with God. You can't do His will if you can't hear His voice. Every religion prays. What makes our prayers any different? God speaks back. God doesn't need us to talk to Him, but one word from Him changes us. Prayer is about us hearing from God."

Suddenly I felt uncomfortable. The words sounded familiar. I once heard a talk by Erwin McManus where he asked, "How do you know if you're a Christian? You know you're a Christian because you know the sound of His voice." Now Don was saying the same thing. Problem was, I'd never audibly heard from God. I'd never even had an overwhelming spiritual experience. I'm a rational thinker—I like to process and ponder and write. Don't get me wrong—I really want to hear from God, but is it even possible for someone like me?

"So, Don," I asked hesitantly, "how do I hear from God?"

"You know, Jared, it's a still, small voice. The more time you spend with Him, the less you'll ask that question. You'll begin to recognize the sound of His whisper."

Aside from his full-time day job as a prayer warrior, Don also spends about forty-five minutes a day with God on his own. He doesn't have a set schedule or plan—he just reads the Bible until God speaks, then he journals about it, and then he prays it back to God. The next day, he picks up where he left off.

I asked Don if he ever heard any really good answers to prayer. "Oh yes, every day," he replied. "Last week we had an incredible answer to prayer. There's a girl in one of our churches. She grew up in the church, went on mission trips—great kid. She started dating this guy who was far from God, and eventually married him. Now she's far from God."

I knew where this was going.

"In December the husband thought he had stomach cancer. No doctor had diagnosed him; he just really believed he had cancer. So he put a shotgun to his stomach and pulled the trigger."

Okay, I didn't see that one coming.

"Somehow he survived the trip to the hospital, but the doctors didn't think he'd make it. The church started praying for his salvation. Not for his healing—for his *salvation*. The church commissioned their pastor to lead this man to Christ. The pastor goes to the hospital and leads him to Christ on the spot. And, wouldn't you believe it, the man makes a miraculous recovery.

"Fast-forward a few months. The guy is home, and the pastor calls him up and says he wants to start a Bible study in the man's home. The pastor tells the man to invite all his unsaved friends and family. So he does. Thirty people show up the first night. The man's parents and sister now drive three hours each way to attend every week. They've been going for five weeks now, and already several of them have gotten saved and baptized."

These are the kind of stories I want to be able to tell. This is the kind of faith I want to have, living in the midst of a community of people who have prayed with greater power than the brute force of a shotgun. But how can I tap into what Don has in prayer? How can I hear God's still, small voice? What will it look like in my life, without having to become a "prayer strategies specialist"?

In true prayer-expert style, Don ended our conversation by praying. He prayed for Michelle and me, that our journey of prayer would be fruitful, that God would open doors of opportunity, and that we'd learn to pray more and more calling and Kingdom prayers. He prayed that I would find what I was looking for.

I hung up the phone—and hummed a little U2.

CHAPTER 2

New York City

I WAS DANCING IN a circle with two dozen Hasidic Jews. And I was wearing a yarmulke. What had I gotten myself into?

Michelle and I had decided to start our year of living prayerfully by exploring the prayer traditions of the Jewish faith. Starting with Judaism made sense, because Christianity grew out of Jewish roots. While Christianity is definitely wholly its own thing, you get the sense that we still have some Jewish markers in our DNA. Hanging out with Jewish folks would be a bit like visiting my grandparents. While I'm most definitely my mom and dad's kid—a Brock through and through—I'm surprisingly like my grandparents in a lot of ways.[1] Passover was coming up, so I e-mailed eight local synagogues to ask if we could attend their seder supper.

---

[1] For example, my grandfather had a very lusty whistle. I've inherited the predisposition to whistle without ceasing, which drives my wife crazy.

We drove from Hamilton, Ontario, to a local synagogue in my hometown, Guelph. I learned some interesting things at their seder, the most important being that many Jews drink prune juice because the matzo bread "bungs you up like cheese." Overall, attending the Guelph seder wasn't a particularly fruitful experience. Aside from the two rabbis who led the service, I didn't get the sense that there were many devout Jews in the crowd. And despite praying twelve or thirteen different prayers, nothing connected with me. So while the seder close to home gave us a taste of the Jewish prayer tradition, we wanted to go deeper. We decided to go to New York City for the full experience.

We arrived at the synagogue precisely on time. The rabbi greeted us at the front door, shook my hand, and then awkwardly half saluted Michelle as he slowly backed away. It was a direct elbow bend, with the palm facing her in a John Wayne Native American movie sort of way. It screamed, "Please don't come one step closer." Hasidic men don't touch women—except their wives, and even then for only about two weeks each month.

The rabbi showed Michelle to her seat, and then he dragged a wooden divider across the room so she wouldn't distract the menfolk.

The rabbi and I walked around to the male side. I quickly slipped into a seat and grabbed a Bible. It seemed to be backward, and upside down, and was definitely missing the entire New Testament. I skimmed through it. Every time they typed the word God, they left out a letter, so it read "G-d." Saved ink, I suppose.

The rabbi towered above me, suspiciously inspecting my thinning hairline. "I'm going to need you to wear a yarmulke," he said. Then he handed me a bag full of yarmulkes of all sizes, colors, and patterns. It seemed equal parts unholy and unsanitary. I grabbed the first one I saw.

Was I switching allegiances by wearing it? It's the same God, right?

I still felt guilty. I put it on, and it fit my bald spot nicely. It didn't move for the entire service. It must've been black magic. It *did* feel strangely right. In fact, I didn't feel it at all.

People often mistake me for being Jewish. I look very Jewish. In fact, when people ask what my background is, I'll jokingly say, "I'm Jew-*ish*." I love God, read the Old Testament, enjoy a weekly day of rest, and try to avoid pork products (with the exception of pepperoni pizza). But I'm not actually Jewish.

Or am I? I wondered.

The service began. I watched for tardy stragglers, of which there were many. If this particular shul represented the average lateness of the Hasidic faith, then they ranked somewhere below the Pentecostals and Lutherans but slightly above the Baptists.

One of the stragglers was a cowboy. A Jewish cowboy wearing leather boots and a cowboy hat. Apparently that was kosher.

The rabbi was chanting his prayers, but everyone seemed pretty distracted. A young dad walked in with a baby who was wearing a miniature yarmulke. The father walked around, and everyone congratulated him. One of the rabbi's sons started drumming on the altar with his hands. The cowboy shot the breeze with a fellow synagogue member. There seemed to be lots of grace and freedom despite all the rules.

Everyone was reading and praying together now. They were rocking back and forth—hip-thrusting, really. It reminded me of the Mr. Bean dance. Then they took three steps forward and three steps back. The service was in Yiddish, and I couldn't understand the words, but I'd read about this ritual. Hasidic Jews take these steps after praying the *Amidah*, "The Standing Prayer." It's an incredibly beautiful prayer tradition, and it's the main prayer in Jewish services. It's a series of nineteen blessings, broken into three sections—praise, petition, and thanks. Before saying the prayer, you take three steps back to symbolize a withdrawal from the material world and then three steps forward to symbolize approaching the King of kings. It's like a holy line dance, and everyone did it except, suspiciously, the cowboy. Wasn't this his area of expertise?

The service continued in a similar fashion—distractions and chatter, then synchronized prayer and dancing. Almost all the men introduced themselves and shook my hand at some point in the service. On the other side of the great wall, no one said hello to Michelle. Then the rabbi told me to stand.

I was dancing in a conga line with two dozen Hasidic Jews. We were banging our fists on the altar, and they were all hollering something I couldn't understand. I felt the rhythm and moved to the beat. My head covering held on for dear life.

Michelle watched the entire spectacle through a row of lattice in the wooden wall: her husband in a yarmulke, banging on a pulpit and dancing like a Hasid.

The service ended, and we were getting ready to head to the rabbi's house. It was pouring rain outside, and we stood on the porch as we opened our umbrellas. I spotted a Hasidic woman holding a newborn baby, and I offered her my umbrella, which she gladly accepted. Michelle and I shared an umbrella, and the four of us walked down the stairs together.

The rabbi quickly caught up. He whispered something to the woman, who apologized and returned my umbrella. I'd been out of the synagogue for less than five minutes, and apparently I'd already broken a law.

"Rabbi," I groaned, "how have I sinned?"

"To hold an umbrella counts as constructing a tent, which we are forbidden from doing during Passover."

He was totally serious. I was shocked.

He shot me a devilish grin. "But you can hold it for her."

Well played.

"Whoever looks intently into the perfect law that gives freedom, and continues in it . . . will be blessed in what they do."
JAMES 1:25

I e-mailed seventy-eight rabbis before Rabbi Aaron agreed to meet with me. Hasidic rabbanim are a rather private bunch, but I knew I'd stumbled across a cool guy when I received his reply:

> Come for a service and then join us for dinner?
> From rabbiaaronsfakeemail@aol.com. Sent from my iPhone.

The clash of past and present was fantastic. Hasidic rabbis had iPhones? People still used AOL?

I read the online listing for his synagogue:

> Modern orthodox congregation, with Rabbi Aaron as the
> spiritual leader. Members are mostly in their 20s–40s. Serving
> Brooklyn Heights and Brownstone Brooklyn. His wife, Shternie,
> has six children, but still manages to run a preschool and hosts
> 25+ people for lunch every Sabbath. Rabbi Aaron is the coauthor
> of *The Rabbi and the CEO*, and you can find over 100 of his
> sermons at www.Jewish.tv.

It sounded like their synagogue was a happening place. They ran morning and evening services every day plus ten classes a week. While Michelle and I wouldn't be able to attend the "Bagel and Talmud" class, we were excited to attend a service and have dinner with the rabbi and his disciples.

As I entered the rabbi's house, I was immediately confronted with something I'd never seen before. I turned and greeted the rabbi's wife. "Okay, Shternie, I'm going to be really honest, this is weird to me: why does your kitchen look like a spaceship?"

I couldn't help myself.

The kitchen looked like a science project. Everything was covered with tinfoil. The counters, the microwave—everything was completely sealed. Even the sink was lined with foil, and the taps were individually covered. The bottom cupboards were taped shut. The top cupboards were strung shut by what appeared to be a long skipping rope.

The rabbi's wife laughed. "I don't even notice it anymore," she confessed.

In order to fully please the Lord during Passover, a good Jewish family must completely purge their home of yeast. They start with a thorough cleaning, and then they pour boiling water over everything. Then a rabbi who specializes in yeast-busting thoroughly inspects the home, even checking the cracks between floor tiles.

Then, for good measure, the family covers everything in tinfoil. The kitchen goes on lockdown. Each family owns a separate set of dishes and silverware, which they keep double-sealed year round, only busting them out for Passover. I refrained from telling them the bad news that microscopic yeast is everywhere.

I moved to introduce myself to an older Hasid. The name on my birth certificate is Jared. It's a nice, classic Old Testament name. But with the exception of my friends Karyn and Catherine, everyone calls me Jay. It's what I call myself. So while my given name is Jared, it would be cowardly to refer to myself other than Jay.

"Hi," I said. "I'm Jared."

The older Hasid was so happy that my name is Jared. "I've always liked that name. If I had been blessed with a second son, I would have named him Jared."

Yes, I pandered.

Here was my chance to drop some serious biblical knowledge. "Jared was the second oldest man to ever live—962 years, just seven shy of his grandfather Methuselah."[2]

---

[2] Not much is known about the biblical Jared, except that he's also going to be the second-oldest *Jared* when I pass him in the year 2949 (subject to massive technological advancements).

The man beamed from ear to ear and nodded in surprise. In a thick Jewish-Brooklyn accent he said, "Very good, Jared. I'm impressed!"

I was so in.

We took a seat at the table. "So, Rabbi, I hear that you come from a long line of rabbanim," I said. "Any idea how many generations?"

The rabbi's wife tried to hide her rightfully proud smile, but the rabbi answered very matter-of-factly, "We have traced my family lineage all the way back to King David."

I almost choked on a matzo ball. So not only were we having dinner with the coolest rabbi in Brooklyn, but it was possible that he shared the same genes as Jesus. They were basically cousins. Was this what Jesus looked like?

This fact continued to blow my mind throughout dinner. I found myself staring while he went through ritual after ritual, prayer after prayer, and reading after reading. As he ate and laughed and talked with his disciples and whispered to those at his left and right, I pictured Jesus with His disciples. I pictured myself reclining at the table with my Lord. It was easy to imagine I was sitting beside tax collector Matthew and beloved disciple John. I got into arguments with Peter, aka "The Rock," and I secretly confessed to Thomas that I was a bigger doubter than he was. I wondered if this was what it was like to eat with Jesus.

I'm not a fan of the one-cup communion policy, but there I was, drinking from a cup that had been touched by a dozen other people.[3] We were singing, and the rabbi held a cup of wine that was overflowing onto a silver plate. He continued to pour as he prayed, and this signified that life was good and abundant.

Like the dancing synagogue service, this evening was an odd mix of strict tradition and lax rule breaking. One of the rabbi's sons

---

[3] I don't want to blame the rabbi and his disciples, but a day after we arrived home from New York, I was alternating between bone-aching bouts of colds and fevers. I had definitely contracted some sort of Brooklyn bug, so I feel justified in being hesitant at one-cup communion services.

accidentally shattered a glass in the middle of a prayer, and everyone just kept going as if it hadn't happened.

Without a working knowledge of Hebrew Scripture (our Old Testament), Michelle and I would have been completely lost. It was sort of like speaking France French versus Quebec French, or Spain Spanish versus Mexico Spanish. Most of the time all of us understood each other. But every few minutes Michelle and I had no idea what our hosts were saying.

There's a certain Jewish prayer called the Shema, they told me, which they pray with their right hand over their eyes. For devout Jews, it's their first and final words of the day. Jewish parents use it as a bedtime prayer with their kids. It's often used as a deathbed prayer. In *Man's Search for Meaning*, Viktor Frankl writes, "We have come to know man as he really is. After all, man is that being who invented the gas chambers of Auschwitz; however, he is also that being who entered those gas chambers upright, with the Lord's Prayer or the *Shema Yisrael* on his lips."

In Mark 12:28 a religious person asks Jesus a question: "Of all the commandments, which is the most important?" Jesus starts His answer with the Shema. At that time, the prayer only had one verse—Deuteronomy 6:4—"Hear, O Israel: The Lord our God, the Lord is one." It's a powerful declaration. As Jewish CEO Charlie Harary says, "It is the mission statement, the pledge of allegiance for Jewish people."

Since the time of Jesus, the Shema has grown in length—to about twenty verses—as Jewish prayer traditions tend to do.

Then, if you're to believe my new rabbi friend, it gets a little funky. Each word of the Shema represents a body part, and if you pronounce each word carefully, it strengthens that particular limb. And every time you slur a word, God creates a crippled angel.

"What!" I exclaimed. "Run that by me again, please."

Everyone laughed, and the rabbi explained that you must be

careful not to slur your words when speaking the Shema, for to do so would create a crippled angel. Then the angel would come and give you a hard time because you permanently injured him. To which one of the rabbi's kids said, "He will beat you, son, for real."[4]

But it wasn't all bad news. Apparently every well-pronounced word you say creates a healthy angel. Plus, I think that Christians need to be reminded of our great allegiance to Christ. In a world where loyalties shift like sand in a windstorm, maybe we should start praying the same Shema that Jesus prayed.

I could get used to Rabbi Aaron's version of Jewish culture. He and his disciples argued a lot, so I fit right in. An older fellow named Moshe provided the contrarian's view on almost every subject. He explained that it was well within his right to do so. "Jewish tradition permits . . . encourages . . . *demands* debate!"

Controversy and dispute were encouraged. The process of understanding required voicing diverse opinions. We experienced more than a few heated discussions around Rabbi Aaron's table. Yet I sensed a deep freedom and care for each other as everyone struggled to figure our spiritual matters as a community. I liked this. A lot.

One heated discussion was about backup wives. According to their law, a Hasid can take multiple wives, but New York sees it otherwise. The merits of polygamy were debated, and the rabbi settled the discussion: "Two Jewish women—who can handle such a thing? You have to supply each of them with a tent, camels, clothing, so on and so forth. In modern terms, that means their own house. In Brooklyn Heights? No man can afford such a thing."

For once, all seemed to agree.

I asked question after question, and the rabbi and his disciples excitedly taught me their ways.

I asked why they do the Mr. Bean hip-thrust dance when they

---

[4] Here's how I suspect this story came to life. One ancient rabbi had a lazy student and threatened to sic a peg-legged pirate angel on the poor boy if he didn't shape up.

pray. They explained that the movement imitated the flicker of a candle as it sought the source of light. Prayer brought them closer to God. It lifted them higher. They saw themselves as the flame that tried to lift the candle. They were trying to become enlightened. They were trying to ascend.

I asked about a tradition I'd read about called a minion. "When ten people pray together in a room, it's called a minion," the rabbi said.

"Is that why everyone has such big families?" I asked.

They all laughed. "You can still pray on your own or with a few others, but it's better with ten."

"But why ten, specifically?"

"Every gathering of ten is a gathering of holiness," the rabbi explained. "God created the world with ten utterances of speech, there are Ten Commandments, and they are connected. Ten is a whole number, a complete number. Then there are the ten spies. And the ten brothers of Joseph." (There were actually eleven, but I didn't get a chance to ask who gets left out in his calculation.) "Abraham negotiated for ten righteous men at Sodom. The Ten Commandments are comprised of 620 letters, representing the 613 mitzvot and the 7 Noahic laws."

I thought that minion prayer was a great idea, but I wasn't as sold on their rationale. Thankfully, there was a far deeper community aspect to minion prayer.

"Where one lacks, another supplies," the rabbi continued. "We complete each other. Rather than simply praying, each minion tries to help each other with real action. We help each other get jobs, find apartments, start businesses, and so on. Everyone helps everyone else."

It reminded me of the quote "Pray like work won't help, and then work like prayer won't help." Or as Shane Claiborne says, maybe it's time to become the answer to our own prayers.

I thought back to my own community. We were working jobs and trying to get ahead. But we were all doing it on our own, and honestly, it was pretty lonely. Sure, we were there for each other in times of crisis, but we were not really in each other's lives. The early church met on a daily basis; we were lucky if we saw our closest friends twice in one month. Everyone was just so busy. What if we actually "did life" together? What if we shared our possessions? What if we traded our skills and talents? What if we actually helped each other?

I really liked the minion concept. But it raised the question—if a community could meet each other's needs, why bother to pray at all?

"That's an excellent question," said one of the rabbi's eldest disciples. "We believe there are three types of prayers. Most people know the first one, gratitude. We say thank you. Next is supplication. Everyone knows how to say 'gimme gimme.' But praise? We've lost the art today. When you meet someone famous for the first time, what do you say? 'I love your book. I really enjoyed your talk. Your work has influenced me greatly.' Why do you say this? Does his ego need you to tell him these things? No. Will he survive and thrive without them? Yes. Then why do it? Because you're trying to make a connection. You think Henry Kissinger needs you to say something nice about him? Do you think he cares? No. We do it because *we* need it. God doesn't need our praise at all. *We* need it. We need the reminder."

The rabbi interjected, "Prayer is not about asking for your needs; it's about connecting with God. The reason we ask is so that we appreciate it more. It's like a son asking his father for bread. You'll be more grateful when it arrives, and your relationship will grow. We ask God for our needs so that we can serve Him more."

I grew up in a series of churches that lied to me. I'd always heard that Jewish people followed 613 rules and that their faith was bossy and religious. We proudly proclaimed that *our* faith isn't about religion; it is about relationship.

But as I'd researched Judaism over the weeks leading up to our Brooklyn visit, I'd discovered something interesting. Those 613 rules are more than rules and laws—they are mitzvahs. *Mitzvah*'s root word literally means "connection." Mitzvahs are "connections to God."

"Rabbi," I asked, "you follow 613 commands. Doesn't that seem like a lot?"

The rabbi nodded. "The 613 mitzvot may seem like a lot. Some people see our laws as rocks in a backpack—a heavy load to carry. We see each mitzvah as a diamond. A bag of diamonds seems far lighter. We're richer with more laws. And 613 is just the beginning. Just as there is an infinite number of worlds, so, too, is there an infinite number of ways for a Jew to connect to God."

I thought about this for a moment. I pictured myself carrying a bag of rocks up a mountain. Then I envisioned myself carrying a bag of diamonds. He was right—diamonds did seem lighter. The diamond metaphor was beautiful, but it seemed to me to contain a subtle flaw. I was still lugging a heavy bag up a steep incline. I was still a broken, sinful person. I couldn't go two hours without sinning in thought, word, or deed. I couldn't carry the burden of perfection. I was irreparable. Rocks or diamonds—either way, the weight would kill me eventually. I needed someone to carry it for me.

One of the rabbi's female followers continued. "People think that God is some evil guy who wants to control their lives. But He's your father. He's your daddy. You don't have to be afraid of Him. Prayer is really about intimacy. It's about becoming one with God."

I looked around the room with new eyes. I'd been seeing it all wrong. All my beliefs about Judaism became apparent for what they were: stereotypes. These people truly loved God. I had assumed that my "Jewish family" would be just like my grandparents—kind, devoted people, but still bound by rules and religion and tradition. In a way, both are. But there was far more heart than I'd expected.

The rabbi summed it up nicely. "Let's be honest—none of the

laws matter if you don't love others. Our faith is not about religion, it's about the relationship."

I thought about my own prayer life, which consisted almost exclusively of asking God for things. That wasn't a relationship. Maybe I was the one who was guilty of "practicing religion" instead of living faith.

"Blessed are You, . . . our God, King of the universe, who fashioned man with wisdom and created within him many openings and many cavities." SIDDUR

One of the rabbi's disciples emerged from the bathroom, grabbed a book, and sat down beside me. "This is the siddur, our prayer book," he explained. I'd read a beautiful quote about the siddur by a rabbi named Benjamin Blech: "The Torah is God's gift to us; the siddur is our gift to God." I really liked that idea. God has written us a book, and now we have the opportunity to respond with our words and actions.

"I'd like to read you a passage," the disciple continued. "It's the prayer we say after going to the bathroom."

I almost spit out my purple cabbage. "You know I'm still eating, right?" He laughed and continued.

"Blessed are You, HaShem, our God, King of the universe, who fashioned man with wisdom and created within him many openings and many cavities. It is obvious and known before Your Throne of Glory that if but one of them were to be ruptured or but one of them were to be blocked it would be impossible to survive and to stand before You. Blessed are You, HaShem, who heals all flesh and acts wondrously."

I remembered Michelle's grandfather, who miraculously recovered from a life-threatening bout with bowel cancer. Knowing what he went through, this prayer was incredibly meaningful to me.

"That's the prayer that you pray after relieving yourself when you do the ritual hand washing called Netilat Yadayim. You know, religion isn't something floating around in the ether somewhere. It's here and now."

I agreed with the sentiment, but I preferred not to talk about things "floating around" directly after a conversation about the bathroom. While not every Jew prays for every occasion, I got the sense that this fellow did. While it's probably a little too religious for my personality, I can definitely see the benefits to a structured commitment to pray without ceasing.

It was almost midnight. The rabbi grabbed a coffee and sat down at my right hand. He continued chatting happily, but I was nervous. What did this mean? Rabbanim did everything intentionally, and this was one of the smartest rabbis alive today. Surely he knew that his seating choice signified me as the person in a position of power. Or was I just reading into it? He was probably just trying to make me feel like a big man. Or maybe it was the only empty chair.

The rabbi's daughter had been silently serving us all evening. She was fifteen years old, and she lived a pretty sheltered life. She attended a five hundred–member all-girl Hasidic school and split the rest of her time between home, the synagogue, and various kosher shops.

She sidled up to Michelle. "What's your name?"

"Michelle."

"Are you married?"

"Yes."

She looked confused. We were also confused until we realized this girl's question was actually a question about Michelle's hair.

Hasidic women, you see, have perfect hair. It's perfect because it's fake. All of it, fake. They wear wigs. According to Jewish law, married women are supposed to wear head coverings. So Hasidic women simply wear other people's hair as a covering.

The girl looked directly into Michelle's eyes and asked very seriously, "Michelle . . . how do you do your hair?"

Michelle's heart melted. The rabbi's daughter was just like every other fifteen-year-old girl. So rebellious.

After Michelle explained her technique, the girl unloaded a series of questions about the outside world. She asked about our jobs and our faith and was delighted to hear that we actually worked together, as equals. She was glad we'd started our year of living prayerfully with Judaism, but she was interested to find out what we thought of all the other world faiths. I silently prayed that we hadn't just wrought havoc upon this fine family, but I also prayed that she'd meet Jesus someday. I hoped they'd all meet Jesus someday.

As we got ready to leave, I was cornered by the rabbi's wife and two of her older friends. The eldest woman peered at me quizzically and said, "Jared, what's your heritage?"

"Why do you ask?" I responded.

"We think you're Jewish." All three nodded in agreement.

I explained that my family came from the Channel Islands in France. "Ah . . . lots of Jews in France!" one lady chimed in.

I appreciated her enthusiasm, but I wanted to set the record straight. "Yeah, but my ancestors were actually Huguenots, French Protestants who were fleeing from Habsburg religious oppression."[5]

"Ah yes, religious oppression, we Jews know all about that. Maybe our ancestors and your ancestors crossed paths at some point in time?" I tried to protest, I really did, but it's never wise to argue with Jewish housewives. "Our people took the same route to get here. Maybe you're a mix-breed somewhere in there." French and Jewish, eh? I tried to imagine what Jerry Seinfeld and Marion Cotillard's baby might look like. Apparently, that was me.

---

[5] I've traced my lineage all the way back to Scotland in 1797. The Huguenot piece is based on my great-grandmother's oral recollections, but I haven't yet been able to make the French connection. I'm praying for a brilliant genealogist's help.

These women were so well-meaning and very kind. One got stone-cold serious. "Jared, it's more than just the way you look. There's something about the way you hold yourself. You have a presence." The other women nodded. "You have a Jewish spirit."

I didn't know what to say. Never mind conversion; they'd already rewritten my ancestry. I wondered if they were sensing the Holy Spirit. I wondered if they saw Jesus in me. He was a Jewish rabbi, after all.

We said our good-byes, exchanging many hearty handshakes and awkward touch-free salutes in Michelle's direction.

What a night. What a wonderful community. They helped each other. They completed each other. Their entire lives were built around daily invitations to connect with God—mitzvahs. I wondered, *How can Michelle and I create small invitations to connect with God in our own lives?*

As we walked back to the car and Michelle and I talked about the night, I recognized that I had just done a terrible thing.

Earlier in the evening, Michelle had used the restroom. When she had finished, she turned off the light. A few minutes later, one of the women asked her to turn the light back on, since they were forbidden from doing work during Passover. Michelle happily complied.

I, however, knew nothing of this encounter until after we left.

Problem was, I had used the bathroom just before we left. And turned off the light. And now we were gone, leaving precisely zero Gentiles to flip the switch back on. Now ten Jews would spend the next week using the bathroom in the dark, thanks to yours truly.

"I will not drink again from the fruit of the vine until the kingdom of God comes." LUKE 22:18

I was at my third Passover meal in less than a week, and I didn't know if I could stomach it. We were attending a Jews for Jesus seder, the Christian version of the Jewish tradition. Generally speaking, a Messianic Passover differs from a Jewish Passover in two ways.

First, a Messianic Passover is all about Jesus. It's totally focused and centered around Christ, which you'll see in a minute.

And second, since it was a good Christian party, we drank kosher grape juice instead of wine. I grabbed the giant bottle and checked the label. One hundred fifty calories and thirty-seven grams of sugar per serving. We had to drink four glasses of the stuff. My belly cried out for mercy.

The worship leader was a Christian Jew with an Australian-Brooklyn accent. It was unique, to say the least.

And since I'd had so much experience with Passover meals in the last week, I was starting to get religiously bossy about it. I kept correcting the other people at my table. I told one of the men he needed to have at least 3.3 ounces of juice in his glass. I told a fourth grader not to lick her finger after we dipped it in the cup. I pointed out a slight discrepancy in a nonbiblical story involving salt water and tears. It's crazy how fast you can slip into legalism. I'd been to two Passovers, and now I was an expert.

And then we ate horseradish. It symbolized the bitterness of Israel's time in Egypt. Technically, Jewish law required me to ingest a whole teaspoon, but in my previous two Passovers, I had taken only a small amount. Tonight I was going full-dose.

I didn't know it, but this wasn't standard horseradish. I swallowed the full teaspoonful.

I caught a whiff and accidentally back-snorted it up my nose. A single tear rolled down my cheek, followed by four more. I was caught up to the seventh heaven. I was suspended in an alternate reality, unable to see, hear, or feel anything in my earthly body. I was frozen in time, totally paralyzed, and about to retch.

The bitterness of Egypt? Consider yourself remembered.

Dinner finished, and the ceremony got serious. We were about to drink the third cup of Passover—the Cup of Redemption—and the seder leader read Matthew 26:27: "Then [Jesus] took a cup, and when he had given thanks, he gave it to them, saying, 'Drink from it, all of you.'" This third cup was that cup. Jesus gave wine a new meaning—now it represented His blood and a new agreement between God and the people who belong to Him. Jesus fulfills the Law. For Jews, this would have widespread implications. No more seders. No more wigs. No more walking in the rain without an umbrella. No more fancy clothes or unshaved sideburns. No more tinfoil countertops or Mr. Bean dances. No more synagogues. No more kosher. It's all about relationship from here on out.

Jesus changes everything.

"Very truly I tell you, no one can enter the kingdom of God unless they are born of water and the Spirit." JOHN 3:5

After our time in New York, my exploration of Jewish prayer traditions reached fever pitch. I always get that way when I'm really interested in a subject. I won't stop until I've experienced it fully. In my search, I discovered the most fantastic Jewish tradition. It's called *mikvah*, and it's a ceremonial ritual involving a bunch of prayers and a giant bathtub.

I e-mailed a few local mikvahs and asked them if they would allow me to experience the cleansing waters. After receiving a number of embarrassing replies, I did a little more research. It seems that mikvah is for women only—to purify themselves after their menstrual cycle.

This immediately ruled me out, owing to the fact that I'm a male. My wife, however, is not.

I shot Michelle a quick e-mail and asked her when "it" would happen next. I assured her that it was research for the pilgrimage.

Mikvah, it turns out, is serious business. While it's not technically in the Bible anywhere, Jews consider mikvah their most important rule.

So important, in fact, that devout Jews are commanded to sell their synagogues and their holy scrolls in order to build a mikvah. To me, this seemed overmuch—until I found out that a Jewish couple is forbidden from having sex until the wife purifies herself after each cycle.

It all made sense.

I called a rabbi and asked him about mikvah, and he gave it a slightly different spin. "What is more important—the Torah or another Jewish child? It's all about the potential for life. The first thing the Nazis did was destroy the mikvahs. Some Jews had to travel twelve hours to visit underground mikvahs."

It turns out a mikvah can be used by men, too. For women, mikvah is mitzvah—a command and a connection to God. For men, it's just a trip to the spiritual spa. Mikvah also serves as a Jewish version of baptism—that is, a Gentile can convert to Judaism by entering the waters of mikvah. I also found out that a mikvah can retroactively cover your kids with a spiritual blessing. In response to this information, one Jewish woman said to her rabbi, "So you mean I can get five kids covered for the price of one mikvah? That's a good deal!"

I met with another rabbi and asked about the power of mikvah. "Mikvah transforms someone from his previous state to a state of holiness. If a mikvah can transform a non-Jew into a Jew, imagine what it can do for someone who's already Jewish!"

I still hadn't heard back from Michelle, but I did find a mikvah app. It's called "My Mikvah Calendar," and it helps couples maximize their window of "eligible days" by reminding women to visit the mikvah as soon as they're eligible.

The rules surrounding mikvah are exhausting. A woman cannot enter the waters before sundown. The mikvah must be built into the ground or the structure of the building. The depth must be such as to enable an average adult to stand upright and have the water reach at least eleven inches above the waist. The mikvah tank must contain at least two hundred gallons of water. The water has to be "living" water. While one could argue that all water is living water, mikvah water must find its source from naturally flowing water, such as an ocean or river or rain or melted snow.

Married Jewish women have to attend mikvah every month using a formula based on their cycle. This might sound like a lot of work, but it's really not as bad as it seems. Women don't have to visit mikvah while pregnant or breast-feeding, and the average Hasidic woman has eight to ten children, since birth control is forbidden. If a woman's lucky (or unlucky, depending on your point of view), she'll go only around ten times in her entire lifetime.

Michelle got home from work and we had "the mikvah conversation." She was unimpressed.

I tried to spin it like a rabbi. "Mikvah is like a Gentile retreat. Think of it as a puri-vacation!" She rolled her eyes.

A quick Internet search for "mikvah" returned 636,000 results. Interestingly enough, when I searched for "Gentile mikvah," I got 1,510,000 results. The heathens want in.

I faced eleven rejections and countless deflections. Rabbanim were particularly good at saying no without saying no. It was frustrating, but I'm a rather persistent fellow.

Only one rabbi was sufficiently blunt for my liking. "Mikvah is not the first step. It's the last to understanding Judaism."

Michelle and I eventually found one mikvah that would give us a tour but not a dunking. It was closed during daylight hours, so we could walk freely through the building. It looked like a standard house from the curb, but it was a high-class spa on the inside. We explored the waiting room and the changing rooms, and then we checked out the mikvah itself.

It was a square hole in the basement, and it had a slight layer of pond scum on the surface of the water. I asked if these two hundred gallons were pure, from a living source. The tour guide nodded. "Well, actually, there's a second tank under this one, and that one contains the living water. In order to maintain sanitation standards, we refill this top tank with tap water every day. But there's a hole that connects the two tanks, so technically it's all pure."

I thought this was cheating, but I also couldn't imagine trying to collect two hundred gallons of rainwater every day.

"He who finds a wife finds what is good and receives favor from the LORD." PROVERBS 18:22

You need to understand a few things about my wife. Without me, she would spend her entire life eating plain macaroni and cereal. Without Michelle, I would do laundry every two months. My beard would be a foot longer than it already is, and I would live in the woods with a giant pile of books. Together we're trying to approximate one normal human being.

Marriage has stretched both of us. I've had to become somewhat domesticated, and she's had to deal with my neuroses. She does my laundry, and I provide an endless stream of drama, excitement, and adventure. I also do all the cooking, and she takes all the Jewish baths.

I'm so proud of my wife—she's talented and beautiful and brilliant and patient enough to live with me. I love her deeply, and I know that she loves me too—I can't think of any other woman who would go along with my ridiculous plans. Especially a mikvah. But Michelle understood deep down that this prayer quest was serious business for me. I wanted to experience the roots of Christian prayer. As a follower of Jesus, I am a follower not only of the Son of God but also of a first-century Jewish rabbi. How did Jewish men experience prayer? How did their wives experience prayer? It had to be a little different from the hurried prayers I had been mumbling in the last couple of years. The answers to these questions, I imagined, would change the way we would pray for the rest of our lives. It seemed worth a dunk in an icy lake.

"Wash away all my iniquity and cleanse me from my sin." PSALM 51:2

My wife was buck naked and about to get tossed into a freezing lake.

Despite my best efforts, I couldn't find a single mikvah that would allow a Gentile to enter the waters without converting to Judaism. While I toyed with the idea for a moment, Michelle quickly shot it down and agreed to take the more natural route we were on now.

It was early spring, and the water was running at a temperature of sixty-six degrees Fahrenheit. It's important to note that my wife has some experience with frigid water. As a true-blue Finn, she has visited saunas and then willingly jumped into an ice-drilled hole in a lake in the Arctic Circle. This mikvah business was small potatoes.

We sat in the car in an empty parking lot near the lake. I assumed this was what being a drug dealer felt like, though I doubted they experienced the irrational happiness I felt in that moment. My Gentile wife was about to get purified from her unholiness.

I would serve as her *balanit*, or mikvah overseer. We'd tried to follow all the rules as best we could. I ran through the checklist one more time:

_ Remove all jewelry
_ Remove contact lenses
_ Remove false teeth, bridges, and retainers
_ Remove clips, barrettes, and elastics
_ Remove nail polish
_ Use the toilet
_ Take a shower
_ Shampoo your hair, but do not use conditioner
_ Clean all crevices
_ Wash your ears
_ Clean your navel
_ Slough your knees, elbows, and feet of dry skin
_ Clean off all makeup

_ Wash your face
_ Clean pierced ears, nose, belly button, etc.
_ Clean the corners of your eyes
_ Blow your nose
_ Brush and floss your teeth
_ Remove Band-Aids and any remaining adhesive
_ Soften scabs and remove dried blood
_ Cut or file your finger- and toenails
_ Clean underneath your finger- and toenails
_ Check your hands for stains
_ Remove unattached loose hairs
_ Remove any foreign substances

In case you're wondering, you can't use conditioner because it coats each hair and is considered a head covering. Knots, tangles, and dreadlocks are also forbidden because each hair isn't free and separate.

I inspected Michelle's lips to ensure they weren't chapped. Dry skin is considered a covering. But you can't use lip balm because that's *also* considered a covering. You have to rip the dry skin off.

Mikvah poses quite the problem for women with water phobias. Technically, you can hold a railing—as long as you don't grip too tightly. But some rabbis just suggest behavior therapy.

Cartilage piercings are a contentious issue too. You're supposed to remove them before entering the mikvah, but since this can lead to infection, most rabbis suggest that you avoid getting them in the first place.

Temporary fillings also cause quite the debate among rabbanim. Most recommend either delaying your appointment until after your mikvah visit or getting the filling set so tight that "theoretically" it could stay in forever.

Thankfully, Michelle didn't have dry lips, a water phobia, cartilage piercings, or any temporary fillings. She only had an impurity problem, which we were about to remedy.

It was dark outside.

Michelle said the official "Prayer before Entering Mikvah": "Blessed are You, O Lord, our God, King of the universe, who has sanctified us with His commandments and commanded us concerning the immersion."

Michelle looked both ways and darted to the lake. She jumped in, and I inspected her dive to make sure she went all the way under, including her hair. The goal was to have maximum water contact with her skin. To that end, Michelle kept her fingers and hands spread open, and her arms were slightly bent. She lifted her feet off the bottom of the lake. I deemed it a good dive and proclaimed the word *kosher*. She came up gasping from the cold.

She emerged from the water and crossed her arms over her chest. I held a towel over her head while she prayed the "Prayer after Immersion": "O God, You are the Fountain of Life! I enter this mikvah as an expression of my commitment to immerse myself in the faith of Israel and in the waters of Torah. Even as our ancestors crossed the sea on their pilgrimage to Sinai, may my immersion nurture my resolve to take shelter under the wings of the Shekhina and seal my devotion to a life of learning, worship, and deeds of justice and kindness."

To cover all the bases, she prayed an alternate prayer too: "I am now before You like a creation newly created. From the earth I have now been formed. The earth, the waters have just been collected together, and it has just appeared. A new creation stands before You, a new creation in a newly created world."

Most women repeat this process once. Some do it three times, and a rare woman will do it seven times. I counted as Michelle dunked seven times. Technically we should have done the same thing with every utensil she had touched in the past two weeks, but we both agreed that this water's purity was questionable at best.

Michelle emerged from the water, shivering, and I wrapped her in a towel. Tradition teaches that the person who descends into the mikvah as a Gentile emerges from its waters as a Jew. Was Michelle a Jew now? Had I accidentally converted her? She didn't look any different.

I asked her how she felt.

"So basically," she said as she toweled off, "if you're a Gentile, mikvah is just skinny-dipping with more rules."

"Repent and be baptized, every one of you, in the name of Jesus Christ."
ACTS 2:38

I thought back to my baptism as a teenager. As I recall, I was clothed at the time. It has been almost a decade since that day. Not much has changed, to be honest. I'm ashamed. I thought I'd be a giant spiritual oak by my late twenties, but I'm still a dwarf sapling.

I reflected on the similarity between mikvah and baptism. Both symbolize a spiritual rebirth and a total transformation. For Michelle, mikvah was a good reminder of God's ability to completely surround us with His presence. "I like physical reminders like communion and baptism," she said. "Those are always pretty powerful for me."

Mikvah was a good reminder to me of how hard transformation truly is. It means cleaning out every pore of your being, removing everything that hinders your relationship with God.

"There's something about being surrounded by a purifying force," Michelle said. Looking back on it now, I can see that we were about to enter a season of immersion. Like learning a new language, prayer isn't an easy discipline to acquire. It takes time and effort, and it is best received through total immersion. I was looking for transformation in my prayer life, and it was going to take a total dunking. Maybe seven.

"In the morning I earnestly seek for God." ISAIAH 26:9, NLT

When we were in New York, I learned that devout Hasidic men will go to the synagogue every morning and spend at least forty-five minutes reading and thirty minutes praying. They start with reading so they have a connection to God. I decided to attempt it for the first time. It was a big commitment, so I started with a one-week trial period. I thought I'd be fine with the reading, but I was nervous I wouldn't make it through prayer time without getting distracted. Or falling asleep.

To give you an idea of my former prayer life, it wasn't unusual to go for weeks without more than a few quick "arrow prayers" when I needed help. I was a bit better at reading my Bible, but my prayers just seemed to echo off the walls.

I made it through my trial week. The reading was easy, and it definitely put me in the right frame of mind for prayer. I felt free to be more honest and heartfelt, and I was far more focused than expected. Apparently reading trumped my fruit fly attention span.

Each day the following week, I read for forty-five minutes and prayed for thirty minutes. It got easier and easier; time flew by. I needed to drum up more prayer requests, so I e-mailed some friends to ask if there was anything I could pray for them about. One of them wrote back, "Besides my husband, you are the first person to ask me that in a long, long time."

And she is a pastor's wife.

A week later, the training started to pay off. I suddenly felt an overwhelming need to pray all day long. I don't know where it came from—it kind of just snuck up on me. I was also starting to feel a much deeper connection to God. Maybe I felt less guilty now that I was praying a lot. Or maybe I sensed that He was listening. I was listening too.

I e-mailed Michelle at her office job to tell her how I was feeling, and she wrote back, "I'm feeling the same thing. I've been praying and praying all day for everyone and everything."

"For everyone and everything." I liked that.

Thirty minutes of prayer simply wasn't enough. There were far too many things that needed the covering of Christ. I needed more time. I found out that really devout Hasidim pray for about forty minutes in the morning, fifteen minutes around noon, and fifteen minutes in the evening. It was time to step up my game.

"Go where your best prayers take you." FREDERICK BUECHNER

My mom's dad is an awesome dude. From the day he found out that my mother was pregnant, my grandfather prayed for me every single day of my life. In fact, he has prayed for all of his kids and all of his grandkids every single day of their lives. And every one of us knows

God because of it. Every morning before work, he would make his way down to the basement, to his favorite chair, and pray for us. Every single day of his life.

Until he lost his memory.

It happened just a few months ago, and it happened so fast. I stayed over for a visit, and it was obvious that while my grandpa knew I was family, he couldn't remember my name. At one point in the conversation I said, "Grandpa, do you remember my name?"

He grinned. "Of course I do!" he said.

"Well," I replied, "what is it?"

He put a hand on my shoulder. "Just a minute now," he said. "I know this. I—I want to say it's Jared, but I know it's not!"

I could see he was embarrassed. "It's okay, Grandpa," I reassured him. "Everyone forgets, eventually."

"I'm sorry, buddy," he said.

Jared is my name, and Buddy was his nickname for me.

I sobbed like a baby that night.

My grandpa used to pray five times daily, on his knees. I was now praying multiple times per day, but I rarely lasted more than five minutes in the kneeling position. I have a bad foot and a bad lower back, and it hurts my knees, too. I was praying for healing, and I was trying various pillows and positions, but nothing worked. Was I a bad Christian? I wondered if praying while pacing was acceptable.

And I was pretty sure I was allergic to the couch.

When I was a teenager, my grandpa made a prayer carpet for me. I had mentioned that I aspired to his level of prayer, and he took it upon himself to equip me for the deed. He acquired an old remnant, cut it into a rectangle, and paid for it to be bound with nice, new edging. Then he drove six hours round-trip to deliver it. I thought that maybe if I had a carpet like his, I'd pray like he prayed. I think I used it twice. Somehow I lost it, and I've always regretted it.

I was praying for well over an hour each day now, but I still wasn't satisfied with my progress. I wished I were more connected to God. I wished that I could audibly hear God, or maybe sense His presence all the time. I wished I knew that my prayers were making a difference. I was moving forward on my prayer journey, but I still had the same nagging questions: *Why is God so silent? Why can't I hear Him or sense His presence? Am I talking to myself? Do my prayers really make a difference?*

I still wanted to pray like my grandpa.

The Jewish prayer traditions were cool, and through learning about them, I was noticing small invitations to connect with God. I was developing a habit of praying more. I needed the reminder that our faith is rooted in Judaism and that we are part of a long and rich history of prayerful men and women around the globe. I was realizing that I was just one person in that huge story. *His* story.

Yet I was still looking for more from my Jewish experience. I needed something a little more authentic and original. I needed something closer to the source. And by source, I mean Jesus. The beauty of the Christian faith is that we serve a God who actually became human and lived among us. I wanted to walk in His footsteps. I wanted to pray prayers in the places where Jesus prayed them. I wanted to talk to Him and hear from Him in the very places where He spoke to people. How did Jesus and His disciples pray? Where did they pray? Why did they pray?

So I decided to visit Jerusalem.

CHAPTER 3

Israel

AS THE BUS DROVE FROM Tel Aviv to Jerusalem, I noted my first impressions in my journal. "Smells of dust and diesel," I wrote. "A thin skin of dirt on a rubble pile." Israel, it seems, is a series of hills and valleys, which means great views and strong leg muscles. Jerusalem, like her history, is a series of highs and lows, with no level ground in sight.

I stayed at the house of a man I met through the grapevine.

"How was your trip?" he asked.

"Pretty good," I said.

"Did you take a bus from Tel Aviv?"

"Yes, sir," I said.

"Glad you made it safely." He nodded. "They bombed a bus in Tel Aviv last week."

I didn't get a chance to respond.

"That reminds me." He motioned for the stairs. "First things first—let me show you the bomb shelter."

"The *what*?" I asked.

He grinned. "Welcome to Israel."

My host did, indeed, have a bomb shelter. Complete with a gas-proof, metal-covered concrete door, it's similar to what you'll find in most Jewish houses, my host informed me. He claimed they're mandatory, but I never confirmed this statement.

"You said you're from Canada, right?" he asked.

"Yes, sir, born and raised!"

"That's good." He nodded again. "Canada has oil because it supports Israel."

"Say again?"

"Help yourself to whatever's in the fridge."

On the surface my host appeared to be a friendly retiree, but upon closer examination, it became apparent he was a highly affluent, highly paranoid Messianic Jew. He had run a business in America for decades but sold everything just before the 2008 crash, investing heavily in Israeli shekels and Jerusalem real estate. It seems he made the right call—today he claims a net worth of over $5 million.

I opened the fridge. The door rattled with vials of insulin next to Mars bars and cartons of chocolate milk. "Uh, it doesn't look like there's much here."

"Oh, that's right!" He snapped his fingers. "Let's go grocery shopping!"

As we made our way to the bus station, he informed me about who all was Jewish. "Basically everybody important is Jewish," he said. "The Rothschilds, the entire cast of *Seinfeld*. Almost everyone in the banking industry—the Salomon Brothers, Lehman Brothers, Goldman Sachs, Bear Stearns—same for J. P. Morgan and John D. Rockefeller."

I wasn't so sure about those last two. Using JewOrNotJew.com—

which may or may not be accurate in any way—I checked them out. Rockefeller gets a Jew Score of 4 (out of 15). He was a Baptist, after all. And Morgan, though born Jewish, was a lifelong member of the Episcopal church.

Our first stop was a gorgeous little bakery. "This used to be a pizza joint," my host said. He pointed at the old sign. "But it got blown up." I purchased a loaf of bread—*quickly.*

We wandered through the market, stopping for fish and eggs and fresh produce. "So when was the last time this market was blown up?" I joked.

"Oh, it's been about four or five years," he responded.

"That's good!" I replied.

"So I guess we're about due . . . ," he trailed off.

By the time we got home, my host had informed me that President Obama would continue to reign after the conclusion of his second term, that America would fall in the next eighteen months, and that every Jew would flee back to Israel. He calls his kids every day and tries to convince them, and he certainly tried to do the same for me.

Despite my host's constant fear of bombs and his questionable prophetic abilities, the view from my bedroom was unquestionably worth it. I was staying in the Hinnom Valley, directly facing Mount Zion and the City of David, with the Old City of Jerusalem in the background. To the right was Gehenna (the garbage dump and the word often used in the New Testament for "hell"), and beyond that was the Kidron Valley. To the far right were Bethany and the Mount of Olives. Not a bad view at all.

"Prayer is the difference between the best you can do and the best God can do." MARK BATTERSON

Early the next morning, I walked from my host's house to the Old City, the ancient part of Jerusalem where Jesus walked, performed miracles, and was crucified and resurrected. I entered the Old City through the Jaffa Gate, the starting point of the road to the ancient city of Hebron, where Abraham, Isaac, Jacob, and David had lived.

The Old City is split into quarters, with a giant wall around the whole thing. Going counterclockwise from the Jaffa Gate, there's the Armenian Quarter, the Jewish Quarter, the Muslim Quarter, and the Christian Quarter—which is actually around 80 percent Muslim; the rest is a mix of Catholic, Orthodox, and a few mainline Protestant denominations, but not much in the way of evangelicalism.

There are not more than a few thousand residents in each of the three other quarters and well over twenty thousand residents in the Muslim Quarter. I've been told that Muslims can sell their houses in the Old City to other Muslims for around $200,000–$300,000, but Jews will pay $2 million or more. But it's not like they can't afford it—Israeli home buyers are funded by people all over the world who donate in an attempt to reclaim the homeland. This included my host, who paid $2.3 million for his home.

I started in the Armenian Quarter, working my way toward the Zion Gate. I visited an Armenian church with a sign of rules that included no bare bellies, no firearms, no putting hands in pockets, and no crossing your legs. There's not much else to see in the Armenian Quarter—most of the district is taken up by a giant monastery, and the monks aren't much for company.

A tense peace exists in the Old City. Pickpocketing aside, crime and violence are rare. It is the merchants, interestingly, who keep the peace, since bombs are bad for business. Merchants are everywhere, selling food and clothing as well as cheap trinkets and souvenirs from all the predictable places. And they're not afraid of cross-selling religious items. I found booths in both the Muslim and Jewish quarters that sold witty T-shirts that read Guns 'N' Moses; Don't Worry, Be Jewish; and Super-Jew.

The Jewish Quarter is the nicest in the Old City for two reasons.

First, it's the wealthiest. Second, it's quite new, having been bombed to smithereens during the Six-Day War. I sat in Hurva Square and ate a hamburger[1] while I listened to a man playing a guitar on the steps of a synagogue. Suddenly I realized I was humming along to his tune. He was playing "My Way" by Frank Sinatra.

I joined a tour group and visited the Chapel of the Ascension, the spot where Jesus is traditionally believed to have ascended into heaven. We even touched the supposed rock on which He rose, worn smooth from centuries of faithful hands touching the spot. I stood on the rock, but nothing happened. Originally Crusader-built with an open roof, the Chapel of the Ascension now has a domed rock ceiling. It is currently controlled by Muslims. A nearby minaret blasts Muslim prayers five times per day.

I will be honest. At first I was quite angry that a group of Muslims was getting rich by charging faithful Christians five shekels to visit a Christian site. I have no interest in charging Muslims to visit Islamic holy sites. But God changed my heart before I even stepped off Ascension Rock. Maybe this was a great opportunity for Muslims to meet Christians, to regularly interact with people who love Jesus. Can you think of a better way? I silently prayed that this place of ascension would continue to be a place where people are raised to life in Christ. As I exited the little dome, I thanked the Muslim guard.

"Prayers are prophecies. . . . The transcript of your prayers becomes the script of your life." MARK BATTERSON

That afternoon the tour group I joined visited the Church of the Pater Noster. It's a church dedicated to the Lord's Prayer, and it contains the spot where, according to tradition, Jesus taught the prayer to His disciples. For a refresher on the Lord's Prayer, here's Luke 11:1-4:

---

[1] I wanted a cheeseburger, but it wasn't an option on the menu—it's heartbreakingly unkosher. There's an Old Testament law that forbids the cooking of a goat in its mother's milk, and somehow that means you can't put cheese on beef. It might be the greatest (and least tasty) biblical misinterpretation of all time.

One day Jesus was praying in a certain place. When he
finished, one of his disciples said to him, "Lord, teach us to
pray, just as John taught his disciples."

He said to them, "When you pray, say:
"'Father,
hallowed be your name,
your kingdom come.
Give us each day our daily bread.
Forgive us our sins,
for we also forgive everyone who sins against us.
And lead us not into temptation.'"

Matthew's Gospel adds "your will be done, on earth as it is in
heaven" and "but deliver us from the evil one," and Eastern Orthodox
Christians later added the mini-doxology "for thine is the Kingdom,
the power, and the glory, forever and ever, Amen."

Let me proceed with a confession: a few years ago, I decided to
simply obey Jesus. I prayed the "Our Father" three times a day for
about nine weeks straight, and I really made a point of actually meaning the words I was saying. It was the worst two months ever. I felt
like I had opened a Pandora's box and had given God permission to
wreck my comfortable life. I applied for over sixty jobs and got a total
of just three callbacks. I lived in a cold basement room, far from my
family and friends, and I was dead broke. I tried to start a business
but couldn't get it off the ground.

So I stopped praying the Lord's Prayer.

Earlier in my year of living prayerfully, my Jewish sources told me
that some people try to focus for seven seconds on every word in the
Amidah, the Jewish "standing prayer" with nineteen blessings. I tried
this practice with the Lord's Prayer, and it took me more than eight
minutes. I got distracted easily, and the combination of egg timers
and verbs like *art* sent my mind soaring. I decided not to make a habit

of this particular prayer practice. It wasn't helping me connect with God. Strike two for the Lord's Prayer.

And now here I was, at "a certain place." The *very place* where Jesus had taught His disciples to pray. I could feel that, like the disciples, God wanted to teach me how to pray. And I wanted to learn. As I surveyed the church and looked up at the ceiling, I wondered what Jesus might say to me right now about prayer. What would be His first lesson for me? What was I doing wrong? What was I doing right? How should I—a twenty-first-century spiritual descendant of Jesus' disciples—pray?

As I toured the church grounds, I decided to start praying the Lord's Prayer again. I wanted Jesus to teach me to pray, even if it meant being uncomfortable.

The walls of the Church of the Pater Noster contain paintings of the Lord's Prayer in over one hundred languages. Our guide asked our group which languages we could read, and about a dozen people prayed the Lord's Prayer in their native language.

I read it in English. "Father, hallowed be your name, your kingdom come . . ."

I was praying as Jesus had taught us to pray.

"Prayer is not a check request asking for things from God. It is a deposit slip—a way of depositing God's character into our bankrupt souls." DUTCH SHEETS

The next morning I visited the Via Dolorosa, the road upon which, according to tradition, Jesus carried the cross from Pilate's Praetorium to Golgotha and the road that led to the Aedicule—the tomb of Christ.

Sometimes called "The Way of Sorrow" or "The Way of the Cross," it is Christianity's most sacred route. Much to the chagrin of some Christians, the Via Dolorosa starts in the Muslim Quarter. But they really shouldn't be offended—people didn't start walking the route until the Byzantine period, and the route wasn't totally established until sometime around 1342, when the Franciscans took custody of many of Jerusalem's holy places. And the current route didn't appear until the eighteenth century.

Nonetheless, it was a wonderful experience. I walked the Via Dolorosa a number of times, noticing different things each time. I contemplated the torture and murder of Jesus, a political move by the religious elite in a tumultuous time in a city known for upheaval. Even after all these centuries, very little has changed. God's peace remains elusive. The human heart is full of violence. I often struggle against God's Kingdom in my own life.

As I walked along the ancient crucifixion path, I prayed the Lord's Prayer. I also prayed for shalom.[2]

"The disciples, faithful Jews who prayed daily, asked him, 'Teach us to pray.' They sensed something different in the way Jesus approached the Father personally and intimately." PHILIP YANCEY

"Sorry, folks," our guide said, "it doesn't look like we're going to be able to visit the Temple Mount today." The group let out a collective groan.

"Wait," snapped one of the more fiery Jewish women in our group. "Are you telling me that I can't visit the holiest site in the world, in *Israeli-controlled Jerusalem*, because a *bunch of Muslims* are taking a holiday?"

The Temple Mount is pretty important to Judaism for a whole host of reasons: at the center of the mountain is the Foundation Stone of the world (though it's not mentioned in the Bible), where Adam came into being (which is geographically questionable), where the Ark of the Covenant rested (likely), and where the two Temples were built (definitely—one was built by Solomon, the other rebuilt by Herod).

---

2 *Shalom* is a Hebrew word that means peace, prosperity, and blessing. It's like a one-word all-encompassing "props." Jewish people use it as a hello and a good-bye, and it connotes a sense of completeness. It's the best one-word prayer ever.

Jews *and* Christians additionally revere the site because it's where Abraham almost sacrificed Isaac (the hill was formerly known as Mount Moriah). And it was the site where the altar rested in the Holy of Holies.

According to Islamic tradition, Muhammad miraculously traveled over 750 miles from Mecca to Jerusalem one night. There he stood on a rock and was lifted to heaven, where he received his teachings. It was the same rock where Abraham almost sacrificed Isaac.

I looked up at the Temple Mount and thought about the stone that rests under the Dome of the Rock. A thought occurred to me: *What are the chances that of all 1.59629 quadrillion square feet of physical land on planet Earth, three major world religions are literally fighting over one single rock?*

I believe that people are holy because they're made in the image of God, and a place can be holy when God is present—but no place is so holy that it's worth shedding the blood of those who bear the image of God. Hundreds of thousands of people have starved to death within the walls of Jerusalem. At least one hundred thousand have been enslaved. At least one million have been murdered. The city of God is one of the most consistently violent places on earth. As one British fellow in my group said, "I didn't come here to find religion, but this certainly doesn't restore my faith in humanity, either."

I had to agree with him. As I stared up at the giant walls, it suddenly occurred to me: *the Temple lives on.* As Paul reminded the Corinthians, we Christians—individually and collectively—are the new temples of the Holy Spirit. The Kingdom of Heaven wants to rest in our hearts. Now how do I rid my life of the unrest that I see all around me?

"The Western Wall is where the Divine Presence always rests."
A SIGN IN JERUSALEM

I stood at the entrance to the Western Wall, the focus of prayer for Jews all over the world. I surveyed a large square with white plastic chairs and brown wooden pulpits littered about. The wall is a big deal in Jewish circles. Muslims control the Temple Mount, so Jews are relegated to the base of the hulking foundations of the former Temple. They pray, without ceasing, for the restoration of the Temple—*the* place where their sins are forgiven.

There were probably around one thousand people on the men's side when I visited. The women were fenced off to my right, at least four hundred over there. Two big parties were taking place at the fence line—bar mitzvahs. It was like celebrating New Year's Eve in Times Square.

There were Jews of every kind there—folks in all black, others in all white, some with furry box hats, some with black caps. And yes, there was a Jewish cowboy, dressed in red plaid.

No matter the denomination, all were praying toward one thing— the giant rock wall. Measuring 62 feet high and 187 feet long, the huge section of stone comprised less than one-eighth of the retaining wall of Herod's Temple Mount. The original Temple complex must have been absolutely enormous.

My group was told to approach the wall with reverence—to always wear a head covering and to never turn our backs to the wall—to always back away. I grabbed a free yarmulke, compliments of the

Western Wall Heritage Foundation, and made my way into the square.

But despite all the warnings and instructions my group received, the Western Wall wasn't marked by reverence. Many were praying, but just as many were chatting, laughing, and texting. I quickly spotted a Hasidic napper, sleeping on his suit jacket, his hat pulled over his face.

One man, however, stood out more than any other. He was leaning over a

pulpit, with one hand on his head, and his head resting on the wall. He was praying fervently, getting louder and louder. I moved in for a closer look. His prayers reached a fever pitch. And then I realized that he wasn't praying at all.

He was screaming at someone on his cell phone.

"In Gethsemane the holiest of all petitioners prayed three times that a certain cup might pass from Him. It did not. After that the idea that prayer is recommended to us as a sort of infallible gimmick may be dismissed." C. S. LEWIS

Later that afternoon, I crossed the Kidron Valley and joined a walking tour of the Mount of Olives

We passed by the supposed tombs of the prophets Haggai and Malachi on our way to the Mount of Olives, as well as the Jewish cemetery. The guide told us that plots can currently sell for over $1 million each, but they're more likely to fall in the $10,000–$50,000 range—depending on your proximity to a prominent rabbi. But it's worth it either way. If you're buried on the Mount of Olives, apparently you'll be the first to get raised from the dead at the end of days.

We entered the Mount of Olives. The sign was simple: No Shorts.

There weren't many olive trees here anymore—land goes for a premium, and there's a lot more money in the burial business. While more fertile than most other places in the city, it is, like the rest of Jerusalem, still pretty dry. The view from the Mount of Olives that day was quite gray—buildings and cemeteries, mostly.

We visited the garden of Gethsemane. It's also not very big anymore, maybe an acre at most. Stewarded by the nature-loving Franciscans, they use oil from the olive trees in the garden to light the garden's lamps and turn the olive pits into rosary beads. It's a small plot containing white pebble paths and a few dozen trees, including *the* tree where Jesus prayed and sweat drops of blood. Scientists recently discovered that several of the garden's trees are among the oldest known to man. Olive trees typically live for five hundred to eight hundred years, but the church claims that one tree is over two thousand years old—its life prolonged by Jesus' tears.

Christ's tree was an epic, gnarled old giant with an ugly brown fence around it.

My tour group went inside the church while I remained to contemplate whether I should hop the fence to get to the tree. Ruling it out, I meditated on the scene. It's nine o'clock at night. Jesus knows He will be arrested in a few short hours. His disciples fall asleep, but Christ is desperate. He kneels under an olive tree and begs God to let Him escape the horrible torture of crucifixion. He runs back to His disciples. "Please," He begs them. "Please pray with Me. Just one hour. I need you." They roll over. He goes back to the tree. He continues to pray, but now He is freaking out. He cries out to God, begging for mercy. But God isn't answering. Jesus goes back to His disciples. "This is our last hour together," He cries. "Please—let's spend it in prayer together." No dice. He goes back to that olive tree again and continues to pour out His soul. He is under such duress that, despite the chill of the night, Luke notes that Jesus sweats "great drops of blood." The scientific term for the rare occurrence is *hematohidrosis*. Tiny capillaries burst during times of extreme anxiety, causing bloody sweat to ooze from the forehead and fingernails. It's often accompanied by bloodstained tears and serious nosebleeds.

Jesus needed His disciples to pray with Him.

As I stood by that old olive tree, so many questions ran through my mind. *Why didn't Jesus just run away?* He could have crossed the Mount of Olives and escaped to the desert by morning, never to be seen again. *Why didn't His disciples pray with Him?* I knew the answer to that one—because they were just like me. *Why didn't God answer His prayer?*

It is comforting to know that even Jesus didn't get all His prayers answered. I thank God that He didn't answer Jesus' prayer in the garden—otherwise I'd still be on the hook for my own salvation.

Our little group climbed to the Church of Dominus Flevit, the traditional place where Jesus wept over Jerusalem. As the sun set over Mount Zion, a young man in our group asked me, "What do you think Jesus would do if He came back today?"

I looked at him and thought about my time so far in Israel. "I think He would do the exact same thing as last time."

I looked back at the city. Jerusalem is the unhappiest city I have ever visited. Three religions, dozens of languages, frantic pilgrimages—but with iPhones. People pray while smoking, texting, and munching on Doritos. No one smiles. No one is happy. The khaki-panted, Tilley-hatted tour guides direct starry-eyed pilgrim tourists, each looking for a revelation, for an epiphany, for miracles and a touch from God. But the bustling streets are an endless sadness, an exhausting sorrow.

"I think He would weep over Jerusalem."

"A vacant chamber of prayer means that a believer has gone out of business religiously." E. M. BOUNDS

It was nightfall by the time I got back to the Western Wall. I wanted to go by myself, to fulfill an old Jewish prayer tradition. One of the guides had told me that pilgrims will often write a prayer and stuff it in one of the cracks in the wall. Every few days a caretaker collects all the prayers and stuffs them in the next coffin to be buried in the Mount of Olives cemetery. Thus, your prayer becomes an eternal prayer. The tradition has become something of a bucket-list thing to do, and even Pope John Paul II placed a note in the wall.

I wrote my prayer on a piece of paper that was about the size of a quarter. It was a huge prayer, but I write small. I stuffed the prayer in the wall, prayed silently, and then started to back away. I walked backward to about the midpoint of the square. I stood in prayerful silence and reflected on the scene.

Suddenly, a Hasidic rabbi shoved an iPhone into my hands. "Take a picture of me," he demanded. I awkwardly scrambled to take his photograph. He inspected the outcome. "No," he said. "Get another." I complied. He came back. "Try it the other way," he instructed. "Vertical instead of horizontal." I complied. He came back, inspected the photo, and shook his head. "It needs a flash. Get two with a flash." Again, I complied. He came back, inspected the photos, and walked away without a word.

So much for a prayerful moment of reflection.

I walked to the back of the square and sat on a stone bench. I thought about how Jesus was the fulfillment of the law, how He sacrificed Himself so that we could be free. . . .

The rabbi interrupted my thoughts. "Come with me." He motioned. "I need some close-ups."

I looked at my canteen and sweater, which I had placed on the bench beside me. "Leave your canteen," he said impatiently. "No one will steal it." As we walked, I asked him where he was from. "Brooklyn." He grinned.

The rabbi walked me all the way back up to the very front of the

wall. "Just keep shooting," he said as handed me his camera. "I'll tell you when to stop." The rabbi approached the wall and raised his hands in pretend prayer. I wanted to capture the sheer hilarity of the situation, so I took the liberty of capturing the moment on my own camera. I figured twenty for him, one for me.

The rabbi turned around. "Great, now let's get some face shots."

He placed a hand on the wall, closed his eyes, and turned his face toward heaven. I couldn't wipe the grin off my face. "Thanks a million," he said as he walked away briskly. *No, no,* I thought. *Thank* you.

I've since thought about this encounter and how it reflected the reality of Jerusalem. Many people visit Jerusalem in search of answers. It appeared that the rabbi was only in search of snapshots. Rather than praying, he was posing. His quest for the perfect photo added to my growing impression that Jerusalem was a bit of a spiritual sham. It reminded me of how much further I still had to go—because like the rabbi, I'm prone to practice the right poses without pursuing the relationship that should accompany them.

"It was liberating to me to understand that prayer involved a learning process. I was set free to question, to experiment, even to fail, for I knew I was learning." RICHARD J. FOSTER

I wandered around the Old City for eight to ten hours each day for almost a week until I knew it by heart. I enjoyed my few days of bachelorhood—I stayed up late every night and ate tons of hummus. Michelle is an early riser, and she's allergic to chickpeas. I'm such a rebel.

I found all the best and worst hummus and falafel joints, including one not-so-great restaurant that locked me in their bathroom. I went in, closed the door, and then realized there was no handle on the inside. I banged on the door and yelled for a few minutes and eventually heard a guy yelling back in Arabic. I assumed he was saying, "Back away from the door" (which I did), because seconds later he laid a shoulder into the door and smashed it open. I thanked him, and he shrugged like it was a regular occurrence.

I found the comically large tomb of King David. The room was divided by a fence so that the womenfolk wouldn't distract the rabbis, but from what I saw, that wasn't going to happen anyway. One rabbi was praying so intensely he was pouring sweat, even with a fan going full blast.

I found the center of the four quarters of the Old City and prayed a circle around it.

I stumbled into one church, somewhere in the Christian Quarter, I think, and followed a stone staircase deep underground. At the bottom was a big cave and a large pool of water. It was eerie. I ascended the stairs and looked around the church. A friendly pair of church ushers approached me. "Did you get a chance to see the pool?" they asked excitedly.

"Yes." I smiled. "I did indeed."

"That will be twelve shekels," the woman said.

"Pardon?" I responded.

"Twelve shekels," the man explained. "For entering the pool."

"Not a chance," I said.

The woman protested. "But you saw the pool! That's twelve shekels." They showed me the wall-mounted box where I was to deposit the money.

"Show me a sign that says it costs twelve shekels to see the pool," I said and folded my arms.

They didn't have one. "Don't you think it's a little deceptive to invite people to see the pool and *then* charge them for it?" I continued my courtroom examination. "Is this a Christian church?"

"Yes," the woman stammered.

"Well, I don't think this is a very Christlike thing to do," I said. "Do you?" I could see they felt ashamed, and I wanted to save face for them. "If I donate twelve shekels, do you promise to put up a sign?"

"Yes." The man nodded meekly.

I stuffed twelve shekels in the box. Next time I'm in town, I'll let you know if they followed through.

"It's time to quit playing church and start being the church."
KEITH GREEN

A number of Messianic Jews had told me not to visit Bethlehem. None of them had ever been there themselves, but all warned me it was dangerous. Why would Christians not want me to visit the birthplace of our mutual Savior?

Because it's on the Palestinian side of the wall.

I boarded a rather weary bus, driven by a young Muslim Palestinian driver. Our guide was a Palestinian Christian, and it was nice to see that two men of different religions could do business together in peace. Twenty minutes south of Jerusalem, we entered an entirely different world. We stopped at the border checkpoint while a troop of young Israeli soldiers scanned the bus and checked our driver's credentials. We passed through the wall—a twenty-six-foot-high concrete monstrosity, topped with barbed wire and video cameras. The difference, from one side to the other, was stark. Whereas the Israeli side was clean and serene, the Palestinian side looked like a war zone, a total wreck. Rubble and garbage lay strewn about, buildings were crumbling, and the people were obviously held in the grip of poverty.

The Palestinian side of the wall was covered in graffiti, including mottoes like "Make Hummus, Not Walls" and the more sinister "To Exist Is to Resist." There was also a large installation, called Santa's Ghetto, that featured the work of urban street artists like Banksy and many others. One piece of graffiti depicted a giant circular wall surrounded by barren land and tree stumps. Inside the protected circle was a giant Christmas tree and lots of presents.

Our guide, Jabar, attended the Baptist church in Bethlehem. I was surprised there were any Christian churches in Palestine, but Jabar set me straight. "Ah, my friend, you forget Acts 2:11. Arabs were Christians before they were Muslims! It wasn't until AD 640 that they became Muslims. Today Bethlehem is about 85 percent Muslim and 15 percent Christian."

We arrived at the Shepherds' Field, which actually has two claims to fame. The first, and far more famous, is that it is the supposed site where the angels appeared to the shepherds on the night Jesus was born. It's a few miles from Bethlehem, and it's as plausible a site as any in the area. The second is a far more ancient claim to fame. In a generous act of geographical serendipity, it's the traditional site of Boaz's threshing floor, where Ruth snuck in one night and "uncovered his feet"—whatever *that* means.

The field sits within a lovely little walled compound, a sea of green in an ocean of sand. The field is actually more of a forest today, carefully stewarded by those nature-loving Franciscans, of course. We visited the small church that marks the traditional spot of the angelic appearance. In the center of the room is an altar with a large maple leaf on it, and the word *Canada* below. He who donates the goods gets the glory.

After touring the church, we headed to Boaz's threshing floor. We approached the rock entry, surrounded by Nativity lights. As we neared the door, we heard an English voice preaching in an unmistakable Southern drawl. It was a pastor of some sort, telling his small group the story of Ruth and Boaz. As we tried to enter, he literally turned and slammed the metal door shut.

What? How could anyone do that to a fellow Christian? I felt angry and disappointed—we'd spent good money and time to come all this way, and Boaz's cave was kind of a big deal.

As a concession, our guide quickly shuffled us into an overflow cave. It was supposedly an equally ancient cave, but I knew stucco walls when I saw them. We sat there for a few minutes, hoping the pastor would wind down his sermon. Or perhaps meet Jesus.

As we waited, Jabar told us a story. "There once was a man who peeled a banana, threw away the banana, and then ate the peel," he said with satisfaction. We waited for the punch line.

"That's it?" asked another man in our group.

Jabar nodded. "Denominations don't matter. They're just the peel, but we treat them like the fruit. The peel doesn't matter. The only thing that matters is the center—Jesus."

"Wait, Jabar." I grinned. "So what you're saying is—"

He grinned and finished my sentence— "Yes, I suppose I'm saying that Jesus is the banana."

We reboarded the bus and drove to Bethlehem, passing a coffee shop called "Stars & Bucks" on the way.

"O little town of Bethlehem, how still we see thee lie. . . . Yet in thy dark streets shineth the everlasting Light." PHILLIPS BROOKS

While folks today are accustomed to the modern Nativity scene, it's far more accurate to say that Jesus was actually born in a backwoods, rural, small-town, first-century cave barn. As the story goes, there was no room at the "inn," so Mary laid Jesus in a manger—a barnyard feeding trough.

I hadn't expected the cave to be so big, with the ceiling upwards of ten feet in some spots. The cave had been repaired over the millennia, which was to be expected, but it was still sufficiently rough. It was cold and bare and quite mean—it was a bedrock barn, after all. "This was where the animals stayed," our guide explained. "Jesus was actually born near the back." He pointed to a stone wall. "On the other side of that wall."

To reach the other side of that wall, one must enter the Church of the Nativity. It was an incredibly run-down building, in the middle of a much-needed restoration. The Church of the Nativity was a gaudy affair, with shiny baubles strewn about. We patiently waited in line to go down the stairs to the "official" birthplace of Christ.

When we finally reached the front of the line, after about twenty minutes, we could hear yelling from inside the little cave. It was our turn to enter. The actual spot of the birth was marked by a rusty metal star on a marble slab, surrounded by fancy candles and incense burners. I bowed my head to pray. One of the women in our group, a faithful Catholic in her late fifties, attempted to kiss the star. As she knelt, she was lifted to her feet and pushed out the door. I couldn't believe my eyes. We had literally been in the cave for less than ten seconds when a small group of Armenian priests started shoving people out of the birthplace of our Lord so they could perform a ritual prayer. I quickly hopped back to avoid the fray and asked our guide what was going on.

He nodded knowingly. "The Armenians lay claim to a piece of this church, and it entitles them to one hour of private prayer every day." I couldn't believe it. Hundreds of people wait in line every day so that four men can perform a religious routine. It seemed so very undemocratic. And so very un-Christlike.

"Lord, teach us to pray," indeed.

"There is a mighty lot of difference between saying prayers and praying." JOHN G. LAKE

Our final stop in Bethlehem was a delightful bonus—the Milk Grotto. While you won't find the tale of the Milk Grotto anywhere in Scripture, here's how the story goes: Joseph and his family hid in a cave before they escaped to Egypt. At some point in their underground habitation, Mary decided that Jesus needed to be breast-fed. As she finished feeding Jesus, a few drops of milk fell to the floor. The cave, miraculously, turned white.

Over the centuries, women with lactation problems have visited the cave, broken off a chunk of the wall, ground it into powder, and consumed the frothy beverage in hopes of being able to produce more milk.

It gets better.

As time went by, women struggling with infertility started visiting the cave in the desperate hope that Mary's milk might make them mothers.

It gets worse.

Somewhere along the line, some devious monk decided to turn the whole thing into a for-profit business venture.

We entered a small shop with white walls covered with photographs of babies. A large friar with a white beard sat behind a large white desk. In his hand he held a small selection of dime bags filled with white powder, each on sale for a usurious sum. To his right was a table covered with cardboard binders. I opened the first one. Each page contained a thank-you letter from a newly minted mother and a photograph of her newborn milk baby. I looked around. The little room contained thousands and thousands of letters.

After declining to purchase a crack bag of milk powder (for fear of getting stopped at the border and of getting my wife pregnant), I descended the steps into the actual grotto. It was remarkably white, but not as spectacularly white as advertised. Our group got a quick tour, and then people started touching the walls. The cave was pocked with finger holes, worn deep after centuries of swiping.

I found a spot on the low-hanging cave ceiling that seemed rather untouched. I ran my finger along the chalky surface. I looked at the substance on my finger. It looked like powdered milk.

I sniffed it. It *smelled* like powdered milk. I looked both ways and then licked it. It *tasted* like powdered milk. I convinced one of the other young guys in our group to do the same. He agreed.

It was, undoubtedly, the Milk Grotto.

"Lord, teach us to pray."

"He who prays most receives most." ST. ALPHONSUS MARIA DE LIGUORI

King of Kings is a Messianic ministry based in Jerusalem, and they're doing some of the best work in town. They hold their service at five o'clock in the evening because Sunday is a workday in Israel. The first people I met when I arrived at King of Kings were a Finnish couple, which was providential, because Michelle is Finnish.

The congregation hovers somewhere around five hundred, but they have over thirty-five people on staff because they're such an enterprising outfit. They rent the basement and top floor of a mall, and their influence is large. They produce over one hundred conferences each year, distributing a hundred thousand CDs in the process. They run a delicious restaurant, a counseling service, a media school, and a bookstore. They've held concerts with Steve Green and Casting Crowns, and they run the most epic Prayer Tower in the city.

I chatted with a few folks before the service started, and one in particular stood out—mainly because of his striped vintage jacket. "That's a sweet jacket you've got on there." I extended my hand to an elderly gentleman.

"It better be." He grinned. "I've had it for over thirty-five years." John was an engineer from California who had sold everything and moved to Israel for the specific purpose of speaking Bible verses over the Knesset, the Israeli government building. He lived three blocks from the Knesset and prayed at least fifteen hours per week. He also "prayed the news," as he called it. "The news is full of bad news and fear," he told me. "So I watch it, then mute the commercials and pray." He told me that he writes down every prayer. One can only imagine that stack of paper.

The service started, and we took our seats. Ushers passed around iPads for newcomers to register on, which I thought was very trusting. Much to my chagrin, the preacher was a visitor. From Canada. I had come all the way from Canada to hear some sweet Israeli preaching, and I was stuck with a Canuck from back home. Thankfully, I hadn't come for the sermon.

I had come for the Prayer Tower.

ISRAEL

"Persistence purifies our prayers. If I'm not willing to pray for something more than once, it's a whim, not a real desire." RICK WARREN

The Jerusalem Prayer Tower at King of Kings had one of the best views in the city. From it you could view the Israeli Knesset; the supreme court; Ramallah; Judea and Samaria; Amman, Jordan; the mountains of Ammon and Moab; and the Bridge of Strings, also known as the Chords Bridge, at the city's entrance. The church is working toward becoming a 24/7 prayer house.

I attended a "soaking watch," which was far drier than you'd think. Basically, it was a room full of people lying all over the floor on giant body pillows, listening to worship music from an iPhone. It was all so very hippie and cool, which reminded me of Keith Green, and I planned to reenact the setup with friends back home. Rather than the rigid "standing worship" of most churches, there was a freedom to move and relax and connect with God without having to sit in neat little rows.

After I left the soaking watch, I went to the "Healing Pool," which also involved no water. This was the church's name for their healing room. I met a profoundly kind couple with the spiritual gift of healing. Healing is something I knew very little about.

You see, my body doesn't heal. As the years have progressed, I've gained a collection of problems that won't go away—my left ear, left wrist, left foot, neck, lower back, elbows, throat, abdomen, right shoulder, right groin, and stomach are in constant pain. I've seen dozens of specialists, and I have had multiple X-rays, MRIs, EKGs, and CAT scans. I've been discharged from multiple years of chiropractic work, massage therapy, physiotherapy, and acupuncture. Nothing has ever worked.

While I didn't know much about the gift of healing, I knew that I had body pain and that if God wanted to help it, I was open to His touch.

"So how long have you been healing people?" I asked.

"Well, we don't actually heal people," the wife corrected.

59

"God does," the husband interjected.

They were the type of couple who finished each other's sentences, and God had been using them to heal people for over twenty years. There was nothing flashy about their ministry—no fanfare, no private jets, none of the stuff you see on TV. As volunteer intercessors, they had seen hundreds of healings over two decades, ranging from the elimination of diabetes to the disappearance of cancer to the regrowth of fingers. *That's pretty epic,* I thought. It raised my hopes that maybe God could use them to heal me.

We talked and prayed for about twenty minutes, but at the end of it I wasn't healed. "What's your 'shooting percentage' when it comes to healing?" I asked.

They both laughed. "We figure it's been about 50/50 over the years," the wife answered. "But some prayers take a long time to be answered," the husband added. "Sometimes up to ten years."

I prayed my healing wouldn't take that long.

"The early Church didn't have a prayer meeting; the early Church was the prayer meeting. In fact, in the early Church every Christian was a prayer-meeting Christian." ARMIN GESSWEIN

That night I went out for dinner with a lovely couple named Mary and Joseph, whom I had met through a mutual Messianic friend. We hit it off right away, especially after the husband told a joke about "Cheeses of Nazareth."

"So, how's your time been in Jerusalem?" Mary asked.

"Did you rent a cross?" Joseph joked.

"Wait, what?" I sputtered. "That's a *thing?*"

"Oh yes," he continued. "The rent-a-cross business is a big money-maker here. People pay forty or fifty bucks to carry an olive-wood cross down the Via Dolorosa."

I hadn't heard of this practice, but it didn't surprise me. I shook my head. *Anything for a buck.* We dug into plates of food that I couldn't pronounce and hadn't seen before.

"I have a question," I asked. "I know that Muslims pray five times a day, but why do they blare it on the loudspeakers all over the city? Isn't prayer supposed to be a private affair?"

"Political reasons," Mary said, shaking her head. "It's ridiculous, really, but I wonder what would happen if Christians prayed five times per day. Maybe we should use their broadcasts as a reminder!"

It wasn't a bad idea. If Muslims could pray five times per day without fail, surely people in love with their Savior could do the same.

"Where did you say you were from?" Mary asked. "Is your background Jewish?"

I laughed and thought back to Brooklyn. "Nope," I said. "Just a good old Canadian."

"There's a future call on Canada to be a healing of the nations," Joseph said.

"Why's that?" I asked.

"It's just a sense I get," he replied. "You know, Canada is the only flag with a leaf on it, and it always reminds me of the verse in Psalm 1 about a tree planted by streams of water, who yields its fruit in season and whose *leaf* doesn't wither. . . . Maybe I'm wrong, but who knows?"

God knew, we all agreed.

"I have another question," I said. "I don't want to sound rude or anything, but it seems like Jerusalem is full of crazy people."

"Research *Jerusalem Syndrome*," Joseph said and gave me a large nod of understanding. "Look it up. People come here from all over the world, and then religion 'takes over.' They become Moses or Jesus or Muhammad. We have an entire hospital just for people like that."

But it was more than just certifiably disturbed people that occupied the city. It was as though all the most fundamentalist people of all three religions had descended upon the Old City, leaving no room for even simple things like politeness and common courtesy. There was no love in the city of God. There was an inbred contempt for any version of humanity not identical to their own. But what good is faith if it causes pain for another? What good is religion if it does no good? What good is any belief that leads to hate?

If someone's faith is true, they should let their god decide the fate of the unbeliever. Must we play God? Can't God defend Himself? A man of true faith should never kill for his belief, but he should certainly be willing to die for it. That's what set Jesus apart. He loved His oppressors, prayed for His detractors, forgave His torturers, and died for His enemies. If there's ever been a real God on earth, my money is on Jesus of Nazareth.

"Are the things you are living for worth Christ dying for?"
LEONARD RAVENHILL

If you exit the Old City from the Damascus Gate and head north on Derech Shchem Street past a big construction mess, you'll soon come to a small sign on your right marked "The Garden Tomb." Whereas the Church of the Holy Sepulchre is the traditional (albeit gaudy and religious) site of Christ's crucifixion and burial, the Garden Tomb is what most people would hope the historic site looks like.

Discovered in 1867, the same year that Canada became a nation, it's a parklike oasis surrounded by a big stone wall. It's managed by the British-based Garden Tomb (Jerusalem) Association.

It seemed like one of the only sane places in Jerusalem. Unlike most of the town, they made very few absolute claims.

My tour guide's name was David, a kindly British volunteer in his early sixties. He and his wife live on the property, receiving free housing and a small stipend in exchange for giving people tours all day.

He had a ceaseless smile and a very winsome way, and he never tried to convince anyone of anything. He gave us a tour, explaining what each thing may have possibly been, always saying "perhaps" or "maybe."

Whereas the Church of the Holy Sepulchre has been considered the traditional site since the fourth century, the Garden Tomb has a number of factors that make it an equally solid contender.

First, it's outside the walls of Jerusalem. It's near a gate and on an ancient road, which was a typical place to crucify people—crucifixion was meant to be a crime deterrent, and the Romans wanted everyone to see.

Second, the Bible mentions that there was a garden nearby. The Garden Tomb complex contains an ancient winepress, suggesting nearby agriculture.

Third is the matter of Golgotha, "the place of the skull." No such thing can be found at the Church of the Holy Sepulchre, but a creative eye can easily spot one from the Garden Tomb. It's not actually on the property—it sits behind the parking lot of a Muslim bus company. Two minarets are in sight, and there's a Muslim cemetery on top. Whereas the focal point of most skulls is the cranium, the most distinct feature of the Golgotha skull are the eyes and nose. I've included a photograph, and I leave it up to you to determine whether or not this is *the* skull.

Last, but certainly not least, is the presence of an actual ancient rock-cut tomb. A small entry has been carved into a large rock face, and there's a trough in which a stone could theoretically sit to be rolled in front of an occupied tomb. The guide explained that, in biblical times, people weren't actually buried in tombs. Bodies were basically placed in tombs to rot for a few years before their bones were collected and placed in a small box called an *ossuary*. Thus, a tomb could be used again and again.

I went inside the tomb, which contained two small rooms, maybe one hundred square feet in total. The first room as I entered was a preparation room, where bodies would be prepared for burial. The second room, to my right, was where the body of Christ was possibly placed on top of a rock table. The tabletop was missing now, and there was a worn white gate that protected the room, but you got a fairly good idea of the scene. I paused in prayer and thanked God for the miracle of resurrection, that what was dead could be made new. True transformation could happen. It wasn't just a hope that was enacted in a religious washing ritual. Soul transformation was real, and I prayed it would occur in me.

"Is this the place of Jesus's crucifixion and resurrection?" asked the guide. "I don't know for sure. But what I do know, for sure, is this: Jesus died for my sins, conquered death, and is coming again. The spot where Jesus died really doesn't matter. What matters is that His Spirit is still alive, in my heart."

As I left Jerusalem, I couldn't shake the deep sadness that had taken residence in my soul. The Holy Land was anything but. It was a crass mix of commercialism, political maneuvering, and religious infighting. It was exactly the environment in which Jesus turned over the tables of the money changers, and it was exactly the environment in which Jesus was crucified. Not that Jerusalem had been all bad—it was there that I fell in love with the Lord's Prayer and that I came to appreciate my faith's Jewish roots and to further understand where our paths diverged. It was there that my Lord and Savior lived and died.

As my time drew to a close, I reflected on the prayer I had placed within the Western Wall: *"Peace in Jerusalem. Peace in the world. Peace in my heart. Shalom."*

Shalom is the prayer I placed in the Western Wall, and shalom is the medicine I'd prescribe for Jerusalem—a deep, God-breathed indwelling of peace and prosperity and blessing. An end to the unrest and a sense of wholeness is what the Holy City needs. It's what the Middle East needs. It's what I need.

CHAPTER 4

Mount Athos, Greece

"ARE YOU GOING TO MOUNT ATHOS?" I asked the bearded monk in the all-black robe at the bus stop.

"Of course." He smiled.

"Great—me, too!" I gushed. "How long have you lived there?"

"Thirteen years."

"May I ask why?"

"Why?" He laughed. "Why *not*? Where else would I want to live? Maybe Jerusalem."

"Trust me," I told him, "Greece has better weather."

I had left Jerusalem the previous day and turned my prayerful attention from Judaism to focus on another stream of the Judeo-Christian faith tradition—Greek Orthodoxy. While Judaism is where all Christian roots originate, Greek Orthodoxy is the most ancient surviving "strand" that links us to early Christianity. At least that's what the Orthodox will tell you. Catholics assert that the line of popes stretches all the way back to Jesus' disciple Peter, and Protestants are happy to report that we stuck it to both traditions.

The mecca for Greek Orthodoxy is Mount Athos, an autonomous polity on the Chalcidice Peninsula in Greece, surrounded by the Aegean Sea. According to Homer, it was the home of the Greek gods before they moved to Mount Olympus. At one point in history, Athos was home to forty monasteries and over twenty thousand monks. Today the number hovers around twenty monasteries, hundreds of *sketes* and hermitages, and around two thousand monks in total.

And no womenfolk. For over one thousand years, women have been forbidden from visiting the mountain. Even female animals are forbidden, with one exception—cats. Rodent problems, you see.

I first learned about Greek Orthodoxy in the best possible manner—while attending a big, fat Greek wedding. My wife's childhood friend Heather was getting married, and I was obliged to attend.

By some stroke of chance (or divine appointment), I was seated at a table with three of the groomsmen—all former Greek Orthodox monks. Over the course of our four-hour dinner, I peppered them with questions about their former life as celibate servants of the Most High. I was hooked. The idea of monasticism (minus the celibacy) really appeals to me, and the notion of a manly, all-dudes mountain proved irresistible. No technology, no advertising, no relational struggle. Just a rustic retreat from the rushing world. What a place to connect with God!

The groom himself, Father Philotheos,[1] was also a former Orthodox monk. To his knowledge, he's the only former monk to be ordained as a priest in North America. It was something of a scandal for the monastery, but the groom was certain of his calling. It was to

---

[1] His name literally means "friend of God."

him that I turned for advice in preparation for a trip to Orthodoxy's most holy mountain.

We met for chicken wings at Father Philotheos and Heather's house in Ontario, and he was, predictably, giddy about the idea. He asked—practically begged—his wife if he could go with me, but she gently yet strictly forbade it. Heather knew that if she let him go, he might never return. Despite my best attempts to promise to bring him back, she knew it was too risky. One could say that the Holy Mountain is his greatest temptation.

Greek Orthodoxy has some interesting marriage rules—people are allowed to marry up to three times. The old saying is that the Orthodox Church "blesses the first marriage, performs the second, tolerates the third, and forbids the fourth." The church also permits divorce for the sake of *theosis*—union with God—so long as the spouse agrees. Which Heather will (rightfully) never do.

Father Philotheos and I wrote back and forth for many weeks before my departure, and he made it quite clear I was in well over my head. On top of his practical advice, I loved the reverence with which he approached the subject of prayer. In one e mail he wrote, "The Orthodox monks consider prayer to be *the art of arts, and science of sciences*."

I was about to get schooled.

Michelle, for her part, took my decision to visit Athos in stride. While many women might be mad or jealous that their husband was about to spend a few sun-soaked days on the Aegean Sea without them, Michelle kept the proper perspective. "You do what you need to do," she said. "I have no interest in hanging out with thousands of bearded men. And I bet the food will be terrible."

Not that she would eat any better—I do all the cooking, and she was holed up at a friend's place in California, house-sitting.

Just ten non-Orthodox are allowed on Athos at any given time. Hermits have lived on Athos since the seventh century, and women have been forbidden since AD 1060. From what I can tell, some monks got in trouble for cavorting with women, which would suggest that perhaps it was the men who should have been given the boot.

Regardless, women can't go within five hundred meters of the republic. Yellow signs on the shoreline shoo away female "intruders." Since Greece joined the European Union, there has been pressure to allow women to visit, but I'm more of the opinion that they should just create a woman-only island and then separate from the EU altogether.

It's important to note that "the man mountain," as my friend Beth calls it, isn't actually antiwoman. On the contrary, the peninsula exists to venerate one very special woman: Mary, mother of Jesus. Though not recorded in Scripture (or pretty much anywhere else), Orthodox monks believe that the perpetually virgin Mary traveled to Athos in her old age. In the year AD 49, she decided to visit Lazarus in Cyprus, but her boat was blown off course. As she stepped foot on the shores of Mount Athos, all the ancient idols and statues crashed to the ground.[2]

"My sword I give to him that shall succeed me in my pilgrimage, and my courage and skill to him that can get it." JOHN BUNYAN

The bus arrived in Ouranopolis, which should immediately be renamed *Mantown*. I don't know why it came as a surprise, but I hadn't expected such a male-dominated metropolis. The city was relatively quiet, but small groups of men were everywhere—the hotels, the street corners, the restaurants. Mostly Zorba types, they were friendly and relaxed.

It was dark by the time I arrived, but I felt safe. Ouranopolis is the kind of town where people don't lock their doors. Many don't even bother to shut them. Someone left their suitcase at the bus stop, and it sat there all night until its owner claimed it the next morning. I walked by a closed restaurant that had left dozens of bottles of wine

---

2 There was an earthquake in Greece in AD 49.

on display. The only sounds were the crashing waves and the occasional dog bark. Truly, God was in this place.

I was booked to stay at two monasteries for one night each. My criteria for choosing these monasteries were, I admit, quite shallow. I chose the oldest and the richest.

To book a stay was a complicated process. I had to get a fax machine. Yes, that's how far behind the monks of Athos are—you have to fax them your reservation requests. Since I was on the road for most of the year, rather than buy a physical fax machine, I signed up for an online fax service at the rather repulsive rate of $14.99 per month. I canceled the plan two months later.

The friendly monk at the bus stop directed me to my hotel. The front door was wide open. Keys hung on a board, a laptop rested on the counter, and no one was in sight. I found the hotel owner on the patio, drinking wine while getting his hair cut by a mobile barber. He reluctantly got up to check me in. There weren't any Gideon Bibles in the room, but there were Bible verses and paintings of Jesus on the wall. I got a map of the town—which, it turned out, was little more than a bend in the road—and made my way "downtown."

I went to scout out the visa office. In the morning I would return here to pick up my *diamonitirion*, the visa that would allow me to stay on the mountain.

The monasteries each have their own set of rules, in addition to peninsula-wide rules such as "No scuba diving." Oddly enough, you're not allowed to fish with a rod or swim at many of the monasteries, but you can spearfish to your heart's content.

I spotted a sign on the wall containing photos of men in various states of dress. From what I gathered, the rules that had to be followed on Mount Athos were no tank tops, no shorts, no khakis, no tracksuits, no earrings, no sandals without socks, possibly no fat people, and definitely no women and no nudists.

Duly noted.

"God loves us more than a father, mother, friend, or any else could love, and even more than we are able to love ourselves."

ST. JOHN CHRYSOSTOM

I awoke to a beautiful sunrise over the ocean. I had been instructed to pick up my visa at 7:30 and board the 9:45 ferry. I hurried down to the visa office shortly before the appointed time. I joined the line of around one hundred men, a cloud of cigarette smoke hovering above their collective heads. The door to the visa office opened, and a man informed the crowd that the ferry would be delayed due to poor weather. We all turned toward the ocean-blue sky. Not a cloud in sight.

I waited for three and a half hours to get moving. Around eleven o'clock, Marko—a Serbian man who was seeking healing for his son on Mount Athos—approached me. "We missed the ferry," Marko said. "But I think we can catch a private speedy boat." *Speedy boat.* I liked that. We bought our visas, sprinted to the dock, and were the last to board.

We passed enormous monasteries as we cruised along the south side of the peninsula. The hills were marked by tiny *sketes*, the woodland homes of hundreds of solitary hermits. We arrived at the Port of Dafni, which is just a block of concrete with one hundred men on top.

I stood on the pier, surrounded by noise and confusion, not knowing what to do. Suddenly, my ear caught the word *Karyes*, and I ran to the monk from whose mouth the word had come. Without saying a word, I paid him five euros and hopped in his van.

The van climbed higher and higher, on a mix of dirt road straightaways, cobblestone corners, and brand-new concrete switchbacks. There were no stop signs anywhere, no traffic lights, no guardrails, and no speed limits. Bring on the bacon—this was a man's paradise.

The monk driver switched on a CB radio. I assumed he would play something manly, but he tuned in to an Orthodox prayer program so he wouldn't miss a moment of monastery life. As we climbed, I spotted Mount Athos for the first time. Its sheer hulk was incredibly impressive, far better than any photograph I had seen. In ancient mythology, the mountain was the seat of Zeus.[3] Athos rose like Mount Doom from the water's edge to the clouds, the peak rarely visible to the mere mortals below.

"The monk in hiding himself from the world becomes . . . not less of a person, but more of a person, more truly and perfectly himself: for his personality and individuality are perfected in their true order . . . of union with God." THOMAS MERTON

We arrived in Karyes, the New York City of Mount Athos. Population 233, all dudes, it is basically a handful of streets that constitute the center of the peninsula. Here, men do all the cleaning, cooking, and washing. The flagstone main square consists of an empty parking lot and a male-only public bathroom, which smells horrible. The town seems very old and very quiet. Above all it seems tired, in need of lots of work. Piles of debris hide behind many of the buildings, and the buildings themselves are in various states of disrepair. Everything needs a woman's touch.

From what I could tell, loitering was practically encouraged. Too much movement was met with suspicion. I sat down against a wall and began journaling. *The monks walk around like they own the place—which, of course, they do.*

Karyes was an excellent town for people watching. More specifically, for dude watching. The gun-free police spent more time praying and drinking espresso than investigating crimes or giving out traffic tickets.

---

[3] To get an idea, Google image search The Colossus of Mount Athos, Macedonia, by Dinocrates, the architect of Alexander the Great. It's pretty ridiculous.

Four young monks went singing from store to store, and I assumed it was so the workers wouldn't lose the spirit of prayer. It turned out it was a daily shakedown for tips, which the shop owners reluctantly paid. Protection money, in a way.

A portly hobbit-sized fellow named Larry approached me and immediately started chatting in a cheery British accent. "I live in England, but I was born in Greece. I'm Orthodox, and I've been here eleven times," he informed me. "And I've walked the whole thing twice." I was impressed.

Some days he had to walk for ten straight hours. His excitement was so palpable I couldn't help but grin. "And then I visited a monastery that contains a piece of Christ's cross," he told me. "The largest piece in the world." He told me about his visit to the monastery that held the gifts of the magi—the original gold, frankincense, and myrrh. He also mentioned something about a piece of a saint's forehead, but I was too weirded out to ask for more details. He held up a clanging bag of spoons and cups and pots and pans. "I've brought my utensils for a blessing!"

I asked Larry about the hermits. "They're all over the place." He waved his hand toward the mountain. "Some live in caves and forage for food. All they do is pray. Some say there are just seven to nine truly holy monks on Mount Athos, who only talk to God. Some say the angels feed them, and when they die, no one knows because they simply disappear."

Interesting.

"There was one monk, they say, who was completely naked except for a massive beard," Larry continued. "And he was so much like the angels that he grew feathers."

I immediately had a brilliant movie idea: Paul Rudd plays a Greek American chef who visits Athos and goes undercover as a monk-cook in order to find the father who abandoned him as a child. After spicing up the bland food, he eventually discovers his feathery hermit father, who will be played by a naked (but mercifully bearded) Will Ferrell.[4]

I said good-bye to Larry and wandered into the corner store. Among other things, the store stocked camping stoves, Red Bull, and panini presses. I wrote a postcard to my Greek friend Richard,[5] stocked up on vitamin C, and checked the timetable on the bus station window.

The bus to the monastery left at a set time every day, unless it was full, in which case it would leave early. If it was not full, it would wait until it was full and could end up being very late, if not postponed until the next day. "Hurry up and wait" was the name of the game on Athos, and it was starting to get to me. I had started my day at seven thirty, and I wouldn't arrive at the monastery until three thirty. In total, I had traveled maybe twenty miles.

At least I didn't have to walk.

I waited a few more hours, and eventually got into a large white van. I was finally on my way to Great Lavra, the oldest and most powerful of the Greek Orthodox monasteries.

"In all the paths that men walk in in the world, they do not attain peace until they draw nigh to hope in God." ST. ISAAC THE SYRIAN

I got off the bus at Lavra along with Larry the Hobbit, Marko the Serbian and his son, and a dozen other Orthodox men.

Situated high above the water, overlooking the gorgeous Aegean, Lavra occupies a commanding spot near the southeast tip of the peninsula. Built by Athanasius the Athonite in 963, it's the oldest monastery on Athos.

We entered through a pair of thick red metal doors into a world so positively medieval I was giddy with excitement. Everything was made

---

[4] Producers: I'm available to write the script. Call me.
[5] The postal system is a miracle. I didn't know his postal code or house number, so I just wrote his name, street, and city. For about sixty cents, it somehow landed at the right place.

of stone—the walls, the ceilings, the floors. We entered the receiving room. A tiny monk scurried in, carrying a large silver tray. We were greeted with Turkish coffee, shots of ouzo, and Turkish delight. He toasted our arrival and then quickly got to work on the rules.

"The gates close at sunset," the monk explained. "So you'll definitely want to be inside by then." He didn't speak English, so I relied on body language and a few whispers from Larry. "Silence is enforced from sundown to sunrise, so please be considerate." Bells started ringing. We hastily signed the guest book and went directly to the Katholikon, the monastery's church building, for prayer.

The Katholikon was very dark—no artificial light, just a few candles and a gas barrel stove. It took a few minutes for my eyes to adjust. The monks were seated in little mini-pew stalls with built-in elbow rests. I went to take a seat, but a bossy monk pushed me back to my feet and pointed to another seat farther away. He wanted the extra elbow room.

I found another seat and tried to settle in, but two minutes later he hissed at me to stand, and I complied. A friendlier monk motioned that I could ignore the grumpy monk henceforth.

The room itself was very old and very gaudy. Brass and copper and silver and gold adorned all the instruments, icons, and candles. Peeling paintings clung to the walls. The Katholikon is where Athanasius died, along with six other workers, when one of the domes collapsed during construction. I prayed no one else would be crushed by the crumbling building.

Most of the monks prayed quietly but aloud, a hum filling the room. A few monks took to reading prayers and Scriptures. They repeated one phrase hundreds and hundreds of times: *Kyrie eleison*. I didn't know what it meant, but I could tell it was important. I wrote it down and made a note to look it up when I got home.

A monk walked past, swinging a glowing incense pot. Sparks and coals fell to the floor. It was a miracle no robes went up in flames.

"Do not forsake prayer, for just as the body becomes weak when it is deprived of food, so also the soul when it is deprived of prayer."
ST. GENNADIUS OF CONSTANTINOPLE

Leaving the Katholikon, all the monks congregated in the courtyard outside the chapel. Pilgrims who had previously visited Lavra greeted those they knew. It was like an old boys' club but without the politics and financial schemes.

A monk hammered on a plank of wood with a wooden mallet. Bells for church, wood for dinner.

We lined up in rows and entered the dining hall. Marko informed me that breakfast and dinner were served four days per week at Lavra. Monday, Thursday, and Friday were dinner only.

Despite the lack of meals, most of the monks looked quite similar—not unlike portly penguins. Average weight: 250 pounds. Average age: sixty-eight. Average beard length: seven inches. All the monks had long hair.

We took our seats around ancient gray-and-white marble tables, which reminded me of Aslan's stone table. Each table had built-in stone benches, mercifully covered with wooden planks to ward off the cold, which my mother affectionately calls "numb bum." We sat in semicircles, eight men per table.

Dinner was already on the table when we arrived. Judging by the temperature, it had been sitting there for quite a while. Each metal plate contained five to six chunks of oily potato, a piece of bony fish, and a bowl of chopped lettuce. Not salad—plain lettuce. In the middle of each table was a basket of rock-hard bread and a bowl of oranges and lemons. I glanced around the table. From the looks on their faces, it was obvious which men hadn't prepared for this experience.

A monk prayed, and we were seated. The fifty-odd monks quickly dug into their dinner, but the pilgrims proceeded slowly. We ate the meal in silence while a monk read Bible verses. You had to rely on hand signals to get what you needed, but there was really no way to say, "Don't drink the wine—it tastes like jet fuel."

The food wasn't all bad, however. The oranges were fantastic. I saw a monk drink a beer, and another squeezed mustard onto his crusty bread. They must have said extra prayers.

About nine minutes later, a small bell rang. The abbot stood, as did everyone else, and the meal was over. This was the reason the monks ate so quickly—when the abbot was finished, everyone was finished, whether they liked it or not. A faithful monk dropped a half-peeled orange. A pilgrim tried to nab an apple off another table and was scolded by a bearded brother.

"Although the body becomes exhausted and wants to lie down on a bed, even while lying in bed the soul longs for the Lord."
ST. SILOUAN THE ATHONITE

After dinner I had a few minutes to explore the surroundings. Around the monastery were a handful of little fountains with animal spouts. I found a bull, a goat, and a rooster, but oddly no fish.

I learned that the little monk who had welcomed us *did*, in fact, speak English, and he told me about common life at Lavra. "Monks pray from 3:30 until 8:00 a.m.," he said. "And then from 2:30 to 4:30 p.m. and then 7:00 to 8:00 p.m. most days. Work goes from 8:00 a.m. to 2:30 p.m., and then again after dinner. Some fathers who work in the church don't work after dinner, because they get up at two o'clock to prepare for service."

"What time do they go to bed?" I asked.

"We are usually in bed by eight o'clock in wintertime and ten o'clock in the summer."

"So when do you sleep?" I asked.

"In another life!" He smiled.

I continued my walk around the grounds. Many of the monasteries run some sort of business, and here I spotted olive groves and beehives, which I avoided. For these monks, the life of prayer was not an easy road. Prayer at 3:30 each morning can't be a picnic. And, from where I stood, it looked like it involved a lot of waiting around.

I stood at a fair distance and looked up at Lavra. Around the top of the walls were little wooden additions, perched precariously on wooden stilts jammed into the stone walls.

Great Lavra had traditionally been the most powerful monastery, and it was the oldest, but it was crumbling. Two construction cranes stood near the wall, and judging from a dated photo I had seen, the cranes had been standing there for at least six years.

"It's such a shame," said a man as he came up to me. "These buildings were once the pride of Greece." I greeted the two men who had approached me. "I am Marcos, and this is Nikos." We shook hands. "Nice to meet you."

It turned out the two men were posing as pilgrims but were actually undercover engineers working on a proposal to strengthen the structures. Sneaky fellows. "We don't want one of these beautiful buildings to collapse and kill anyone," Marcos explained. "We want them to last another thousand years."

"When we bravely and quietly endure the afflictions sent to us, we participate a little, albeit not fully, in the sufferings of Christ."
ST. MACARIUS OF OPTINA

We checked into our rooms as the sun went down. Each room contained eight wooden beds with a firm mattress, a small pillow, and a pair of slippers. There were no towels, because no one showered—making Lavra the manliest, nastiest hostel ever.

I'd heard a rumor that many monasteries actually forbid bathing, but I've been unable to confirm or deny it. More than likely, providing water for hundreds of people each day proves an immense challenge, especially at the monasteries that don't even have electricity. Lavra, however, did have electricity, and I managed to find a single shower stall. It was dry as a stone and remained that way for the duration of my stay.

Although my room contained eight beds, only two of us occupied it—we were the only non-Orthodox pilgrims. People had said the accommodations were Spartan, but I rather liked the firm beds and small pillows. As the monk mentioned earlier, silence was requested from sundown to sunrise. It was six fifteen when I turned in for the night.

Sadly, no one *enforced* the silence-after-sunset rule. A small group of pilgrims stayed up for hours, talking and smoking just outside my door. I wanted to toss them into the Aegean, but alas, it was against the rules.

In addition to this disturbance, my fellow occupant took three phone calls throughout the night and went out for four smoke breaks. He evidently came from a part of the world without doors—he wasn't familiar with the concept of push-button door handles and knocked each time to get back in.

Lastly, there was a mouse in the room.

Mercifully, the man in the room, the mouse on the floor, and the men in the hall all retired to bed shortly past midnight. I didn't know how they would be able to function during prayer the next morning. We had to be in church by three thirty.

Upon waking just three hours later, it immediately became apparent how the men had planned to get through morning prayers. They slept right through them.

At three thirty, I was the only pilgrim in attendance at the church, along with just six monks. By four o'clock, there were ten monks. When I left, there were only twelve monks in attendance—not a single Orthodox pilgrim had bothered to show up. I wasn't mad—I was too tired to think straight. I don't drink coffee or tea, so I need about nine hours of sleep each night (in this life) to fully function. Mix the lack of sleep with incense and echoes, and it was all Greek to me.

Still, it was great to spend time in a place that felt so holy. Perhaps I was just romanticizing the centuries of tradition. Or maybe all those prayers had left a spiritual residue. For some reason, time flies in an Orthodox sanctuary. Each hour and each half hour passed quickly, and I could only imagine how easily years on Athos could become a blur. I didn't speak Greek, so I couldn't follow any of the monks' prayers. As a non-Orthodox pilgrim, I was largely left to myself, able to pray as I saw fit. I took time to pray for those I loved and to meditate on the Lord's Prayer. "Father, hallowed be your name, your kingdom come . . ."

I was starting to mean it again.

"Give thanks to God for everything. Try to be manly."   ELDER PAISIOS

It was still dark when the bus arrived later that morning. We boarded quickly and then sat there for thirty minutes. Hurry up and wait.

As we bounced back toward Karyes, Larry the Hobbit had an idea. "Excuse me, driver," he asked in Greek. "Can we stop at the Spring of St. Athanasius?" Everyone cheered in agreement.

The Spring of St. Athanasius was created after Athanasius performed the Moses-style miracle of cracking his stick on a wall of stone so hard that it opened up a five-foot-high and three-foot-wide hole in the rock—quite the impressive blow. The water was refreshing, but as the son of a former Culligan Man with a keen sense of taste, I can tell you there was a little too much algae to make it a salable product. Nevertheless, many of the men filled multiple bottles.

We reached Karyes, and I headed back to my favorite sitting spot, where I met a kindly man named Emmanuel. "I was baptized Orthodox," he told me. "But I walked away from God for forty years. I immersed myself in politics and philosophy, but I was alone and empty inside."

"So how did you come back to faith?" I asked.

"One day I started thinking about the seven mysteries, and that was it," Emmanuel explained. "I came back to God, and I've never been alone since!"

The seven holy mysteries are the sacraments of the Orthodox Church—the way in which humans participate in God's grace. The seven mysteries are Baptism, Chrismation (baptism of the Holy Spirit), Eucharist, Confession, Holy Unction (healing with oil), Marriage, and Ordination.

It was a beautiful list, and I thought about these mysteries—until my thoughts were interrupted by the unmistakable sound of digital chirping. Someone was playing Angry Birds.

My stay at Lavra hadn't been the *Wild at Heart* experience I had expected. I summarized it in my journal: *I thought Athos would be more rugged. Alas, cell reception is strong here.*

"I will go back to the monastery, for patience and the help of God are necessary everywhere!" ANCIENT PATERICON

In the 1980s, Vatopedi was virtually abandoned. As Michael Lewis puts it, the monastery "was a complete ruin—a rubble of stones overrun with rats." Today, under the brilliant guidance of Father Ephraim, Vatopedi is the richest monastery on Athos.

The monastery is located near the water, but it is more of a sprawl-

ing complex of buildings than a single block. There are thirty-seven chapels within the monastery's wall. They even have their own private cove and seaport.

I arrived at the Guest Services Center shortly after three o'clock in the afternoon and spotted Larry the Hobbit.

"Hello again!" I said.

"Why, hello there!" He smiled. "Nice to see you again."

I took a seat beside him. "Larry," I whispered, "where does Vatopedi get their money?"

"Olive oil," he whispered back. "And Russian billionaires."

He wasn't far off. The Orthodox Church is the largest landowner in Greece, and the monasteries are particularly well-endowed. A recent investigation suggests that Vatopedi has been running a real estate swap scam for the past ten years, and some economists think they're partially responsible for bringing down the Greek government. Lawsuits are pending.

I looked around the room. The color red dominated the exterior color scheme, but yellow was the name of the game inside. The steward arrived with a silver tray containing shots of ouzo and various flavors of Turkish delight. I asked a number of people why the monasteries serve Turkish delight instead of some Russian or Greek delicacy, but no one knew.

There was a bit of a commotion. One of the pilgrims, a Quebecois, got ushered out of the room. Rumors circulated immediately. "He snuck onto the island," one man whispered. I was tempted to remind him that this was a peninsula, not an island, but I let it slide. The pilgrim returned a few minutes later wearing different clothing. He had been caught in track pants and flip-flops. Sinner.

We waited for almost an hour to be assigned room keys. Unlike Lavra, Vatopedi didn't separate Orthodox from non-Orthodox. I didn't mind. By that point I'd crossed paths with many of the other pilgrims, and they were mostly good dudes. I was assigned to the same room as Larry the Hobbit, along with five others.

We were on the fifth floor, in the attic. It might as well have been the tenth. I counted seventy-six steps in total. Most of the guys were huffing and puffing. I was one of them.

The room had eight beds. The attic was under renovations, and I could hear a Skil saw buzzing down the hallway. Everything smelled like varnish.

I heard someone knock on wood. Dinner time. I prayed it was edible.

We made our way down to the courtyard. The monks were a bit thinner and much younger than those at Lavra, with marvelous plumage—the longest beards by far. We entered the dining hall. Vatopedi's tables were also stone semicircles. Dinner was served communally from a giant pot instead of individually plated as at Lavra. The menu? Raw onions and tomatoes, eaten like apples. And lentil soup.

We all thanked God for the lentil soup.

We marched directly from the dining hall to the sanctuary. I looked around the room. There were at least eighty monks and thirty pilgrims present. Lots of them were walking around. It looked like they'd added some movement to their prayers, like spiritual circuit training. They rotated from station to station, kissing icons, lighting candles, standing, kneeling, sitting, bowing. I liked it. As a non-Orthodox, I wasn't allowed to join in the main service in the "holy of holies," so I hung back. The service let out in just thirty minutes.

A young monk approached me. "Are you the Canadian, then?" he asked in an unmistakable Australian accent.

I grinned and shook his hand. "An English-speaking monk!" I said. "Nice to finally meet you!" Despite the interactions I've written about, I had spent most of my time on Athos either not understanding what was said or in silence. Meeting another English speaker—and especially a monk—was refreshing.

He laughed. "There are at least three of us here. Would you like a tour?"

The monk's name was Terry, and he was indeed from Australia. He was in his early thirties, and he'd already been there for over twelve years. His English was fraying at the edges.

"There are over 120 monks here now," Terry said. "Twenty-five years ago, there were only three, but Father Ephraim is a wise man."

I learned that the monks at Vatopedi prayed about four hours per day. Morning prayer continued to boggle my mind—it started at four o'clock. Why did these monks make prayer so hard?

They ate twice per day—breakfast and dinner—seven days per week, which was nice. Their schedule seemed *relatively* light, compared to the other monastery. I asked how much the monks slept. "It depends on their needs," Terry explained. "And how much they must . . . struggle." Terry said the average Vatopedi monk slept four to seven hours but added that a famous monk once said, "You're not a real monk unless you only sleep one hour per day."

I'd never be a real monk.

"Would you like to see our miracle-working icons?" Terry asked.

Icons are a big deal in the Orthodox Church. While one could certainly make a case against them[6]—especially considering that the

---

[6] "Thou shalt not make unto thee any graven image" (Exodus 20:4). I love the King James. The Orthodox supposedly skirt this commandment by insisting that their icons may never be more than three-quarter bas-relief.

word *icon* comes from "image"—Eastern churches are icon-heavy. No, really—some of their icons literally weigh a ton. These sacred objects serve as symbols, reminders, and waymakers that (hopefully) point the way toward God. I can see the appeal—sometimes it's nice to have a physical representation of a spiritual reality.

Vatopedi contains seven supposedly miracle-working icons, including Mary's belt, a piece of the cross, and some dude's ear. Terry set several items on display.

"People receive a blessing when they rub their special objects on these icons," Terry informed me.

"Tell me about Mary's belt," I said as I pointed to a fancy jeweled box.

"This is the belt of the Holy Virgin Mary, Mother of our Lord Jesus Christ," he explained with reverence. "It recently healed a boy from diabetes, and it helps women who can't have children."

"Thus," I joked, "lock it up where women can't go." Terry laughed.

"We took it to Russia recently, and some people waited more than twenty-four hours in line to touch it." In total, over one million people kissed the belt, making it the filthiest belt on earth.

Larry the Hobbit arrived with a clanging bag of utensils. "Can I still get my items blessed?" he gasped.

"Prayer is exhaling the spirit of man and inhaling the spirit of God."
EDWIN KEITH

Terry and I walked to the courtyard. I noticed a black knotted bracelet on his wrist. I'd seen these before, and I knew they were part of an important Orthodox prayer tradition. "Terry," I asked, "what's the bracelet about?"

Terry took the bracelet off his wrist. "This is a *metanie*," he explained. "It is for personal prayers. It is for praying the five-word prayer."

"What's the five-word prayer?" I asked.

"Lord Jesus Christ, Son of God, have mercy on me, a sinner," he said.

"That's twelve words," I said.

"I know." He laughed. "But it was originally only five words in Greek."

"So how does the metanie work?" I asked.

"The metanie has many knots. Each knot is one prayer. As we breathe in, we say, *Lord Jesus Christ, Son of God*, and as we breathe out, we say, *Have mercy on me, a sinner*."

He shifted the bracelet slightly, his thumb resting on the next knot. "Then we do it again, all the way around the entire metanie."

Terry continued, "Sometimes we pray this Jesus Prayer out loud, which helps us to focus, but often we just pray it in our minds. Our aim is a heart that prays without ceasing—that every breath becomes a prayer to God."

It is a beautiful tradition. But it felt incomplete. "Terry, if you're doing all the talking, when does God talk to you?"

He shook his head. "Once we have been fully sanctified, that is normally when God communicates directly or audibly. The metanie itself isn't sacred. It's just a tool to help you keep track of how many prayers you've done. Each monk prays the Jesus Prayer a certain number of times each day."

"How many times do you pray it each day?" I asked. "One round? Twenty rounds?"

Terry smiled and said nothing.

"What, is it a secret or something?" I asked.

"No. It's not secret, it's just . . . personal."

I asked how many times a standard Vatopedi monk prays the Jesus Prayer each day. He wouldn't even give me a ballpark.

"Last question." I grinned. "Tell me about Prince Charles."

"I hope you receive this before some frightful undercover agent stabs me in the left buttock with a poisoned umbrella."

PRINCE CHARLES, IN A LETTER TO A FRIEND

Despite his reputation as a somewhat dour individual,[7] Prince Charles is, to me at least, the most interesting member of the Windsor family.

Born in Buckingham Palace in 1948, he's been a prince for over sixty-five years—and the heir apparent for longer than any other person in human history. Despite this depressing fact, he hasn't wallowed or complained—and has instead busied himself with a vast array of princely endeavors. He has started an organic cookie company. He has created over a dozen charities, which raise almost $200 million each year. He has championed the use of organic farming. And then, of course, he has fostered his love of classic architecture.

While the modern architects of the United Kingdom would love to turn London into Tokyo, Prince Charles has almost single-handedly fought for the preservation and restoration of the stone buildings that make England what it is. After viewing a proposal for an addition to the National Art Gallery, he declared it a "monstrous carbuncle on the face of a much-loved and elegant friend." For this we should be grateful—if we believe Ruskin, we know that architecture is one of our strongest links to our past.

Terry filled me in on the story. "Prince Charles started visiting Mount Athos back in 1997," he said. "He arrived at Vatopedi just a few days after Diana's death."

I was just a kid when Princess Diana and her boyfriend died in a car wreck. My neighbors drove to the SkyDome in Toronto for a live cast of the funeral at five o'clock in the morning. Elton John's "Candle in the Wind," rewritten for the occasion, became the second-bestselling single of all time.

---

[7] He's not dour—he's *British*.

"Apparently Prince Charles visited Mount Athos three times in 2004 alone," Terry continued. "Vatopedi is his adopted home."

Prince Charles used to visit at least once per year, I was told, but he suddenly stopped visiting about three years ago. "What happened?" I asked.

Terry shrugged. "I guess someone put two and two together and figured out that he's the future head of the Anglican church!" He laughed and shook his head. "Such religious fraternization wouldn't do, apparently."

I thought about it for a moment. Beyond architecture, why would the future head of the Church of England, Defender of the Faith, regularly visit the Orthodox world's holiest site? For a retreat from the media? For a wild adventure on the man mountain? For a sacred time of silent prayer and meditation?

The answer, it seems, is in his bloodline. One of his relatives, the Grand Duchess Eugenia, was murdered in Moscow after she built a monastery and was eventually proclaimed an Orthodox saint. His grandmother on his father's side, Alice (otherwise known as Aliki), was an Orthodox nun for most of her life. Apparently she spoke excellent Greek and even maintained an Orthodox chapel inside Buckingham Palace. Prince Charles's father, Philip, was born in Corfu. As an honorary member of the Friends of Mount Athos, he had to convert from Greek Orthodoxy to Anglicanism in order to marry Queen Elizabeth.

The prince himself is something of a painter. A few years ago he auctioned off some watercolors and used the money to help restore Vatopedi. He attended the grand reopening and supposedly promised to work hard to ensure that each of Athos's twenty monasteries would be restored to their former splendor.

"Perhaps he still visits," Terry added with a glimmer, "but it's all rather hush-hush."

Terry had to go, so we shook hands. "Thanks, Terry," I said.

Terry pointed to heaven. "Thank God," he instructed.

"The more you pray the more you dream—and the more you dream the more you have to pray."   MARK BATTERSON

That evening I headed to the gift shop to buy a metanie. They had them in all shapes, colors, and sizes. I bought the simplest one I could find, a small black bracelet. I counted the knots. There were thirty-three in total.

The gates were already closed, so I wandered the monastery until I found a small English section in the library. One book was titled *The Hermitess Photini*. It was about a woman who disguised herself as a monk, lived in a cave, and became a clairvoyant. Maybe that was the key for women to make it to Athos.

I borrowed the book and climbed to the attic. I grabbed my journal and a sleeve of Oreos and found a nice spot to read. I read for about five minutes before a monk interrupted me. "Hey." He motioned with his hand. "Can you help me with something for a minute?" I put down my book and marched back down four flights of stairs. I entered a workroom and immediately realized I'd been suckered.

The monk pointed to a massive stack of flattened cardboard boxes. "Fold along the edges, two staples in each end, and pile them in these bags." He walked out of the room.

I was staring at thousands of little white containers that needed assembling, incense boxes that would later be filled and sold in the gift shop. He returned with a jug of cold water and a bowl of Turkish delight, bribery following deception. I begrudgingly got to work, wishing I was reading about a psychic she-monk instead.

Minutes later, an elderly man walked into the room. He was an Orthodox priest from Greece. We exchanged names and pleasantries, and he sat down to start folding boxes with me.

Pretty soon the priest started chanting. "What are you saying, Father?" I asked.

"*Kirie Ihsou Xriste Eleison Me*," he explained. "'Lord Jesus Christ, give me favor.'" He folded another box. "Now you say it. In Greek." He wrote it down on a piece of paper, and we chanted together for a while.

Eventually my voice gave out.

"Jay!" he yelled playfully. "Pray!"

I explained that, among my other bodily problems, I had a chronically sore throat.

"Eat Turkish delight," he said. "It's good for your throat!"

Two more men joined us. The elderly priest immediately recruited them to chant. Whenever one of us got tired, one of the other workers would sub in. The chanting continued for hours, with some conversation and other interruptions occasionally breaking it up. We must have prayed it five hundred times. At first it drove me nuts. It didn't feel like prayer—it felt like work. Eventually, though, I gave up—I was a guest on Athos, so who was I to get annoyed at their traditions? I settled into a box-folding routine, and the time passed quickly. I really started to like the rhythm of the prayer. It was beautiful.

I didn't know it at the time, but my prayer for favor that evening would be answered soon, and in a most ridiculous fashion.

I reclimbed the stairs, collected my books, and headed for bed. I was probably going to be the first person to steal a book from a monastery, but I wanted to see how it ended. If I got caught, I'd explain that I tried to read it on-site but a devious monk forced me to fold incense boxes for him.

I got under the thin covers of my bed in the attic. The rest of the guys were already asleep. I slipped off my metanie and moved my thumb to the first knot. "Lord Jesus Christ, Son of God, have—" My prayer was interrupted by a large emission of flatulence from the man beside me. I started again. "Lord Jesus Christ, Son of God, have mercy on me, a sinner." I heard another fart from across the room. I was trying to concentrate on prayer, and I was interrupted by rumblings of all kinds.

I stifled a laugh as I realized what was happening. By some sort of cosmic joke, our earlier lentil dinner was kicking in. I opened the skylight to ward off asphyxiation at the hands of gassy pilgrims. Needless to say, my first attempt at the Jesus Prayer was a "moving" experience.

"God will have the last word." ELDER PAISIOS

It was around seven the next morning, and I was once again waiting at the curb. I sat on the bench, thinking about the old priest. "Lord Jesus Christ, give me favor," I whispered. I thought about Terry and the Jesus Prayer. "Lord Jesus Christ, Son of God, have mercy on me, a sinner," I prayed. The Jesus Prayer seemed a bit depressing. If you repeated it your whole life like these monks did, I suspected you'd be pretty down in the dumps.

I decided to change it up a bit. (Don't tell the monks on Athos.) I grabbed my metanie and placed my thumb on the first knot. I did a full breathe-in-breathe-out prayer per knot, but I alternated prayers with each new knot:

> *Lord Jesus Christ, Son of God, have mercy on me, a sinner.*
> *Lord Jesus Christ, Son of God, have favor on me, a son.*[8]

Because here's the thing—I'm not just a sinner in need of mercy. I'm also an adopted son of God in need of my Father's favor.

I prayed my new prayer thirty-three times, and then lapsed into silence. My time on Athos had been disappointing. I had spent a lot of time in Spartan rooms and on creaky buses—but not much time in prayer. I had hoped to learn from lots of monks, but so far I'd met only two who could speak English. Aside from Larry the Hobbit,

---

[8] Many months later, I taught this prayer to a friend who was eight months pregnant. She decided to use the prayer during her breathing exercises as she went into labor. She brought her baby into the world while praying for mercy and favor.

Marko the Serbian, and the two undercover engineers, there hadn't been very many English-speaking pilgrims. I realized I should have brought Father Philotheos with me after all.

A large monk in his late thirties sat down beside me. "Are you the Canadian?" he asked. I nodded. "Father Terry said I might find you here. My name is Anthony. I'm one of the other English-speaking monks."

"Nice to meet you!" I replied.

"So, have you had a nice time on Athos?" he asked. "Did you find what you came for?"

"No." I shook my head. "Not at all."

"And what is it that you seek?"

"I wanted to learn how to pray," I said. "To really, truly know how to pray."

"Ah, my friend!" He patted me on the shoulder. "What you search for is not taught in any book! It is given, not taken."

He saw my look of disappointment.

"But we can talk about it if you like," he said. "I have to make a couple of quick stops, but you're welcome to come with me."

I figured I probably wouldn't be leaving for at least another five hours. So why not? I looked at my bag. "Throw it in the back of the pickup," Anthony instructed. "No one will steal it."

We hopped in the pickup. Neither Anthony nor the driver fastened their seat belts.

"Anthony," I scolded, "put on your seat belt."

"There are no rules on Mount Athos!" he replied.

"Yes, but there is *wisdom* and *safety*!" I shot back.

"Then we will pray for our safety and for the driver's wisdom!" He hopped out of the truck before I could respond.

Anthony returned and we moved on to another work site. I spotted a man pounding a rock with a hammer and chisel. "What's he doing?" I asked.

"Making cobblestones," Anthony replied.

Talk about literally hand hewn. "Wow, won't that take forever?"

Anthony grinned. "He has all the time in the world! And do you hear him? He's not just chiseling; he's praying, too."

Father Anthony explained that Orthodox monks often turn repetitive tasks into a time of prayer. They choose or create a mantra and repeat it over and over again while they work. It alleviates the stress of manual labor while focusing them on God. I remembered the old priest from the previous night and then recalled my first "real job" as a young teen. I prayed constantly as I loaded frozen patties into the broiler machine at Burger King. It was a great way to turn a mundane task into something of lasting spiritual value. Rather than waste precious moments of life, I prayed for friends who eventually came to know Christ.

Anthony and I arrived back at the waterfront and sat on the stone dock. There was a little sandy beach, and the water was gorgeous. You could see down at least twenty feet. The great tragedy was that monks were forbidden from swimming.

"Prayer starts with humility," Anthony explained. "And humility comes when you are filled by the Holy Spirit. When we first start to pray, we pray with our lips." He touched his hand to his mouth. "As time goes by, and we grow in faith, we start to pray with our minds." He touched his temple. "After decades of discipline, the Jesus Prayer can enter your heart." He touched my heart. "Then your soul is all peace, like a glassy lake."

This idea resonated with me, in a way. I knew that I'd moved past spoken prayers, so to speak, and spent most of my prayer time in my mind. But I'd love to truly engage my heart in the process. Did it have to take decades? Maybe, if you only prayed the same prayer a few hundred times every day. I especially liked what Father Anthony said about having a peaceful soul. I was reminded of the prayer I'd stuffed in the Western Wall in Jerusalem.

I wanted my prayer life to be a place of total serenity, like a glassy lake. But how would I get there?

As if to answer my question, Father Anthony continued. "You need a spiritual father to show you the way, to model prayer and to guide you in the formation of humility."

"And where do I find one of those?" I asked.

"Well, in the Orthodox Church, we have abbots for monasteries and priests for laypeople. You will need to find your own way."

I've been praying for a spiritual father ever since. I have a few "godly grizzlies" in my life, but not many. I don't know very many men who pray a lot, let alone effectively. Though Scripture admonishes older men and women to train up younger men and women, I've always had to go searching, and searching hard, for someone to train me.

Father Anthony said good-bye as the ferry arrived.

We pilgrims made our way west along the north shore of the peninsula, docking at Ierissos. I caught a taxi to the airport, stopped for gyros along the way, and boarded my flight a few hours later. The gyro was a glorious gift after three days on Athos. As I devoured the savory fry-stuffed lamb wrap, I figured that maybe Father Anthony was a gift from God as well. I needed the peace he described—a transcendent peace. I needed to slow down and shut up. I needed to find shalom in order to develop a heart that prays without ceasing.

After twelve hours of flying and many days apart, I was happily reunited with my wife.

Since women aren't allowed on Athos, I brought a piece of Mount Athos back with me. It was a small white stone, worn smooth by years of saltwater waves. "Here you are, darling, your very own chance to climb Mount Athos." She immediately put the pebble on the ground and stepped on top, satisfied to have been the first female in a millennium to set foot on Athos.

"Prayer is the test of everything. . . . Prayer is the driving force of everything. . . . If prayer is right, everything is right."

ST. THEOPHAN THE RECLUSE

I needed to debrief after my time on Athos, so I called Father Philotheos.

"Okay, first off, who was the bearded monk covered in feathers?" I asked.

Father Philotheos laughed. "His name was St. Onouphrios. He was a hermit in the Egyptian desert in the fourth century. An angel served him Holy Communion every Saturday. St. Paphnutios discovered him in AD 400. St. Onouphrios was totally naked with a beard that reached to the ground. He was covered in hair, not feathers. St. Paphnutios watched him die in prayer the next day."

"So why do men become monks on Athos? Why did you become a monk?"

"I didn't go to the monastery to learn theology," Father Philotheos explained. "I wanted to know God. I wanted to experience God. Prayer is the lifeblood of existence. Prayer is oxygen. It's more necessary than breathing. Prayer is how we can know God."

"So what does prayer mean to you? How do you define prayer?"

"Prayer isn't one thing," he answered. "You can read a whole university library full of books that have been written just on the Jesus Prayer."

"Okay, let's talk about the Jesus Prayer," I said. "Why is it such a big deal to Orthodox Christians?"

"This is the pearl of great price in the Orthodox Church," he replied. "If you receive the prayer in your heart, it's like you've won the lottery. You're rich."

"So how do you receive the prayer in your heart?" I asked.

"*Praxis*, then *theoria*," he said. "Practice first, then contemplation. It's like learning a martial art. You do it again and again, and it becomes a reflex. The Bible says to pray without ceasing. Unceasing prayer is the focus of every monk's pursuit. King Solomon said, 'I sleep, but my heart wakes.' I want to be able to pray in my sleep. The Jesus Prayer begins to turn over and over in your heart. Soon you stop praying it, and you listen to the prayer say itself. The Holy Trinity takes abode in your temple. Your heart becomes an altar. This is pure prayer."

"That's pretty intense," I said.

"My elder used to say that 'the name of Jesus is fragrant.' People who have the Jesus Prayer exude a fragrance. You can feel a gust of spiritual fragrance when you walk past them, and it's better than any drug."

"Do you have the Jesus Prayer in your heart?" I asked.

"Next question!"

"Will anyone tell me?" I asked.

"Probably not," he answered. "Monks are reclusive for a reason. They don't want to expose their spiritual walk to vainglory. We don't want to expose what has been hard won."

"One last thing about the Jesus Prayer," I said. "What's the role of the metanie?"

"We usually just call it a prayer rope or *komboskini*," he answered. "They say you have a distracting thought every seven seconds. Probably more when we pray. The prayer rope helps distract from distractions."

"Well, it's working for me!" I had used the metanie almost every day, praying a full round of thirty-three modified Jesus Prayers. It was a great way to keep just focused enough to not get distracted, if that makes any sense.

"Okay, I know this question might sound indelicate, but I've got to ask. What's the point of being a monk? Is it really that effective? Couldn't they do more good spreading the gospel or feeding the poor or defending the helpless?"

Father Philotheos said, "I hear that a lot. 'What have they done for society?' It's kind of ignorant of history. Most universities started as monasteries. The intellectual value of Athos is absolutely massive. At a very base level, it has stored and protected from war some of the greatest manuscripts the world has ever produced. But on a spiritual level, Athos represents the angelic life. One holy father is probably the best evidence of the truth of Christ, better than a million books. Christ truly dwells in them—they have an undeniable apostolic and prophetic grace."

"Athos also acts as a safeguard of the faith," he continued. "Out of some thirty thousand denominations, Greek Orthodoxy is the oldest. If Orthodoxy sees a drift in the Christian church, they can fearlessly accuse it. They're the conscience of the church.

"And then there's prayer!" he added. "Someone once said that one Orthodox monastery is worth four universities and seven hospitals. They pray ceaselessly for the world. I don't think we realize the importance of prayer. God is waiting for someone to ask Him for mercy for this world. The moment the prayers on Athos stop, there's no justification for the earth to exist anymore. Alfred, Lord Tennyson, once said something similar. He said that the world knows little of the works wrought by prayer. Perhaps our very hearts continue to beat because of the prayers of the saints."

"Geez," I said. "That's serious business."[9]

"It is," he said. "More than Protestant or Catholic prayer, Orthodox prayer tries to be God focused. We shouldn't wait until we die to be with God. Union with God is our purpose in life."

"So as a Protestant," I said, "what can I learn from Greek Orthodox prayer?"

"*Hesychasm*," he said. "Stillness. God isn't known in noise in the Orthodox Church. He's rarely found in the confusion of sound and

---

9 I think we have a low view of prayer. I know I do. How powerful is prayer, actually? Powerful enough to redeem a thief on a cross in his final moments of life.

light. He's known in the still, small voice. I was driving in the car the other day, and a comedian came on the radio. He was quite vulgar, but he made a really good spiritual point. He was talking about cell phones and how we're so distracted all the time. He told a story about driving in silence, and how he was overwhelmed by a sense of despair and emptiness and lack of meaning and aloneness. He pulled over and cried. Eventually the tears stopped, and he realized everything was going to be okay. Most people never take time to stop. Noise and distraction keep us from stillness and ultimately from peace and oneness with God. I'm not afraid to be alone anymore. I'm not afraid of silence anymore."

I wanted that. I didn't want to be afraid of silence. Or anything else, for that matter. As an activist, stillness seems counterintuitive. Yet stillness inside might have a far-reaching impact. What if making peace with our warring hearts—peace within—is the first step to world peace?

I thanked Father Philotheos for his time, and we talked about our next chicken-wing date. When I put the phone down, I realized it was a blessing in disguise that there weren't many English speakers on Mount Athos. The days had been filled with waiting for boats and buses, checking into rooms, and attempting to interpret gestures from Greek-speaking hosts. It was deeply uncomfortable. But in the midst of that discomfort, I learned a valuable lesson about prayer.

I learned about silence. But it was more than just a lack of noise— I experienced a great stillness. Staring at the ocean, walking in the forest, looking up at the stars—there was always noise and movement, but there was also stillness.

Quieting my spirit has always been a difficult task for me. When Michelle and I get into bed at night, she knows my brain is still whirring because my feet are jittery. Only one thing helps—she places her hand on my forehead, and the thoughts disappear.

The Jesus Prayer has started to do the same thing. Asking for mercy and favor has allowed me to truly rest in the knowledge that God is both abundantly gracious and ridiculously generous. I'm starting to accept that God has the whole world in His hands and that I'm counted in that number. He's got me.

Thus far, my prayer pilgrimage had taken me from the synagogues of Brooklyn to the Temple Mount in Jerusalem, and from the Garden Tomb to Mount Athos. I had experienced mikvah and metanie. And Michelle could tell it had changed me. As we would drive in our car, she knew I was praying because I was holding my komboskini. We started praying more together, too. I was praying the Lord's Prayer, albeit with a little fear and trepidation. My journey wasn't close to over, and I definitely had more questions than when I'd begun. But somehow I was okay with that. Was this a glimmer of the glassy-lake soul that Father Anthony talked about? Was silence teaching me about peace? I was starting to experience stillness, but I wanted some action to complement all my sitting around. I set my sights on Rome—it had a long history of prayer and action, and I wanted to know more.

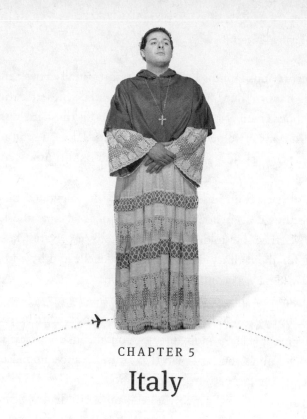

CHAPTER 5

Italy

BORN IN ARGENTINA AS Jorge Mario Bergoglio, the former nightclub bouncer became a priest in his thirties. He became the provincial superior of the Jesuits, then the archbishop of Buenos Aires, then a cardinal in the early 2000s. When Pope Benedict XVI broke six hundred years of tradition and resigned to devote his life to prayer, Bergoglio was elected to replace him in what we may assume was a landslide victory. Bergoglio chose the name Pope Francis, in honor of St. Francis of Assisi.

The way I saw it, if I wanted to learn about Catholic prayer, I might as well ask the head of the Catholic church. I knew he was deeply prayerful, and I wanted to meet the new pope everyone was talking about.

And as usual, I had bitten off more than I could chew.

In the previous months I'd done everything in my power to make a meeting happen, but I hadn't had any luck. I'd sent letters through all the proper channels, made phone calls to all the right numbers, e-mailed dozens of contacts and connections. I'd even sent a fax to the pope's personal aide. Who, besides the monks on Athos, still uses a fax machine?

I heard back from just one person, and he suggested that I try to get on the guest list for the pope's personal Mass at the Domus Sanctae Marthae. He told me the pope holds a private Mass every morning for about thirty-five people. If Michelle and I could get on that list, we'd have a chance of meeting him.

They say you should make all your arrangements before you go on a trip, but I've found that the best pilgrimages can't be planned. There's something crazy and wild and spontaneous about last-minute plans. Some things you can't plan that far in advance, no matter how hard you try. You just need to get on the ground and see what happens.

After three days in Rome, Michelle and I still hadn't heard anything. We waited and waited and waited. Perhaps I had been a little too optimistic.

I decided to take matters into my own hands. I decided to visit the Vatican.

They say Pope Francis is special, and I was about to test that theory. This was our last chance—desperate times called for desperate measures.

I checked out a number of maps online and came up with a plan. I would park near the Vatican, cross through St. Peter's Square, and hop over to Via Paulo VI. I would walk through the Piazza dei Protomartire Romani, past the Ufficio Parrocchiale and the Ufficio Scavi, and knock on the door of the Domus Sanctae Marthae. I'd chat with the security guards, tell them who I was and what I was doing, and ask if I could get added to the guest list for Sunday's private Mass. If they said yes, then there was a good chance that I'd get to meet the pope after the service.

"How to pray? This is a simple matter. I would say: Pray any way you like, so long as you do pray." POPE JOHN PAUL II

Michelle and I stood in St. Peter's Square (which is actually shaped like an egg), and I realized that my plan was completely doomed. One can't simply stroll through the fifty-seven-acre Vatican garden and take photos of fountains and statues in the world's smallest nation. Officially founded by Benito Mussolini in 1929, Vatican City is surrounded by gates and a wall, and Swiss guards *actually* guard the gated entrance.

The official population of Vatican City hovers somewhere around eight hundred citizens, but there were thousands of people in the square—faithful Catholics—and they all wanted to meet the head of their church. Michelle and I didn't have a chance.

We decided to check out St. Peter's Basilica. The words "Templum Vaticanum" were stamped on the threshold. The floors were made of marble, and the ceiling was covered in gold. It was fancy, but far less flashy than I had expected.

At the center of the cathedral was Peter's tomb and the spot of his crucifixion, covered by a giant shrine. As I inspected the structure, I noticed a sculpture to my left. It was a beautiful carving of Jesus carrying the cross, but people barely noticed it. A thought occurred to me. *Peter's tomb is the center of the basilica, the basilica is the center of the Vatican, and the Vatican is the center of Catholicism.* It seemed to me that they missed the true center by about forty feet.

We went on a hunt for tickets to the Sunday Mass. Five thousand tickets are available each week, and once they are gone, they are gone. I approached a Swiss guard. "Halt!" he said. His colorful outfit made him look more like a court jester than a pope protector. I continued walking toward him. He panicked, lowered his spear in my direction, and yelled "Halt!" A real security guard ran up to me. The Swiss guards are more for show—it's the guys in suits with earpieces and handguns that you need to watch out for. "I'm looking for tickets to

Sunday's Mass," I explained. "I was told to ask a Swiss guard." He apologized and broke the news that Sunday's Mass was completely booked. I was crestfallen. Not only would we not be meeting the pope, but we wouldn't even get to attend Mass. As a concession, he let me snap a photo of the Swiss guard.

We walked to the Vatican post office. My e-mails and phone calls and letters and faxes had failed, so I made one last-ditch effort to reach the Holy Father. I purchased three postcards and wrote the same request on each. I handed them to the postal clerk.

"Three stamps, please," I said.

"What country?" he asked.

"To the pope."

The clerk looked at the mailing address. *Papa Francesco, 00120, Citta del Vaticano.*

He looked up at me. "Yes," I nodded. "You literally just need to send these about two hundred yards over the wall."

He handed me three stamps with the pope's face on them. That must be a weird experience, to receive letters from your own private post office, each bearing your own personal stamp. We popped our cards in the bright yellow postbox and prayed for a miracle.

"All the darkness in the world cannot extinguish the light of a single candle." ST. FRANCIS OF ASSISI

We awoke the next morning to the sound of thunder and the crack of lightning. We were about to head to Assisi, a small town 120 miles north of Rome, the hometown of St. Francis, after whom the current pope is named. Even if we couldn't meet the pope, we wanted to explore the rich and deep tradition of prayer in the Catholic church. Throughout the centuries, monasteries and convents have been home to men and women who were totally dedicated to prayer. Imagine a city full of intercessors. Assisi was the first stop in the Catholic portion of my trip—I'd also planned to dig into the lives of Benedict of Nursia, Teresa of Avila, and Ignatius of Loyola, plus the pope, if he'd ring me back. All these folks were legit prayer warriors, and I wanted to learn from the best that the Catholic faith had produced.

It had rained all night, and it was pouring as we packed our bags and said good-bye to our host. Within minutes, we were stopped dead in a traffic jam. We turned on the radio for traffic information. It was all in Italian.

I checked my rearview mirror and noticed that the driver behind me wasn't slowing. I laid on the horn, and she slammed on her brakes, just inches from rear-ending our car. She had a MacBook on her steering wheel.

After a few hours in traffic, cars ran out of fuel. Dozens of people simply abandoned their vehicles, opting to climb the steep slope and hitch a ride back to the bus station.

My host had told me that Italians are some of the most rain-averse people on earth, but they were scrambling all over the highway. Men and women were peeing in the shrubs by the side of the road, unable to hold in their early morning espressos.

A trucker got out and started talking to the folks in line. It turned out that Rome was experiencing serious flooding. We ended up stuck in traffic for seven hours. In total, we counted fifteen ambulances, twenty cop cars, five fire trucks, and hundreds of stalled vehicles. When it was all said and done, it took us over nine hours to reach Assisi, instead of the two we'd budgeted. It felt like I was back on Athos.

"The deeds you do may be the only sermon some persons will hear today." ST. FRANCIS OF ASSISI

The town of Assisi stands atop a large hill in the Italian countryside, with the imposing monastery right in front. It is, by far, one of the most impressive towns I've ever seen.

Born in either 1181 or 1182, St. Francis was christened Giovanni di Pietro di Bernardone while his father was away on business. His father loved French culture, and when he returned from his trip, he renamed him Francis—literally, Frenchy.

Frenchy grew up like many rich kids of his era. He was known for playing pranks and dressing in fancy clothes with sewn-on patches, giving him an almost clown-like appearance. While he wasn't a mean teenager, he did hold his nose and run away from lepers.

At age nineteen he went off to war. He watched hundreds of soldiers die and ended up spending over a year in jail as a prisoner of war. Francis was a wreck when he returned to Assisi, wandering the streets in a state of depression. He had constant nightmares and flashbacks, what we might today call post-traumatic stress disorder.

Then one day he discovered San Damiano, a small church in disrepair. He visited the chapel, and there he had an encounter with God. While he was praying toward a painted crucifix, Jesus spoke to him from the cross: "Francis, go and repair My house, which, as you see, is completely destroyed."

Francis saw this as an order to physically repair churches, and he got to work right away. He quickly lost interest in his father's business, spending his time repairing churches and donating furniture. His father imprisoned him in the family home, perhaps thinking Francis had lost his mind. His mother let Francis escape while his father was out of town on business.

Francis continued his work until his father returned and took him to court. Standing before the bishop, Francis stripped off his clothes and gave them to his father. Standing naked before a room of witnesses, he renounced all but Christ. The bishop, sensing Francis's earnestness, covered him with his own robe and let him go in peace.

For two years Francis wandered the forests and caves around Assisi. He renovated the church of San Damiano and even worked in a leprosarium for a while.

Two others joined Francis in serving those in need, and on April 16, 1208, they decided they needed a collective word from God. The three young men went to a local priest and asked him to tell them God's will. They asked him to perform a mystical divination called *sortes biblicae.*

"Do not conform to the pattern of this world, but be transformed by the renewing of your mind. Then you will be able to test and approve what God's will is—his good, pleasing and perfect will." ROMANS 12:2

Sortes biblicae involves asking God for guidance and then opening the Bible, trusting that He will lead you to the passage of Scripture that offers you the wisdom you need. While it used to be very popular among some leaders in the church,[1] it is no longer widely practiced.

Still, I'm not against trying anything that might bring me closer to God, including a game of chance. After all, the apostles chose Matthias to replace Judas based on lots, and Israel's high priest even had sacred lots to determine God's will. I think back to the method of prayer my wife used in high school. She called it "Lottery Prayer." She put all her friends' names in a box, and each day she'd pick out a few and pray for them. Sometimes the same name would surface for many days in a row, and when she'd tell them she was praying for them, they'd inevitably spill a story about why they definitely needed prayer.

Who knows what God can do?

I decided to give sortes biblicae a shot. I wrote down three questions —they were more "guilty pleasures" than actual deep spiritual questions:

1. Will *A Year of Living Prayerfully* be a success?
2. When should Michelle and I have children?
3. What are my chances of meeting Billy Graham on this trip?

I borrowed my wife's aunt's Bible for this, a large, sturdy hardcover edition of *The Living Bible.* I dropped it on the bed. It bounced on

---

[1] Count Zinzendorf, John Quincy Adams, and John Wesley were among those who used sortes biblicae, and Augustine of Hippo came to faith through it.

the spring coil mattress, and out shot a tiny gospel tract with a photo of Billy Graham on the cover. The title read, "A Message for Fathers."

God has an excellent sense of humor.

I closed my eyes and started thumbing the pages for my first question—will this book be a success? I'm not going to lie—I may have subconsciously aimed for Proverbs, hoping for a verse about blessing without toil. Instead, I landed on a line from Psalm 31: "Rescue me from those who hunt me down relentlessly."

Not a great start.

Verse #2: 2 Corinthians 8:18: "I am sending another well-known brother with him, who is highly praised as a preacher of the Good News in all the churches." I considered calling Andy Stanley or Craig Groeschel.

Verse #3: Leviticus 25:36: "Fear your God and let your brother live with you; and don't charge him interest on the money you lend him." I really hope my brother doesn't read this book. Or my wife.

I attempted a new technique for the next question in order to make sure I wasn't cheating. I stood the Bible upright on its spine and let it fall open and then jumped on the bed to make the pages move.

Verse #1: Psalm 33:22: "Yes, Lord, let your constant love surround us, for our hopes are in you alone."

Verse #2: Esther 3:12: (About Haman dictating letters to secretaries.)

Verse #3: Esther 3:12: *the exact same verse again*. This Bible was clearly rigged. I flipped deep into the New Testament and landed on Romans 7:10. It was a rather depressing verse about the death penalty.

So far, sortes biblicae was not working out. But I gave it one last chance with the Billy Graham question.

Verse #1: Deuteronomy 26:9: I landed directly on the phrase "flowing with milk and honey."

Verse #2: Ezekiel 47:8: a verse about a river flowing from beneath the Temple all the way to the Dead Sea, where fishermen stand by the shoreline and a healthy agricultural industry exists.

Verse #3: 1 Timothy 4:12: "Don't let anyone think little of you because you are young. Be their ideal; let them follow the way you teach and live; be a pattern for them in your love, your faith, and your clean thoughts."

I tried all nine rounds again, using only the New Testament, but the results were equally inconclusive—with the exception of a verse about Mary's cousin getting pregnant and going into hiding for five months.

I started to see why people don't really use *sortes biblicae* anymore.

"The will of God is not something you add to your life. It's a course you choose. You either line yourself up with the Son of God . . . or you capitulate to the principle which governs the rest of the world."
ELISABETH ELLIOT

Because Bibles weren't cheap, Francis's priest only had access to a New Testament. His three verses were, unlike mine, particularly prescient:

Mark 10:21: "One thing you lack. . . . Go, sell everything you have and give to the poor, and you will have treasure in heaven. Then come, follow me."

Luke 9:3: "Take nothing for the journey—no staff, no bag, no bread, no money, no extra shirt."

Luke 9:23: "Whoever wants to be my disciple must deny themselves and take up their cross daily and follow me."

Francis and his friends agreed that they were called to a pretty extreme renunciation of all worldly possessions. They memorized the verses, and those verses shaped the rest of their lives and the core of the Franciscan way of life.

The brothers started small—they lived in a shed, sweeping church floors and laundering altar linens. At the time, monks followed one of two rules: the Rule of St. Augustine or the Rule of St. Benedict. Francis had never liked hierarchy, so he set up a fraternity based on brotherly service and equality.

Francis, in fact, wasn't much of a leader. When one of his first companions, Masseo, heard that Francis was becoming world famous, he asked Francis, "Why you? Why is all the world following after you?"

Francis spent much of his time in prayer. He used to tell his fellow friars that "no one makes progress in the service of God without prayer." He frequently traveled to isolated places for prayer, often for long periods of time.

"If you have men who will exclude any of God's creatures from the shelter of compassion and pity, you will have men who will deal likewise with their fellow men." ST. FRANCIS OF ASSISI

In addition to loving prayer and people, Francis was a great lover of animals. He would rescue worms from the roadways after it rained, set rabbits free from traps, and throw fish back when people caught them for him, and he even traded his jacket for sheep that were going to be sold for meat.[2] He particularly loved swallows, and he preached to them too. "My sisters the swallows, it's my turn to speak now, because you've already said enough. Listen to the word of God. Stay still and be quiet until it's over." To the amazement of those who watched, the birds immediately quieted down and didn't utter a peep until he was finished.

More brothers joined Francis over the following decade, and before long the order started sending out missionaries. In 1219, Francis sent himself, setting his sights on Egypt. But the cardinal in charge of Francis and his band of men said no—Egypt was far too

---

[2] Speaking of meat, the town of Gubbio was especially grateful for Francis's animal-whispering services, because a giant wolf had been eating all their animals. Francis went out to speak with "Brother Wolf" and asked him to stop killing. The wolf promised to stop, and they walked back into town together. Francis told the townsfolk that Brother Wolf was hungry, and they promised to feed him. The wolf lived among the townsfolk for two years, going door to door for his food.

dangerous. So the saint harassed him for days until he finally relented. Francis soon departed for Egypt with the intention of preaching to al-Kamil, the sultan of Egypt and a nephew of Saladin, the great Muslim warrior. Unable to speak the language, Francis kept shouting "Soldan" (meaning "Sultan") until he was given an audience.

Hmmm . . . maybe I should go back to Rome and try that approach with the pope.

At first the sultan thought Francis was the leader of a peace negotiation, but Francis informed the sultan that he represented God, not man. The sultan tried to dismiss him, saying he had no time for theological discussions, but offered Francis a chance to debate with his Muslim religious experts. Francis told the sultan that if he could not convince him to convert to Christianity, the sultan could behead him. The sultan was impressed by his zeal and sat in on the debate.

Francis stayed for more than a year. He didn't convert the sultan, but he didn't lose his head, either. When he left, the sultan offered parting gifts of gold and jewels, but Francis refused. He instead asked for some packed lunches, leaving the sultan even more impressed.

Francis returned home and retired—he had never liked leading in the first place. He spent the next two years writing the Rule of St. Francis, the governing document for the Franciscan Order. It received papal assent on November 29, 1223, making the Franciscans a legitimate order of the Catholic church. Francis himself was never actually ordained, but then again, neither were Jesus or Peter, the first pope.

Less than one month later, Francis visited the town of Greccio to celebrate Christmas. He wanted to help people understand the birth of Christ, so he arranged the first live-action reenactment of the Nativity. He filled a manger with hay, brought in oxen and donkeys, and arranged brothers to hold candles and torches like a starry night. The monks took turns singing. When Francis's turn came to sing the gospel, he lifted up a small doll, and for an instant, legend claims, the doll became a living child.

Francis claimed another major "first" the following year. During a particularly intense forty-day fast, it is reported that he became the first person to bear the wounds of Christ—the stigmata. He never recovered. Francis died on October 3, 1226, while listening to a reading of Psalm 140.

Less than two years later, he was pronounced a saint by Pope Gregory IX. In 1979, Pope John Paul II declared Francis the patron saint of ecology.

"Remember that when you leave this earth, you can take with you nothing that you have received—only what you have given."
ST. FRANCIS OF ASSISI

The Basilica of San Francesco d'Assisi, the resting place of St. Francis, seemed far smaller than it had appeared from below, and the fading white stone needed a good refacing. The interior, however, was quite impressive. The walls were covered by a series of paintings from Francis's life, and at the front of the church was a replica of his talking cross.

Little plastic "candles" lined the room, and when you inserted a euro, a bulb lit up. Even in Assisi, the times were changing.

I grabbed a welcome pamphlet. The theme of the basilica was written across the top: "May the Lord give you peace." I sat and read the famous Prayer of St. Francis:

> *Lord, make me an instrument of your peace,*
> *Where there is hatred, let me sow love;*
> *where there is injury, pardon;*
> *where there is doubt, faith;*
> *where there is despair, hope;*
> *where there is darkness, light;*
> *where there is sadness, joy.*
> *O Divine Master,*

grant that I may not so much seek to be consoled, as to console;
to be understood, as to understand;
to be loved, as to love.
For it is in giving that we receive.
It is in pardoning that we are pardoned,
and it is in dying that we are born to Eternal Life.
Amen.

We descended the stairs to the basement. There was a little chapel and an altar, and above it, the
tomb of Francis. The closest walls
contained the graves of his dearest
brothers.

It was probably the most beautiful grave I'd ever visited.

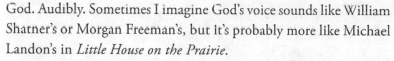

"Love God, serve God: everything
is in that." ST. CLARE OF ASSISI

I've always wanted to hear from
God. Audibly. Sometimes I imagine God's voice sounds like William
Shatner's or Morgan Freeman's, but it's probably more like Michael
Landon's in *Little House on the Prairie.*

I wanted to see if God would use Francis's talking cross to speak
to me.

After two false starts—we visited chapels that contained only replicas of Francis's cross—we were directed to the real thing. Since it's illegal to park outside the church that now holds the original talking cross,
we parked the car, put on our hazard lights, and made a quick dash
inside. There's nothing like breaking the law to hear from the Lord.

The chapel was full of people, and a priest was giving a sermon.
The real cross was nearly identical to the two replicas we'd seen,
except it appeared older. Tens of thousands of people visit the cross

every year in hopes that it will talk to them as it did to Francis. I wondered if any of them have heard anything. Maybe there was too much ambient noise.

It's rare to read in Scripture about God speaking to a large group of people. Abraham left his servants at the base of Mount Moriah. Moses was alone when the bush started to burn and when he ascended Mount Sinai. Samuel was asleep. Elijah was alone by a brook. Paul was the only one of his companions blinded by the light. John was exiled to Patmos. Jesus was alone in the garden.

Maybe the magic wasn't in the talking cross after all. Maybe God just wants to spend time with us, alone, in silence.

"Don't canonize me too quickly. I'm perfectly capable of fathering a child." ST. FRANCIS OF ASSISI

The Cave of St. Francis, his original hermitage, was just a few miles from Assisi. We took a winding road to get there, driving higher and higher into the hills. It would have been quite a climb, back in the day. We continued to drive for hundreds of feet above the clouds, back into the bright sunshine, and eventually found the front gate. Again we were forced to create a parking spot. I put a note on the windshield: "Please don't tow—we're praying!" We walked down a long gravel path and came upon a beautiful stone monastery, perched on the edge of a ravine.

Francis loved to be alone in nature, and even today, the Cave of St. Francis fits the bill. The monastery is completely surrounded by nature, with no signs of humanity. There are miles of walking trails through the mountains, and Michelle and I were intoxicated by the freshness of the forest. We crossed a stone bridge and saw the ancient olive tree where Francis reportedly preached to the birds. The problem, of course, is that the tree is an *oak* in the original story.

We started down the trail and discovered one of the most unique statues I've ever seen. At first I thought someone had knocked it over, but then I realized the pose was purposeful. It was a bronze statue of Francis, lying down. His sandals were kicked off, his feet were crossed, and his hands were resting comfortably behind his head. He basked in the light.

We found the entrance to Francis's cave at the bottom of a steep set of stone stairs. The steps didn't exist in Francis's day, but neither did the monastery. It was in that cave that Francis dwelt with God in prayer. The cave was very small and quite rough. I wouldn't have had a great time with God if it had been my place of retreat.

I thought about how hard life has been for most of humanity and how easy my own life has been by comparison. I often forget that my life is *very* above average. As an educated, Caucasian male in a wealthy nation in the richest time in human history, I'm at the top of the food chain. In the grand scheme of humanity, I am very high in the one percent. I have clean water, millions of food choices, clothes, a car, and a place to sleep at night. My parents didn't abuse me (better yet, they love me deeply), my nation's not in turmoil, my friends love me, I met Jesus as a teenager, and my future looks bright. On balance, I'm thriving. Very few people can claim this. If a destitute monk could give his life to God in prayer over eight hundred years ago, surely I can do the same today.

That said, I won't be joining the ranks of the Franciscans anytime soon—especially if Michelle has anything to say about it. I won't be spending years secluded in a cave, dedicated to prayer. But what would that type of prayerful dedication look like for a twenty-first-century Canadian? While I'm probably going to pass on sortes biblicae, I'm definitely going to plan times of solitude in nature. While it's unlikely I'll start talking to animals, I'm going to be far more intentional about cultivating relationships with the godly brothers around me.

There are hundreds of thousands of Franciscans today, ranging from the strict Order of Friars Minor Capuchin, from whom we got the word *cappuccino*, to the Order of Friars Minor Conventual, who run hospitals, help the poor, and teach in universities. There are Catholic Franciscans, Anglican Franciscans, Lutheran Franciscans, and nondenominational Franciscans.

And now there is a pope named Francis.

"Ora et labora." ST. BENEDICT OF NURSIA

You know you've "made it" when a pope writes your biography, and it is Pope Gregory the Great whom we must thank for leaving us the story of St. Benedict's life.

Here's what we know about Benedict of Nursia: For starters, he grew up in Nursia.[3] While attending university in Rome, he grew horrified by big-city life. He dropped out of school and made for the hills. He secretly lived in a cave for three years, and a friend used a rope to lower him food scraps. In the silence of the cave Benedict prayed to God and fought with demons. To battle temptation, he would throw his naked body onto thornbushes. It probably worked.

Eventually Benedict's cave was discovered, and a neighboring monastery invited him to become their superior. He emerged from his cave, took up leadership, and started to make changes to the monastery. His rule was incredibly strict. It wasn't long before the monks grew to hate him so much they tried to kill him.

Their first attempt involved poisoning his dinner wine. The glass shattered while Benedict prayed a blessing over it. For the second assassination attempt, the monks poisoned his bread. As Benedict prayed a blessing over it, a raven swooped in and made off with the loaf. Poor bird.

Benedict took the hint and returned to his cave, but soon a crowd

---

[3] You're welcome. Also—don't confuse Benedict of Nursia with Benedict of Cumberbatch.

gathered around him. He founded his first monastery in Subiaco, in the ruins of Nero's abandoned imperial villa.

We stopped in Subiaco on our way from Assisi to Monte Cassino. We parked our car and walked up another long, tree-lined cobblestone path. The monastery was perched at the top of a gorge, hundreds of feet above the roaring river below. The building clung to the stone wall, and I wondered how such a feat of engineering could have been possible over one thousand years ago.

The monastery itself was not very large—smaller than Assisi, and far smaller than the monasteries on Athos. The real action was in the basement. Someone in Subiaco must have been an excellent artist, because the walls are covered with beautiful paintings from floor to ceiling. Every square inch is decorated in rich colors. We walked deeper and deeper, discovering chapel after chapel, all of them carved directly into the rock face, all the way down to Benedict's cave. It was in this cave that Benedict spent three years alone with God.

The cave itself wasn't much to look at—it's a cave, after all. All that's left is a large slanted stone face, maybe twenty feet in length, with a statue of Benedict in the middle. It's hard to get a good sense of it, due to all the additions. I can't imagine where Benedict slept. Perhaps he was a "true monk" and only needed one hour per night.

Benedict was a great monk, in the truest sense of the word— he's one of the few people honored in the Catholic, Protestant, and Orthodox churches. Benedict's philosophy is best summarized by his famous phrase "Ora et labora." Contrary to popular belief, it doesn't mean "Work is prayer." The phrase isn't a definition of prayer at all—it's a suggestion about what Christians should actually do with their lives. "Pray and work."

Benedict believed that prayer and work are partners. Prayer comes first, and work follows. It is a potent mix. Ignatius of Loyola summed up Benedict's thought well: "Pray as if everything depended on God and work as if everything depended on you." The combination of meditation and action was powerful in Benedict's life—he founded over a dozen monasteries in his lifetime.

In my life I try to separate prayer and work. I have my work time, and I have my prayer time. Rarely do the two mix. I don't labor when I pray. I don't go about my business prayerfully. I tend to spend seasons in prayer without action, and then I spend seasons in work without prayer.

In looking at Benedict's life, I recognized that I needed to start working at my prayers and praying at my work.

"When they live by the labor of their hands, as our fathers and the apostles did, then they are really monks." ST. BENEDICT OF NURSIA

Monte Cassino was built by Benedict in 529 on a giant hill between Naples and Rome. I have no idea how he managed to haul all the stones up the massive slope. The imposing structure was built over the remains of an ancient temple of Apollo, and it could be seen for miles around. Benedict's first act upon arrival was to smash the Apollonian altar.

It was the final monastery Benedict constructed, and it's easily the most impressive.

Over the centuries, Monte Cassino was sacked and destroyed by the Lombards and the Saracens and by Napoleon's troops, and an earthquake also wrecked the abbey for good measure.

If you ever decide to build a monastery, here's something important to remember: never build a giant fortress on a militarily strategic mountaintop.

During the Battle of Monte Cassino in 1944, Allied troops completely obliterated the hulking fortress. They dropped 1,400 tons of bombs on the structure, which seems a bit much. They didn't eliminate any Germans, but they managed to kill 230 Italian civilians who had sought refuge in the monastery. The remaining rubble provided excellent protection from aerial attacks, which the Nazis discovered as they poured into the ruins two days later. It took four assaults and twenty divisions to drive them out. While overshadowed by D-day, the Battle of Monte Cassino was one of the bloodiest of World War II. Dr. Peter Caddick-Adams, author of *Monte Cassino: Ten Armies in Hell*, claims that almost 200,000 soldiers were killed or wounded in just 129 days.

Thankfully, the Allies *did* drive them out and then had the courtesy to rebuild Monte Cassino after the war.

It was at Monte Cassino that Benedict penned his famous rule, and it was at Monte Cassino that he died. The Rule of St. Benedict set the standard for monastic communities around the world, including the Rule of St. Francis many centuries later. Benedict is widely considered the father of Western monasticism—almost a dozen popes were Benedictines, as well as over one hundred prominent reformers, historians, missionaries, founders of abbeys, scholars, writers, nuns, and martyrs.

"Let peace be your quest and aim." ST. BENEDICT OF NURSIA

Driving to Monte Cassino was a fantastic experience, not unlike rally racing. I sped across long straightaways and geared down for the sharp switchbacks while my wife held on for dear life. We drove for a great distance, well above the cloud line, and I couldn't imagine trying to walk up that road, let alone carrying the construction supplies necessary for such an enormous stone building.

We parked our car in an actual parking lot and walked to the front gate. The sheer bulk of the imposing building was instantly noticeable. The word *PAX* was painted in red paint above the main door. "Peace again," Michelle remarked. "I see a recurring theme."

"Did the monks view that word as a prayer or a command?" I wondered.

The door was locked. I spotted a small sign indicating that the monastery was closed for lunch, but given the length of the closure, I expected they also snuck in a nap. We went back to our car and decided to join them, napping in the sun for almost an hour.

A brother knocked on the door. I woke up and rolled down the window.

"Would you like to tour the monastery?" he asked.

"Yes, please!" I said.

"That will be three euros for parking, please," he instructed.

We entered the gigantic building. The theme was "white"—the stone walls, the stone floors, the stone statues—everything was white. The monastery even had a small flock of domesticated white doves, which was a nice touch.

After paying five euros for entry and a self-guided tour brochure, which included a map to guide us through the dozens of rooms and courtyards, we started with the sanctuary. It was impressive, although it looked unfinished. On the way out of the cathedral we spotted *The Glory of Saint Benedict*. We really couldn't miss it—painted by Pietro Annigoni in 1983, the giant fresco measures 430 square feet. In the painting, Benedict is surrounded by monks, nuns, abbots, and bishops who followed his rule. Three popes bow at his feet. It was positively jar-

ring, and I wasn't sure Benedict would have approved. Benedict was reticent to lead the Subiaco monastery in the first place, and I doubt he would have allowed popes to bow at his feet.

We exited the cathedral and walked to the library. The doors were locked. We located the museum, but those doors were also locked. We noticed that the gift shop was open, so we went to talk to the clerk. "What gives?" I asked. "How do we get into the library and the museum?"

The clerk shrugged his shoulders. "Sorry, everything is closed today."

"How come you didn't tell us that when you took our entrance fees?"

He shrugged again. "Sorry, everything is closed today."

"Well, can I get a refund then?" I asked.

"Did you enter the cathedral?"

I knew where he was going. "Never mind," I said. "Have a good day."

We had paid twice and had seen a total of two rooms—the sanctuary and the gift shop.

"I don't think Benedict would have approved," Michelle said.

We arrived back at the hotel around ten o'clock that night, ready to return to Rome in the morning before flying to Spain the following day. I logged on to my computer to check e-mail and the weather. I noticed we had one voice message on Skype. I clicked play.

"Hello, this is Father Alfred. I am the Holy Father's personal aide," the voice said. "Come to the Domus Sanctae Marthae at noon tomorrow."

I jumped on the bed. "We're going to the pope's personal Mass!" I howled to Michelle.

"Prayer is a cannon set at the gate of heaven to burst open its gates."
AN UNKNOWN PURITAN

By Vatican law, the pope is entitled to live in the Papal Apartments in the Apostolic Palace. Instead, Pope Francis has chosen to live in a spare bedroom in the Domus Sanctae Marthae. He explained his motivation in a Jesuit periodical: "I cannot live alone. I must live my life with others."

The Domus Sanctae Marthae was built in 1996 at the behest of

Pope John Paul II. It was named after Martha, the servant-hearted sister of Mary and Lazarus. The Domus Sanctae Marthae is the guesthouse for visiting clergy and guests of the Holy See. It's also where the College of Cardinals have their sleepover during conclave, the time of seclusion when they choose a new pope. It was never intended to house the head of the Catholic church, but I couldn't have been happier—we were headed to the pope's house.

I knew exactly where the Domus Sanctae Marthae was located, having scouted it previously. It was drizzling rain when we reached St. Peter's Square, and the street that led to the Vatican was blocked off. A large procession of dancers filled the streets, Latin Americans in colorful dresses. I panicked.

A police officer was redirecting traffic, and I aimed my vehicle at her. She blew her whistle as I pulled up alongside.

"Excuse me, ma'am," I said. "Do you speak English?"

"Yes," she said. "You can't park here."

"Yes, I know." I laughed. "But I need to drive up this street."

She shook her head. "This street is closed until one o'clock this afternoon."

"Yikes," I said. "I have a twelve o'clock meeting at the Vatican. Is there another road I can take?"

She shook her head again. "No, this is the only road in," she said. "The other road is a one-way."

"Hmm." I pondered. "Do you think maybe you could guide me through?"

"No," she said. "Where are you going, anyway?"

"Ah, well, you see," I stammered, "I'm . . . I'm going to the pope's house."

Her look said it all. *Sure you are, buddy.*

"I'm serious!" I grinned. "Twelve noon at the Domus Sanctae Marthae. I was told to ask for Monsignor Alfred."

I think she believed me, but she still wouldn't let me through.

We found parking and quickly walked back to St. Peter's Square, maybe a mile in all. The rain had picked up, so we huddled under a made-in-China umbrella, trying not to get wet. Several thousand people were gathered in the Egg, watching the public Mass on four giant waterproof screens.

Inside the basilica, all five thousand seats were fully booked.

It started pouring rain—pounding drops, reminiscent of a Noahic downpour. We crossed over to Via Paulo VI and walked up to the Swiss guards. I handed them our passports, and one gratefully retired to a dry hut to process our entry. We chatted with the other guard while we waited.

The first guard returned with our passports. "You're good to go," he said. "You'll probably be stopped a number of times, so just mention your names and where you're headed."

We thanked the guards and took our first steps into a new country—the Holy See. As per my original plan, we walked through the Piazza dei Protomartire Romani, past the Ufficio Parrocchiale and the Ufficio Scavi, all the way to the front door of the Domus Sanctae Marthae. We didn't even have to knock.

We did, however, have to go through five security checkpoints in less than two hundred yards, each manned by real security guards. They were courteous but on high alert. Once we stepped inside, the guards were totally relaxed. "May I take your jacket?" one asked. He could. "Would you like a plastic bag for your umbrella?" he offered. I would.

Michelle and I were so excited. We were about to attend a private Mass with the pope! While the odds were slim, I hoped we'd have a chance to say hello and maybe ask him a question about prayer. I had prepared a question, just in case. I had even gone online to see if he spoke English. I'd learned that Francis speaks at least seven languages, including possibly English. I'd seen video of the pope *reading* English, but I hadn't discovered any clip where he *conversed* in English.

The guard ushered us into the waiting room. The room was dated, with white floors and brown tile edging. We sat in wooden chairs covered with fading green upholstery. There was a hardwood coffee table, a few nice paintings on the walls, and a sweet tube TV. "Monsignor Alfred will be in to see you in a moment," the guard said.

"The Church is not Pope Benedict's but Christ's."
MONSIGNOR ALFRED XUEREB

My wife, Michelle, has an uncanny knack for having incredible first-time experiences.

For example, the first time I took her to a county fair, she turned four quarters into twenty dollars by playing the dice game crown and anchor.

The first time Michelle ever watched a football game was on February 3, 2008, when the New York Giants beat the New England Patriots—one of the greatest football games in history.

Now Michelle was about to celebrate her first Catholic Mass—at the pope's house. *With the pope.*

Monsignor Alfred appeared. He wore a long black robe with a white collar, thin glasses, and a big smile. He had perfect teeth. "Welcome to the Vatican!" he said.

We shook hands.

"Jay, so very nice to meet you," he said.

"Monsignor Alfred, I—"

He put up his hand. "Please," he said, smiling, "just call me Father Alfred. And this must be your wife."

As he shook her hand, he started singing "Michelle" by the Beatles.

"Father Alfred," I asked, "I'm curious—how did you hear about us? Did you read my postcards?"

Father Alfred looked confused. "No. I received your fax."

The best thirty dollars I've ever spent.

We heard a loud commotion outside the door. We peeked into the hallway. There stood a group of men, totally drenched from head to toe.

Father Alfred explained that they were Argentine priests, from the pope's home country, and that they had a lunch date with the pope.

"Lucky guys," I whispered to Michelle.

I was reminded that priests aren't allowed to get married and that the men had worked for many decades in order to earn this free lunch.

The men were panting heavily, totally out of breath.

"I see you missed the free parking as well, eh?" I said.

They smiled, so relieved to have made it in time.

"Ah," said Father Alfred. "I was wondering why no cars were parked out front. The city sometimes forgets to tell us when there's a celebration happening outside."

"So, Father Alfred," I asked, "what time does the private Mass begin?"

"I'm sorry?" He looked confused again.

"When does the Father's private Mass begin?" I repeated.

"The Holy Father just finished public Mass a few minutes ago," he said. "Didn't you see it outside on the monitors?"

Now *I* was confused. I had assumed we had been invited to the pope's personal Mass. Apparently it was canceled on days when the pope held a public Mass.

Father Alfred beamed. "He'll be out to meet you in a moment."

"Friendship is born at that moment when one man says to another: 'What! You too?'" C. S. LEWIS

I met Richard Saunders in the eleventh grade. Our mutual hairstyle (dreadlocks, at the time) drew us to each other, and the friendship has grown ever since. I introduced him to his future wife, and he was the best man in my wedding. We've gone on three major road trips together, plus a mission trip to Honduras. My birth date is January 17, the same day as Benjamin Franklin's, and Benjamin Franklin's pen name was Richard Saunders.

Richard is the kind of person who excels at every single thing he puts his mind to. Whether it's in being kind or handsome or theological or smart, he is my equal or better in every way. As a descendant of the ancient Macedonians, his Greek demigod physique makes him particularly adept at athletics. We are both highly competitive creatures. I beat him at racket sports, and he beats me at everything else.

Richard and his family visited Rome a few years ago, and a rather remarkable thing happened. While touring St. Peter's Basilica, they heard the sound of a trumpet. The then Holy Father, Pope Benedict, entered the room. Richard flicked on his video camera as the papal procession strolled past. Suddenly—I've seen the footage—Pope Benedict strayed off course and made a beeline for Richard's wife, who was holding their newborn, Charlotte. He placed his hand on Charlotte's head, blessed her, and carried on.

I had told Richard that I was heading to Rome and joked that I was going to attempt to get the pope to bless *me*.

As I stood in the papal residence and allowed Father Alfred's words to sink in, a grin spread across my face. I realized I was about to one-up Mr. Richard John Saunders.

> *"I thank you, Holy Father, because you thought of me. I promise you right away my obedience; I promise you my prayer for you!"*
> POPE BENEDICT TO POPE FRANCIS

I could see the pope walking in our direction. The near impossibility of our meeting cannot be stated enough. The pope receives thousands of letters every day, from faithful people far more deserving than I, yet I was having a personal meet and greet with less than twenty-four hours' notice. It occurred to me that this was completely God's doing. The old Greek Orthodox priest's prayer was being answered—"Lord Jesus Christ, have favor on me."

Father Alfred explained that we'd have about one minute with the pope and could ask him one question about prayer. He turned to walk away.

"Wait, Father Alfred!" I cried. "Does the pope speak English?"

It was too late. The pope had walked into the room. I could feel my heartbeat thumping in my throat.

Dressed in an all-white robe, Pope Francis wore a little white beanie on his head and a small smile on his face. We shook hands.

"Hello," he said. "So nice to meet you."

He was soft spoken, but not soft. He shook hands with Michelle. He was about my height, with big, droopy, puppy-dog eyes. He maintained steady eye contact—an assured confidence won by decades of trusting God instead of himself.

"Father, may I ask you a question?"

"Yes, of course!" he said in broken English.

"What does prayer mean to you?" I asked.

He looked confused and shook his head. "I don't understand the question."

Gratefully, Michelle managed to cobble together some Spanish. "*¿Cuál es el significado de la oración?*" she asked.

His face lit up. "Ah, yes, prayer!" He smiled. "Yes! Prayer is opening up your heart to God!"

He raised his eyes to the ceiling and opened his hands. "In silence, it is letting God's power come inside you."

We were all silent for a moment, and I don't remember what else was said. I remember being struck by the feeling that Pope Francis was genuinely kind. I do remember that he maintained physical contact with me for most of our short conversation—he shook my hand, held my arm while we talked, then held my hand.

"Please pray for me," he said.

I liked that. Here was the pope—model of Jesus, head of the Catholic church, symbol of infallibility—admitting his great need for God.

I needed to do more of that.

The pope gave us presents. He reached for a silver tray and  handed us two little boxes— a red one for me and a white one for Michelle. Though he knew we were Protestants, each box contained a prayer-related gift—a crucifix and a rosary. Add it to Michelle's list of incredible firsts—her first rosary was a gift from the pope. I wondered if he was trying to convert us. The boxes were stamped with the papal insignia and Pope Francis's personal motto: "Miserando Atque Eligendo." *Lowly but chosen.*

Michelle thought it was a necklace at first. I had attended Catholic high school for a few semesters, so I was familiar with the rosary. Not unlike the Athos metanie, the Catholic rosary is a counting tool to help people keep track of their prayers. Unlike the komboskini, it's far more complicated than praying a one-sentence prayer over and over. A good Catholic will, on a daily basis, use the rosary to recite the Apostles' Creed, pray the Our Father, then three Hail Marys, one Glory Be, and then announce the twenty mysteries of the Catholic faith, with additional Glory Bes and Hail Marys in between. Whew.

Pope Francis said good-bye and moved on to greet the soaking, smiling priests. He turned back quickly. "Please pray for me," he repeated with a smile.

While it's of little importance in the grand scheme of things, you might be interested to know what we wore for our papal visit. We had been on the road for many months at this point, and I didn't have a single collared shirt in my bag. On such short notice, we didn't have time to make a shopping stop, nor did I feel like dragging a suit around the world for the rest of the year.

I had asked our host in Rome if I could borrow a few items. He graciously offered me a pair of black shoes, black pants, and a black shirt. I put on the outfit. The shirt was enormous, reminiscent of billowing ship sails. The pants, on the other hand, were about four inches too short, exposing both my white socks and my pasty white ankles.

I pulled my pants lower, not unlike a Brooklyn gangster whose arrest we had witnessed a few months earlier. I looked in the mirror. I looked like a mafia bodyguard in a parachute at a funeral.

I had kept the shoes and shirt, but switched back to denim. My wife, on the other hand, had no alternate clothing options. They say that success in life is doing the best you can with what you've got, and we had tried our best.

We met the pope in jeans and yoga pants.

"Do not be content to live a mediocre Christian life: walk with determination along the path of holiness." POPE FRANCIS

Father Alfred rejoined us. "I don't know if you have time, but I could add you to my table," he offered. "Do you have plans for lunch?"

Of course we didn't.

As we were seated in the cafeteria, Father Alfred again hummed "Michelle." The pope entered. He smiled and waved at us before taking his seat with the Argentine priests at the next table.

The Domus Sanctae Marthae dining hall was decidedly '90s. It had a green color scheme. The table was covered with white linen tablecloths. The black metal chairs were covered with green padding, and they looked like they'd been stolen from an old conference room. The table setting was pretty standard—two forks, two glasses, plate, knife, and spoon. Each plate was covered by a little cloth napkin,

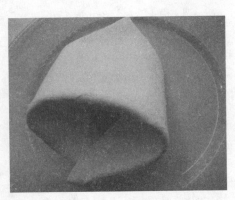

which I believe was unintentionally folded into the shape of the papal headdress.

As we ate lunch, Father Alfred told us his story. The Maltese gentleman had started off as the deputy private secretary to Pope Benedict XVI and moved into the lead role when Pope Francis took over. Father Alfred was impeccable—so obviously kind and caring, attentive, meticulous, and articulate in all the right ways.

"I used to have e-mail," Alfred said. "But it was overwhelming, so I had to go back to a fax machine."

"Yes, I know," I said. "I had to rent a fax number just to call you!"

"Still," he continued, "I get at least one hundred faxes per day."

I did the math. Father Alfred gets around forty thousand faxes per year.

"So why did you choose ours?" I asked.

"Because of how you are loving Jesus," he said. "Your abolitionist work. It helps."

I asked about the pope's daily schedule. As one would expect, his schedule is quite disciplined—he wakes up at four o'clock each morning and runs on the treadmill for an hour.

I'm totally kidding. Nobody's knees have time for that.

The pope gets up at four o'clock and celebrates a private Mass at seven. Pope Benedict celebrated private Masses alone, but Francis invites others to join him five days per week.

Pope Francis and Father Alfred have lunch together every day, and in the afternoon Alfred walks in the garden and prays for one hour.

We heard laughter from the pope's table. Michelle was delighted that the dripping priests were enjoying a moment they would never forget. I reminded her we were doing the same.

"What is the pope's favorite prayer?" I asked.

"Definitely the 'Our Father,'" Alfred informed me.

"He also prays the rosary twice per day," he added. "Often while reclining in a chair."

"Strong prayer is needed, humble and strong prayer that enables Jesus to carry out the miracle." POPE FRANCIS

While I didn't get a chance to confirm it with Father Alfred, Pope Francis is said to have invented a prayer technique many years before he became the pontiff. It's called the Five-Finger Prayer, and you use the fingers on your hand to track who and what to pray for. Here's how it works.

1. The thumb is the closest finger to you. So start praying for those who are closest to you. They are the persons easiest to remember. To pray for our dear ones is a "sweet obligation."

2. The next finger is the index. Pray for those who teach you, instruct you and heal you. They need the support and wisdom to show direction to others. Always keep them in your prayers.

3. The following finger is the tallest. It reminds us of our leaders, the governors and those who have authority. They need God's guidance.

4. The fourth finger is the ring finger. Even though it may surprise you, it is our weakest finger. It should remind us to pray for the

weakest, the sick or those plagued by problems. They need your prayers.

5. And finally we have our smallest finger, the smallest of all. Your pinkie should remind you to pray for yourself. When you are done praying for the other four groups, you will be able to see your own needs but in the proper perspective, and also you will be able to pray for your own needs in a better way.

"Father Alfred," I asked, "What does prayer mean to you?"

"Prayer is the communion of your spirit with God's," he said.

We snapped a few photos together, including one on his papal iPhone. In total, we spent just over two hours in the Vatican, but I knew I would remember it forever. We said our thank-yous and good-byes and promised to stay in touch. Via fax.

Leaving the Vatican proved far easier than getting in. We passed through zero security checkpoints, in fact. We thanked the Swiss guards and reentered St. Peter's Square. The rain had calmed to a slightly less-than-torrential deluge. Thousands of people still waited in line to enter the basilica. I felt that oh-so-familiar sting of Protestant guilt.

On the way back to our parked car, the pope's words rang in my ears: "Prayer is opening up your heart to God." I was really touched by the fact that the pope had asked *me* to pray for *him*. Then it dawned on me: the pope wanted God's power just as much as I wanted it. We were both looking for the same thing.

The pope's prayer life is grounded in a radical sense of dependency on God, the kind I was searching for. The question was, how could I stop myself from drifting from that humility? Why was I constantly tempted to rely on my own power instead of Christ's?

We arrived back at our host's apartment and told him the story, and he instantly e-mailed his girlfriend. I chatted with her later that evening.

"Did you shake the pope's hand?" she asked.

"Yes, ma'am."

"So cool!" she replied. "Feel free to touch everything in the apartment with your pope hand."

I also messaged Richard and told him I had met the pope. He wrote back, "I would've asked you to say hello, but alas, different pope."

Many months later I received a very official-looking letter, addressed to "Jare Brock" from the pope's personal secretary:

Dear Mr. Jared,

   In reply to your fax in which you requested to take part in one of the Papal Private Masses at the Domus Sanctae Marthae . . . I regret to Inform you . . .

CHAPTER 6

Spain

THE CAMINO DE SANTIAGO is the world's most famous pilgrimage route. The trek traditionally starts at St. Jean Pied-de-Port[1] in France, but over the centuries an untold number of pilgrims have journeyed a vast array of routes. All end at the same destination—the resting place of the apostle James[2] in northeastern Spain. The route became famous after Paulo Coelho published *The Pilgrimage* in 1987, and more than 250,000 pilgrims hiked the Camino in 2013.

No matter where pilgrims begin, all routes lead to Santiago de Compostela, the capital of Galicia in northwestern Spain. A *Compostela* is a certificate earned by walking at least 62 miles or cycling at least 124 miles. While the entire route could take over

---

[1] Which literally means "St. John at the foot of the mountain pass."
[2] Let's keep our Jameses straight. The one in Spain is James "the Greater," son of Zebedee. Then there's James—the shorter one—son of Alphaeus. Then there's Jesus' brother James, the "pastor" of Jerusalem, who wasn't one of the Twelve but who likely wrote the Epistle of James.

thirty days to walk, someone could technically earn a Compostela by cycling for just a few days.

The trail is marked by the symbol of a scallop shell. Theories abound as to why the shell is the chosen symbol, but the most common myth suggests that James spent time preaching the gospel in Spain but returned to Jerusalem after seeing a vision of Mary. He was beheaded in AD 44, and his disciples shipped his body back to Spain. The vessel carrying James's body hit a heavy storm off the Iberian peninsula, and the body was lost at sea. A few days later, the undamaged body washed to shore—covered in seashells.

If you're thinking that the Camino is a solitary stroll through the picturesque countryside, think again. Pilgrims along the main route are within earshot of traffic for over 90 percent of the hike. The route is quite commercial as well. The Camino generates a lot of revenue for northeastern Spain. Business is booming for hostels and restaurants. Even the gas stations and convenience stores sell almond cakes with decorative crosses on them.

Due to time constraints and my bad foot, I'd never wanted to hike the full Camino, but I'd always wanted to meet someone who had just completed their 490-mile march. Lots of people do the hike for secular reasons, but I wanted to meet a spiritual pilgrim—someone on a serious prayer quest. To that end, Michelle and I made our way to Santiago to see what all the fuss was about.

"Everywhere is walking distance if you have the time." STEVEN WRIGHT

Michelle and I walked one mile of the Camino—the final mile down the Rua de San Francisco. The road ended at a big square, encompassed by the Cathedral of Santiago de Compostela, the Hostal de los Reyes Católicos, and the Galician Culture Council. The square was completely empty. Though winter was well over, its icy grip hadn't yet let go. I knew we were visiting in the "off season," but I hadn't expected Spain to be quite so cold. I hoped the weather wouldn't ruin my chances of meeting a winter pilgrim.

The front of the ancient church was a rather gaudy affair, made pronouncedly more haunting by the green moss that hung off every crag and corner. The front door was locked, so we had to search for another entrance. I later learned that the front door doesn't open very often, only on Holy Years—years in which the Feast of St. James (July 25) falls on a Sunday, to be precise.

The church was under construction, so we had to enter through a side door at the rear, which actually brought us in at the front of the sanctuary. The first thing I noticed was a giant beehive hanging from the ceiling by a fifty-foot noose. It is the *Botafumeiro*, a dangling ball of incense. I was told that, many years ago, the priest would swing it over the aisles of the church because the pilgrims smelled so bad.

The church was subdued, austere even, without much color. During the spring and summer months, it is regularly packed with pilgrims, but on our visit there were only five attendees at Mass, and none of them were pilgrims.

We had arrived early in the morning and were the first in line to visit the "tomb of the glorious St. James." His tomb is located under the altar at the front of the church, and we waited patiently for a church staffer to open the door. As a friendly security guard unlocked the gate, an old man pushed us aside. He raced into the tomb and bowed his head in prayer.

James's tomb wasn't much to look at—just a silver box set at a distance behind bars. For most pilgrims, this is the end of their journey. If I had just walked almost five hundred miles, I would have been very disappointed by such an anticlimactic lunch-bag letdown.[3]

The church of St. James, though, isn't the end of the Camino. In

---

[3] Now obviously there's way more to hiking the Camino than simply visiting James's tomb. But I hadn't yet met a winter pilgrim who could tell me all about it.

truth, the Camino continues west for another fifty-five miles. Only about 5 percent of pilgrims who make it to Santiago continue to the very end, but those who do get to enjoy a truly magnificent destination—the end of the world.

"The chief danger in life is that you may take too many precautions."
ALFRED ADLER

"It is pronounced FINIS-TERRA," the barista yelled. "FINIS-TERRA. It is Latin. It means 'the end of the earth.'"

Cape Finisterre is a rocky peninsula that juts into the Atlantic Ocean off the west coast of Spain. The Romans believed it was the end of the earth. Once Christopher Columbus (a Spanish explorer whose real name was Cristóbal Colón) rediscovered the Bahamas, people changed their tune and claimed that Finisterre was the westernmost point in Europe. It turns out it's not even the westernmost point in Spain.

Nevertheless, it is the official end of the Camino, and Michelle and I wanted to see it.

We sat in a Spanish coffee shop near Santiago and chatted with the barista and a few other customers. They tried to convince us not to go to Cape Finisterre.

"Read the paper!" the barista said. He showed us the front-page headline. Roughly translated, it read, "Red Alert—140 KPH Winds."

"We call it a European hurricane," the barista explained.

Another woman called it a "ciclón."

"When is the storm supposed to make landfall?" I asked.

The barista shrugged. "Around noon, maybe."

We had an hour to get there.

When he realized he couldn't convince us not to go, he drew us a map.

"The Chinese use two brush strokes to write the word 'crisis.' One brush stroke stands for danger; the other for opportunity. In a crisis, be aware of the danger—but recognize the opportunity." JOHN F. KENNEDY

If you make your way to the very end of the Finisterre Peninsula, you will discover a metal boot anchored to the bedrock. It is upon this spot that pilgrims who have completed the pilgrimage traditionally pray a prayer of thanksgiving for safety on their journey. They also burn their clothes—or at the very least, their boots. It's a tradition that predates Christian times, but I wanted to experience it anyway. As usual, I wanted to participate in a centuries-old tradition to connect with our spiritual past in an attempt to connect with God.

A few years ago, Michelle and I took the 100 Things Challenge.[4] We got down to fewer than one hundred items, combined. Since then, we've tried not to accumulate more junk. Accordingly, I wear all the clothes I own on a regular basis. Because of this, I decided to burn a worn-out pair of socks that smelled like Orthodox incense.

As we drove the road to Finisterre, the weather got worse with each passing minute. Trees bent at alarming angles, and fallen limbs were scattered over the road. We prayed none would fall on our car.

"Pass me the car cigarette lighter," I said to Michelle. "I want to make sure it works."

She looked around for a few moments.

"It's not here," she said. "The car rental company probably removed it so no one would attempt to burn their socks in the automobile!"

"Very funny," I said. "But we need to find a lighter, quickly."

We stopped at a gas station a few minutes later. Michelle leaned into the wind and ran into the shop.

"Do you have a lighter?" she asked in Spanish.

"No," the clerk replied.

---

4 The 100 Things Challenge is an exercise in simplicity. Basically you give away most of your possessions, keeping only what you really need. The goal is to get to less than 100 items. For more on the 100 Things Challenge, see jaredbrock.com/100things.

"Do you have matches?" she asked in Spanish.

"No," he replied. "*No tengo fuego!*" *I have no fire.*

We found another gas station, and Michelle purchased a lighter. For eleven euros.

"What!" I howled. "You spent almost twenty bucks on a lighter?"

"How was I supposed to know?" she protested. "I don't smoke!"

We sped back to the gas station and Michelle ran inside. The attendant grinned and held up her change—a ten-euro note.

The weather worsened. The wind blew the car all over the road. Fortunately, there wasn't much traffic—everyone was hunkered down for the storm.

We reached the end of the earth. The weather was insane. The parked car shook as if a team of football players were trying to flip it. I attempted to open the door, but the wind was too strong. I pushed harder, and it opened. The wind caught the frame and almost tore it off the hinges.

The rain poured sideways—totally horizontal. The wind howled and the giant waves pounded the rocks. The sound was deafening; we had to yell at point-blank range just to hear each other.

"I'm going to find that boot!" I shouted. "You wait in the car!"

"You're crazy!" Michelle yelled back. "Don't get blown out to sea!"

I crouched and made my way down the slippery rocks, all the way to the little metal boot. I tried to light my socks on fire, but I didn't stand a chance with all that rain. I picked my way back to the car. I was drenched. I got inside and wrestled the door shut.

I pulled out the lighter and held up my socks.

"Pause for a moment," Michelle said. "Who tries to light their socks on fire in a hurricane in Spain?"

"Aren't you glad you married me?" I grinned.

I lit the socks on fire, and quickly opened the car door. *Poof.* They were instantly blown out of my hand, carried sixty feet and out of sight. "That's good enough for me!" I yelled at the ocean.

I hadn't quite captured the experience of a pilgrim—I hadn't hiked the five-hundred-mile trip to the end of the world, nor had I burned my boots and all my clothes. I had simply tried to capture a moment, and there was something refreshing about just letting go.

We left Finisterre as quickly as possible, doing our best to outrun the worst of the storm. We prayed we'd make it out alive. Our car was blasted with sheets of rain for hours, but we both relaxed once we realized we were safely in the clear.

I was disappointed I hadn't met a winter pilgrim in Santiago. Thus far, while I had seen the tomb of the apostle James and lit my socks on fire, the Camino hadn't taught me anything about prayer. We would return in a few days to catch a flight, so I had one more shot. I knew my chances were slim, but I was hopeful.

"You pay God a compliment by asking great things of Him."
ST. TERESA OF ÁVILA

After burning my socks, my next order of business was to visit Ávila, the hometown of a very famous shoeless woman named St. Teresa.

And then we hit a blizzard.

We were driving through the mountains when it started snowing. Hard. As a Canadian driver, I usually don't have a problem with snow—unless I'm driving a lightweight Spanish go-kart rental car. We were all over the road. Our brakes were useless. Our tires were a joke. I drove in first gear, doing about five miles per hour, for hours.

Spanish weather certainly wasn't what I had expected—a cyclone and a blizzard in the same day. In total, the 375-mile trip took eleven hours.

If you ever visit the city of Ávila, try to arrive at night. It's the most beautiful city you'll ever see. The entire city is enclosed by stone walls built directly into the bedrock, and the city is lit up at night. Many groups have lived here over the past twenty centuries—Romans, Arabs, Moors, Franks, Celts—and Ávila was our home for two wonderful nights.

We had been driving all day and were ravenous. We found an open restaurant and sat down to order. The Spanish don't eat quite as late as Italians, but they still eat much later than back home. We had asked a Spanish friend what people eat in Spain, and she wrote back one word: "Meat."

Michelle and I both ordered from the fixed-price menu and were delivered an enormous spread—an unfinishable bowl of white bean soup with sausage, a salad topped with tuna and sickly white pickled asparagus, a foot-long steak, a side of chicken and peppers, dessert, bread, wine, and tea.

I truly don't know how the Spanish do it.

We checked into a sixteenth-century hotel just outside the gorgeous walls and collapsed into bed. At breakfast the next morning, the Beatles' "Michelle" played overhead. Michelle saw it as a sign and decided to work from the hotel all day.

"Prayer is nothing else than being on terms of friendship with God."
ST. TERESA OF ÁVILA

Doña Teresa Sánchez Cepeda Davila y Ahumada was the founder (along with John of the Cross) of the Discalced (literally "shoeless") Carmelites.

In her lifetime she was known as Teresa de Jesús, and after her sainthood, she became Santa Teresa de Jesús. Today she is usually called St. Teresa of Ávila.

Teresa was the first woman to be named a Doctor of the Church for her important contribution to Catholic theology and doctrine. She is specifically known as the Doctor of Prayer, and it is for that reason that I decided to visit her home.

I drove to the convent where Teresa spent most of her life, located about half a mile outside the city walls. The gate opened into a little courtyard, which had a cross surrounded by circles of stones. At the foot of the first circle were the words *Las Moradas*—"the mansions."

"The Mansions" was another title for *The Interior Castle*, the spiritual development guide that Teresa completed in 1577. She envisioned the soul as a circular castle containing seven mansions. She believed that every soul was on a journey—each mansion represented a "stage" of faith, ending with a mystical union with God.

I ascended an old wooden staircase and knocked on the unmarked museum door. A lovely Spanish woman answered. I paid my entry fee, was taken back down the stairs, and was ushered into the first room of the museum. The woman said good-bye and locked the door behind me. Immediately, the lights went out.

I knocked on the door. "Uh, excuse me?" I said. "Are you still there?"

I heard the jingling of ancient keys, and the door opened again.

"Can I help you with something?" the woman asked.

"Uh, yeah," I replied. "First, why are you locking me *inside* your museum, and second, why did you turn off the lights?"

"Oh, sorry about that," she apologized. "I'll make sure the lights stay on. As for locking the door, that's for security reasons. When you're finished, just ring the bell."

She pointed to a very old rope on the wall. I looked at her. She was serious. It made little sense from a security standpoint. Talk about a fire hazard. Maybe she just didn't want me to sneak into any nuns' bedrooms.

She handed me a self-guided tour sheet and locked me in again. The room was excellently preserved, with lots of the original abbey furniture and cooking utensils, as well as an original fresco that had been painted by one of the sisters in 1569.

Teresa believed that a nun should never be sad and that music was a cure for melancholy, so there were many fabric song sheets and musical instruments. The museum even had letters Teresa had written, her hand-embroidered towel, and a statue of "St. Joseph the Tattle-tale." According to legend, Teresa would place the doll in her prioress chair while traveling, and when she'd return, it would tell her what had happened while she was away. I suspect that Teresa was a sneaky strategist, and that her story about the doll effectively kept the nuns in line.

Another item that was very casually on display was labeled "Clavo del locutorio de Sabiote." Having lived in Latin America a few years ago, I assumed it meant "one of the nails that crucified Christ." No big deal. I did a translation search in twenty-six different languages and regional dialects, but couldn't find a direct translation. I eventually found the item in Teresa's autobiography. She claimed that Jesus Himself had pulled it from His hand and given it to her in a vision.

I peeked into Teresa's bedroom, the simple cell where she slept for over twenty-seven years. I recalled that Teresa is the patron saint of headache sufferers, and this can easily be explained after seeing her pillow. It is a literal block of wood.

I located the famous steps where Teresa had a vision of baby Jesus,

or so the story goes. I suppose He was more of a toddler Jesus, because He asked, "Who are you?"

She replied, "I am Teresa de Jesús."

"I am Jesús de Teresa," He replied, signifying that He was hers and she was His. I wanted to sit on the steps, but they were locked behind bars.

I discovered another piece of art in the last room of the museum— a tiny sketch by John of the Cross. It's a marvelous little piece. John of the Cross was standing on a balcony when he had a vision of Christ on the cross, and in the vision he saw Him from an overhead angle. It was a totally new concept at the time, and it later inspired Salvador Dalí's *Christ of St. John of the Cross*. I had previously seen prints of the original groundbreaking work, but, like the *Mona Lisa*, I hadn't realized how small it actually is in real life. In fact, John's work is just a thumbnail sketch, barely larger than a watch face.

"On a dark night . . . Without light or guide, save that which burned in my heart." ST. JOHN OF THE CROSS

John of the Cross was born Juan de Yepes y Álvarez. The "Rebel Doctor of the Church" was originally a Jesuit follower of Ignatius, and he had planned to join the super-strict Carthusian Order—until he met Teresa.

At first I thought that maybe Teresa and Juan could have fallen in love, but given the twenty-seven-year age gap between them, theirs was more likely a mother-son relationship. Both Teresa's and Juan's parents were Jewish converts to Christianity. That might explain their personal affinity, and it might explain their mutual attraction to mysticism.

Juan changed his name to John of the Cross on the same day that Teresa founded her convent. John became the spiritual director and confessor for Teresa and the other 130 nuns who lived in the convent.

The Discalced Carmelites were a strict bunch, and a group of less-strict Carmelites didn't like their reforms. They captured John and threw him into prison. He was jailed in a tiny cell, fed a diet of bread and fish scraps, and brought out weekly for a public lashing. It was during that time that he wrote his famous poem "Dark Night of the Soul." He escaped nine months later, after he managed to tear the cell door off its hinges.

The term "dark night of the soul" has been used to describe the spiritual crises that Christians inevitably face on their journey toward God. St. Thérèse of Lisieux, a nineteenth-century French Carmelite, shared with her fellow sisters, "If you only knew what darkness I am plunged into."

I've had at least three "dark nights of the soul." The most recent one, about two years ago, was the worst. I sank into a depression for many months. I felt so far from God. I didn't feel Him or sense Him. It was hard on Michelle, and it drove her to prayer. It drove me to prayer too, of course. What else could I do? I completely and totally identified with the apostle Peter: "Lord, to whom shall we go? You have the words of eternal life." *You alone can save me.* I cried like the monks of Athos, "Lord Jesus Christ, Son of God, have mercy on me, a sinner." I clung to the feet of Jesus and tried to weather the storm.

Eventually, the darkness lifted. I didn't pray a special prayer or do anything different—dawn appears when it appears. I wish I knew the formula for avoiding these "dark nights" in the future. But I don't, and on some level, I'm okay with that. In an age where pain is medicated and sadness avoided at all costs, I want to embrace every season of the soul. Because there is a season for everything under the sun—even when I can't see the sun. Dark nights of the soul rarely last forever, but sometimes they last a long time. Mother Teresa (of Calcutta) had a "dark night" that lasted for almost forty-nine years. Only toward the end of her life did the darkness finally lift.

"Real prayer comes not from gritting our teeth but from falling in love."
RICHARD J. FOSTER

After Teresa's death, John traveled extensively and founded seven monasteries. His reputation spread, and by the time of his death he was
widely known. He died of erysipelas, a nasty skin infection sometimes
known as "holy fire." But that wasn't the end of John's body problems.

Here's how it (apparently) all went down: John was initially buried in a ditch in Úbeda, but then he was secretly moved to Segovia
seventeen months later—with the exception of one leg. As the body
made its way through Madrid, folks lopped off an arm. The citizens of
Úbeda petitioned the pope to return the body, and Carmelite leadership eventually sent back an arm and a leg.

I couldn't decide whether to visit John's arm in Madrid, his other
limbs in Úbeda, or his head and torso in Segovia. I felt torn.

I pulled the rope that rang the bell, and at length the museum
curator let me out.

Walking down the hall, I came to a small parlor with a jail-like
window set into a stone wall. In the room was a small sign that
explained that Teresa and John had been "caught up in ecstasy" on
that very spot. To be clear, this wasn't a sexual encounter—there was
a barred window between them. It was a prayer meeting.

As a mystical Doctor of Prayer, Teresa wrote in her autobiography
that the soul ascends through four stages while praying.

The first stage is mental prayer, a time of deep concentration and
contemplation, preferably on penitence and the passion of Christ.

The second stage is quiet prayer, a state of quietness where the will
is surrendered to God, even if the imagination, memory, or reason try
to create a disturbance.

The third stage is union, a supernatural state where the will and
reason are absorbed in God and only the memory and imagination
are left to wander.

The fourth stage is ecstasy or rapture, a trancelike, out-of-body experience in which human sense ceases to be experienced.

Teresa's depiction of the rapture stage involves a mixture of joy and pain, manifesting at times as a trancelike state of unconsciousness, strangulation, and levitation. In her autobiography, Teresa mentions a "moment of rapture" in which an angel used a fiery iron-pointed spear to stab her in the heart.

I was in way over my head. The mention of stabbings and strangulation totally disturbed me.

And levitation? *Come on.*

I did further research and discovered a number of mystical saints with unbelievable stories. St. Joseph of Cupertino often levitated during Mass. St. Francis Xavier could bilocate—he could appear in two locations simultaneously. St. Martin de Porres could levitate *and* bilocate, *and* he could talk to mice. In addition to his bird-and-wolf whispering, St. Francis of Assisi could also levitate in "ecstatic flight"—up to six feet off the ground.

On one hand, levitation and bilocation and talking to animals seem totally crazy and very "New Agey." On the other hand, Christians believe in *all* these things. If we believe the Bible, then we believe in talking bushes on fire, tongues of fire, walking through walls, and people being transported to different locations. Technically speaking, walking on water is a form of levitation. When Peter walked on water, he shared an intense communion with Jesus. One could argue (though I wouldn't) that levitation might actually be a highly advanced form of prayer.

I believe that—with God—*all* things are possible. But as much as I wanted to learn to levitate, unless it would bring me into a closer relationship with my Savior, it fell outside the bounds of what I was hoping to receive this year. I needed to dial it back and focus on practical things, prayers more suited for a beginner like me. I decided to stick to the first two stages of Teresa's prayer life.

Thankfully, she offered a practical approach in her writings:

> My method of prayer was this. As I could not reason with my mind, I would try to make pictures of Christ inwardly; and I used to think I felt better when I dwelt on those parts of His life when He was most often alone. It seemed to me that His being alone and afflicted, like a person in need, made it possible for me to approach Him. I had many simple thoughts of this kind. I was particularly attached to the prayer in the Garden, where I would go to keep Him company. I would think of the sweat and of the affliction He endured there. I wished I could have wiped that grievous sweat from His face. . . .
>
> This method of praying in which the mind makes no reflections means that the soul must either gain a great deal or lose itself—I mean by its attention going astray. If it advances, it goes a long way, because it is moved by love. But those who arrive thus far will do so only at great cost to themselves, save when the Lord is pleased to call them very speedily to the Prayer of Quiet.

I've reflected at length on Teresa's journey of prayer. She, too, struggled to understand it. In fact, she didn't even truly start praying until she was forty-one years old.

As I read her thoughts on prayer, Teresa helped me get rid of some of my excuses for not praying. I'd often said that if I had more time, I would pray more. To this Teresa would say, "Don't imagine that, if you had a great deal of time, you would spend more of it in prayer. Get rid of that idea; it is no hindrance to prayer to spend your time well." And she is right—if I had a few extra hours to spare, I'd take a nap or throw on a movie instead of heading for my knees. I need to keep it simple, like Benedict and Francis—pray and work.

There's a poem attributed to Teresa (though it appears nowhere in her writings) that I particularly appreciate for its bias toward action:

Christ has no body but yours,
No hands, no feet on earth but yours,
Yours are the eyes with which he looks
Compassion on this world,
Yours are the feet with which he walks to do good,
Yours are the hands, with which he blesses all the world.
Yours are the hands, yours are the feet,
Yours are the eyes, you are his body.
Christ has no body now but yours,
No hands, no feet on earth but yours,
Yours are the eyes with which he looks
compassion on this world.
Christ has no body now on earth but yours.

Sadly, Teresa abused the body that Christ had given her: aside from not wearing shoes, she also believed in self-torture and mortification of the flesh. A certain Madame Calderón visited Teresa and wrote the following: "Round her waist she occasionally wears a band with iron points turning inwards; on her breast a cross with nails, of which points enter the flesh." Calderón also mentioned that Teresa would scourge herself with a whip covered with iron nails. Her weakened state may have made her more susceptible to contracting tuberculosis. It certainly caused extensive nerve damage.

Teresa thought that pain was the best way to feel God's love. She truly believed that inflicting personal pain would draw her into prayer communion with her Savior. She forgot that it was that same Savior who conquered sin and death so she wouldn't have to.

Still, there must be more to the story than what I've described. The Catholic church considers Teresa a Doctor of Prayer, so I'm guessing I've got more research to do. After all, the apostle Paul, in Philippians 3:10, also tells of his desire to participate in the sufferings of Christ.

The motto associated with Teresa is usually "Lord, either let me suffer or let me die." She was granted this request and died in the same year that Catholic nations moved from the Julian calendar to the Gregorian calendar. Her last words were a prayer: "My Lord, it is time to move on. Well then, may your will be done. O my Lord and my Spouse, the hour that I have longed for has come. It is time to meet one another."

Though Teresa of Ávila certainly had some interesting beliefs and questionable practices, one thing is certain—she took prayer way more seriously than I do. Though I have significant questions about her methods, I know I could learn something important from her zeal. It's time to step up my game.

"Pray as if everything depended on God and work as if everything depended on you." ST. IGNATIUS OF LOYOLA

While I didn't have time to visit any sites in Spain that are connected to Ignatius of Loyola, the man is still easily one of my favorite Catholic saints, simply because he was one of the toughest men in history. The sixteenth-century Spanish knight's leg was smashed during a battle—by a *cannonball*. Rather than amputate the leg, he retired to a castle for a series of operations—without anesthesia.

Today there are around sixty Jesuit parishes in America, but the saint's true legacy rests on a book he completed in 1524—*The Spiritual Exercises*. An early predecessor of today's thirty-day devotional, it was written to help readers discern God's presence in their daily lives. It has been used by Catholics and non-Catholics for almost five hundred years.

The exercises are meant to be conducted under the guidance of a spiritual director during a thirty-day retreat in silence and solitude. Each week has a theme, and each day is filled with passages to read, ideas to contemplate, and methods to practice.

Of the exercises, Ignatius believed the *examen* was the best way to continue practicing the exercises after the formal four-week course was completed. The Examen of Consciousness is a daily spiritual self-review. Usually conducted in the evening, it's a chance to reflect on the day—its ups and downs, wins and losses, successes and failures. Most important, the examen is practiced in order to develop discernment—to see where God has been present in the day.

It's a great exercise, one every Christian might do well to practice daily. Examen has started to play a role in my own life, and I suspect it will play a larger part as I develop the discipline to do it daily. Socrates said that "the unexamined life is not worth living." One of my favorite verses is Psalm 90:12: "Teach us to number our days, that we may gain a heart of wisdom." *To learn how to live rightly.* I don't want to live an unexamined life—I want my days to count for something greater than myself. I want my life to *matter.*

Examen helps me stay attentive to the work of God in my life and the world. If we are going to see God move powerfully in our generation, we need to watch for signs. We need to develop a keen understanding of how He is working in us, through us, and around us.

Not only do Jesuits try to cultivate a strong personal walk with God, they are committed to "faith that does justice," often lived out by working with the poor or dedicating their lives to a purpose greater than themselves. Theirs is a contemplative faith, and also a very practical one.

I had previously visited the Jesuit community in Guelph, Ontario, the city of my birth, on many occasions. The Ignatius Centre is a gorgeous retreat within the city—they have hundreds of acres of organic gardens and farmland, an old-growth forest, a retreat center, and a creek stocked with brook trout. Michelle and I love to hike along the stream in the summertime. The Jesuit brothers run retreats throughout the year, where they teach people to pray like Ignatius. People have the option to undergo a three-, five-, six-, eight-, or thirty-day program each year. Each program is spent in total silence, with the exception of a daily one-on-one session with a spiritual director. So far, the Guelph brothers have led over one hundred thousand people through a prayer retreat.

I interviewed a novice, a brother-in-training named Artur. He had been a scholastic (student) for six years and was preparing to take his vows. I had expected to meet an elderly brother, so I was shocked when I saw the handsome twenty-nine-year-old with blue jeans and surfer hair.

"So, Brother Artur," I said, "how do you define prayer?"

"Prayer is facing the reality of who you are before God," he began. "It's learning how to accept it. Prayer is a moment when you realize you're before God. It's being conscious of God's presence so that you can learn to truly live."

"That's beautiful," I said. "When you're leading these prayer retreats, what do you teach people?"

"First and foremost, I encourage them to get to love the silence!" Artur replied. "We need to ask for the grace of openness if we want to hear from God.

"There are three main Ignatian prayer practices," he continued. "The first is Ignatian meditation. I'm currently cycling through the Gospels. I'll read just a couple paragraphs each day. I try to meditate word by word or phrase by phrase. I stop when I hear something that catches my attention. Anything. Maybe it annoys me or excites me. I stop when a phrase moves me. Whatever stands out, that's my word from God for the day.

"The second prayer practice is Ignatian contemplation. I read through a story and use my imagination to enter into that story. Maybe I'm Peter, and Jesus is calling me to walk on the water. Or maybe I'm in the boat. How do I feel? Am I scared? Why can't I step out in faith?"

"That's a really cool idea," I said. "But do you think God speaks to us like that?"

"God wants to speak to us, and He uses creation to do it," Artur said. "The imagination is part of God's creation, and He can use it to connect us to Himself. Obviously, we need to run it past Scripture. Something can be 'real' in our minds, but it doesn't mean it's true."

"What's the third practice?" I asked.

"The third prayer practice is called examen," he answered. "You do it in the evenings, and it's a way of going back through your day and seeing where God was at work in your life. God is calling us all day, but we don't usually pick up. Examen is like checking voice mail.

"You start by placing yourself before God in stillness. You thank Him for all that you've received that day and ask the Holy Spirit to illuminate where you said yes and no to His leadings. You examine your wins and failures and give thanks that God showed you Himself. You end by resolving to be more attentive the next day, and you say the Lord's Prayer.

"So basically, I start my day with Ignatian meditation and end my day with ten or fifteen minutes of examen. I'll do contemplation every few days. I think it's really important to mention that Ignatian prayer isn't just a 'spiritual' devotion. It's a highly practical exercise. The goal isn't some lofty state of ecstasy or rapture. Obviously we want to experience God, but we want to help people, too. We go 'up' for union with God in order to come back 'down' and share it with others."

I've since tried Ignatian meditation. It's like a more disciplined version of sortes biblicae, which is fun. I haven't yet been able to picture myself in the Bible, but I love examen. It's still not a daily ritual for me, but it's on my list. What I like most about Jesuit prayer is that it's so practical.

"Jesuit prayer is mission oriented," Artur explained. "My goal is to bring God to people and bring people to God."

"So I guess it's a great time to be a Jesuit, eh?" I asked. "Now that you have a Jesuit pope!"

"It sure is." Artur smiled.

"It is no use walking anywhere to preach unless our walking is our preaching." ST. FRANCIS OF ASSISI

Michelle and I had originally planned to drive back to the Santiago airport, fly to Barcelona, and then continue on to Paris. When I realized that meant recrossing the snowy mountains by automobile, I decided to cancel our flight and fly from Madrid instead. After thirty-one minutes on hold, the operator informed me, "We can only refund two euros per ticket." How reasonable.

Rather than losing our airfare, we drove back to Santiago to catch our original flight. Thankfully, it wasn't the treacherous trek that our first trip across the mountains had been.

During our time in Spain I had been looking for a real-life person who had recently completed a pilgrimage on the Camino. When I stopped at the Hostal de los Reyes Católicos[5] and asked to see their guest list, the concierge told me, "Pilgrims don't really walk the Camino in winter." No matter how hard I looked, I was coming up empty. It looked like my quest to meet a pilgrim had failed.

The morning we left Spain was full of annoyances. It was early in the morning, and we had trouble finding an open gas station. Then we took a wrong exit and had to reroute. We arrived at the airport terminal, parked the car, and took the elevator to the car rental office. The desk was closed, so we went back down the elevator, searched around for the well-hidden key drop-off, and then reascended to the departure terminal.

We went to the Iberia airline counter. For the first time in my life, there was no line. I handed our passports to the attendant. She informed me that, even though we had booked our flight on Iberia, we would be flying on a different airline, whose name rhymes with "grueling."

"You need to get in that line over there," she said, pointing to the longest line in the terminal.

---

[5] Built in the fifteenth century, the place is described by acclaimed travel writer Jan Morris as "perhaps the most beautiful hotel in Europe."

"Can't I check in here?" I asked. "Since I paid *you*?"

She shook her head and pointed to the other line. We lugged our bags to the back of the several-hundred-person line.

The man in front of us smiled and nodded, and I grumpily nodded back. I complained to Michelle about the line. The man interrupted when he realized we spoke English.

"Can you hold my spot in line while I throw this out?" He pointed to an apple core. I said yes, of course—it's not like his spot was much better than ours anyway. He threw out his garbage, stopped to cough, and got back in line. Within a few seconds I could see this man was *radiating* joy. He kept looking at us, and he clearly wanted to have a conversation. I broke the ice.

"Where are you from?" I asked.

He grinned. "Sweden, you?"

"I'm from Canada," I said. "But my wife's from Finland!"

And they were off, talking about Scandinavia and common words and reindeer and what have you. He asked me questions about my prayer pilgrimage, and we told him stories about meeting the pope and getting stuck in a blizzard.

"So what brings you to Spain?" I asked.

"Oh, me?" he said. "I just hiked the Camino."

Thank God for two-euro refunds and mornings full of annoyances. I had finally found my winter pilgrim!

"Hiked it?" I said. "As in, you hiked the Camino in wintertime?"

"Yes." He nodded. "I had hiked the route four times before, but never in winter. I wanted to 'raise the bar,' so to speak."

"Wow!" I said. "What was that like?"

"I'm not going to lie to you. It was very difficult. I hiked for many days in the cold and in the rain. I crossed over three mountains, too."

I was reminded of our Spanish blizzard. "Did you hit any snow?" I asked.

"Of course!" he said. "Two snowstorms. They lasted four or five days in all. I was totally alone. The snow was knee high, sometimes as high as my thigh."

"That's insane!" I exclaimed.

He nodded. "I also did the whole pilgrimage in silence."

"Wait, wait, wait," I said. "Let me guess—you wanted to raise the bar?"

He laughed and nodded. My winter pilgrim's name was Gustav, and I was only the second person he'd talked to since breaking his monthlong vow of silence.

"Gustav," I asked, "I'd love to buy you breakfast once we get through this horrible line, but I have a question in the meantime. Aside from wanting to raise the bar, why would you possibly *want* to be silent for an entire month?"

His answer was simple but immensely profound. "Because silence is an excellent room for prayer."

"Religion points to that area of human experience where in one way or another man comes upon mystery as a summons to pilgrimage."
FREDERICK BUECHNER

We made it through the horrible line, purchased breakfast, and found an empty table. Michelle and I grabbed Gustav's hands.

"Gustav, would you do us the honor of saying grace?" I asked.

"I would be delighted." He beamed.

We bowed our heads. Gustav cleared his throat, found the right key, and started singing a prayer in Swedish. It was fearless, graceful, and beautiful. Others stared at the three of us. We didn't care. Gustav was happy to be singing. He was happy to have a voice.

"I did this Camino with one question in mind," he explained. "'God, what would You have me do?'"

"And did you receive an answer?" I asked.

Gustav put his head back and laughed. "Oh yes!" he said. "Many, many times over!"

"So," I pressed, "what did He say?"

"The church in Sweden. It doesn't move. I want to bring back the soul-body connection, to reintroduce the church to the *body* in 'body of Christ'!" He leaned forward in his seat. "I want the church to *move*. Get rid of the chairs and pews, greet each other like family, dance off the week's cares, worship with our hands raised, sit in small groups, and discuss!" He trailed off. He didn't need to describe it any further. You could see the vision in his eyes.

"Also," Gustav said with a twinkle in his eye, "I didn't get any blisters the entire time."

"Wow, that's impressive!" I said. "What's your secret?"

"I prayed for my feet every day," he said.

"You *what*?" I laughed.

"I blessed them, thanked them, rubbed them," he said. "At one point I was rubbing my right foot and could feel that my left foot was envious. Then I watched as it turned blue. I started rubbing it, and the right one turned blue! But I didn't have any pain. And not a single blister the entire time." He grinned. "Just jealous feet!"

This guy was too much. Gustav informed me that he had done five Caminos, plus a bunch of other serious treks—the Jesus Trail, five days around Jerusalem, the Israeli desert, Sweden, New York, and I believe he also mentioned Poland.

His first pilgrimage was in the summer of 2008. "I could sense that something was coming," he said. "Then the Lehman Brothers collapse happened."

The market crashed, but Gustav was totally at peace. He closed up his consulting business, downsized to a condo, and dedicated his life to reviving the church in Sweden by making it relational.

"Where are you heading next?" he asked. "Have you heard of Taizé in France?"

We were heading there in a few days.

"I was there just before walking the Camino!" he said. "Do you think you could pass on a letter to one of the brothers for me?"

"Of course!" I said.

He borrowed my pen and notebook and wrote a letter on the spot.

"Please give my letter to Brother Matthew," he said. "Also, do you think you could check the grammar and spelling for me?"

I happily obliged.

"We don't think about pilgrimage in this country. We don't think about meditation. The idea of taking a six-week walk is totally foreign to most Americans. But it's probably exactly what we need." EMILIO ESTEVEZ

We flew to Barcelona and then reunited with Gustav in the airport.

"How was your flight?" Michelle asked. "I think I got high off the jet fumes."

"I coughed the whole time," he replied. "I've had a horrible cough for four days, in fact. I saw a doctor and everything. I coughed all the way to the airport, and I coughed for the entire flight. But it's funny, it immediately stopped when I met you. I haven't coughed once." Weird.

We had been to this airport before, and I knew there was a nice coffee shop in a park on the other side.

"Do you want to grab a tea?" I said. "I know it's a little far . . ."

I trailed off as both Gustav and Michelle gave me "that look."

"Right!" I said. "You just walked across Spain."

Gustav was a handsome fellow in his early fifties, in great shape, and buzzing with energy. "Like most pilgrims, I started in St. Jean Pied-de-Port," he said. "I walked maybe six to eight hours per day on average. But some days I walked thirteen hours in order to really push my body. I wanted to totally trust God."

"You're crazy!" I said. "How did you pray while walking, Gustav?"

"I didn't want to say too much," he said. "I just tried to be open, grateful. I tried to keep my sin nature from creeping in—fear, doubt, sin, greed. I tried to kill my agenda and just be in His presence."

We sipped our hot drinks.

"Prayer is the communion of the soul," he continued. "It's a 'connection,' moving in the stream. I want to be constantly in prayer, and the Camino very much grows that ability."

"So how did you communicate with other people?" Michelle asked.

"I wore a plastic shell around my neck that explained I was being silent," he said. "I would only point and write on a tiny notepad. Many people laughed, but they respected it and entered into that silence with me. They would serve me coffee in silence or show me to my room in silence. Our souls connected."

"Silence helps kill the ego," he continued. "You can't defend yourself. You have to rely on others. You can't spout your opinion. Diminishing your ego is a great way to improve your connection with God."

"You know, Gustav," I said, "it's a divine appointment that we met you." I explained how I had prayed to meet a winter pilgrim and how we'd had a rough morning. He burst into tears when I told him how we had tried to change our flight.

"I was so sick that I had to cut the walk short by almost one hundred miles," he said. "I wasn't supposed to fly out for another six days, but I changed my flight last night!"

He laughed through his tears. "Don't be surprised when God surprises you—because if you're not surprised, you're on the wrong path!"

"Well, Gustav, Michelle and I need to catch a flight to Paris," I said. "Shall we pray together?"

To be honest, I don't remember a word he prayed. I only remember being filled with a radiating sense of joy. I was so grateful to have met Gustav. It completely changed the way I saw the Camino—it gave meaning to the world *pilgrimage*. It wasn't walking five hundred miles or getting a Compostela or visiting the tomb of St. James or even burning your boots at Cape Finisterre—it was about walking with God.

With the exception of a donkey ride in Jerusalem, Jesus walked everywhere. In the desert, in the mountains, on the water, by the sea. He carried His cross to Calvary. Now He invites us to walk with Him.

I've had a song stuck in my head for over fifteen years, and it drives Michelle crazy. It's called "New Way to Be Human" by Switchfoot, and it has become something of my life song. I'm not the only person in my family to have a life song. It's genetic. Like many adorable old ladies, my grandmother has a song for everything. But one song, in particular, tends to resurface again and again. It's called "In the Garden":

> I come to the garden alone,
> While the dew is still on the roses;
> And the voice I hear falling on my ear,
> The Son of God discloses.
> And He walks with me, and He talks with me,
> And He tells me I am His own,
> And the joy we share as we tarry there,
> None other has ever known.

Michelle and I have our best talks when we walk. Come to think of it, I receive some of my best ideas while I walk. Perhaps God still wants to walk with us, just like He did in the Garden. I think He does.

We said good-bye to Gustav and boarded our plane. I would never walk the same again.

CHAPTER 7

France

I DON'T PREFER FRENCH FOOD. I love croissants, baguettes, and caramel soufflé, but overall I think French cuisine is overrated. Boeuf bourguignon isn't great. The name "coq au vin" creeps me out. I've never enjoyed ratatouille. Quiche lorraine is okay, if you skip the bacon. Steak tartare is awful. Foie gras should be illegal. Escargot is just plain nasty.

This is going somewhere, I promise.

Nicholas Herman was a seventeenth-century French cook. Born in Lorraine around 1611, Herman came to faith in Jesus at the age of eighteen. A tree led him to Christ.

Herman saw a bare tree in winter. He stopped and marveled that it would soon be full of flowers and fruit. He was so overwhelmed by God's goodness that he simply fell in love.

Herman fought in the Thirty Years' War and was injured so badly he was forced to retire. Like St. Ignatius in the previous century and St. Francis a few centuries before that, God used Herman's time of recovery to help him ponder the true meaning of life.

Following in the steps of Teresa of Ávila and John of the Cross, Herman became a Discalced Carmelite[1] in his midtwenties. He chose the name Frère Laurent de la Résurrection, or Brother Lawrence of the Resurrection.

Much like myself, Lawrence spent a lot of time in the kitchen. While he is described in modern times as a humble dishwasher, his duties went well beyond scrubbing pots and pans. He was the monastery cook in a bustling kitchen, and he likely had a small staff to help him feed the hungry monks. He definitely was in charge of wine procurement, and it's likely he was in charge of purchasing food as well.

Despite his busy life, Lawrence truly wanted to seek the heart of God. Like many of us today, he read countless books on prayer methods and spiritual life practices, but none taught him what he was determined to find—in his words, "how to become wholly God's."

So he invented a new method, one that has stuck with us to this day—the practice of the presence of God. In the early years of his novitiate, rather than spending time in elaborate meditations and intellectual sentiments, he simply "spent the hours appointed for private prayer in thinking of God, so as to convince his mind of, and to impress deeply upon his heart, the Divine existence."

In a similar fashion to the Orthodox monks on Mount Athos, Lawrence turned repetitive tasks into times of prayer. But instead of repeating a mantra, he simply basked in the presence of God. Like Teresa of Ávila and many others, it was said that Lawrence was so close to God that he could levitate. I imagine this must have made dishwashing far more complicated.

---

1 While we're on the subject of food, let's set a matter straight: the correct spelling is *Carmelite*, not *caramelite*, though the latter sounds far more delicious and creamy.

Lawrence's goal was to continually keep God in his mind and heart, even while he cooked food or washed dishes or unloaded a shipment of wine barrels for the thirsty monks. He admitted it wasn't easy at first. "I found no small pain in this exercise, and yet I continued it, notwithstanding all the difficulties that occurred." After ten years of disciplined practice and struggle, practicing God's presence became his overwhelming joy.

"The time of business does not with me differ from the time of prayer; and in the noise and clutter of my kitchen, while several persons are at the same time calling for different things, I possess God in as great tranquility as if I were upon my knees at the Blessed Sacrament."

This was the kind of prayer life I was looking for.

Brother Lawrence died in 1691 in relative obscurity. All he left behind was a handful of maxims and one enormously powerful book, *The Practice of the Presence of God.*

"It was a great delusion to think that the times of prayer ought to differ from other times." BROTHER LAWRENCE

Weighing in at just a few dozen pages, *The Practice of the Presence of God* is an incredibly simple book, but it's packed with profound ideas that can alter the reader forever.

I had attempted to read it many years earlier, but I confess that I had tossed it aside. I found it confusing. I was confused because it's not very book-like—it's actually a compilation of four conversations and fifteen letters. The version we read today was anonymously[2] published three years after Lawrence's death. The correspondence, in fact, was never supposed to be published. Lawrence makes that point quite clear in his very first letter: "It is with great difficulty that I am

---

[2] It was compiled by Father Joseph de Beaufort, whom Brother Lawrence mentored and who later served as vicar general to the archbishop of Paris.

prevailed on by your importunities; and now I do it only upon the terms, that you show my letter to nobody."

Thank God for a little holy disobedience.

The correspondence took place over a decade, and continued until the very end of Lawrence's life. In his final letter he ends by saying, "I hope from His mercy the favour to see Him within a few days. Let us pray for one another." Two days later he went to bed, and he died within the week.

I decided to read the book again, and my second reading left an entirely different impression—namely, one of great excitement. I had never before read something so groundbreaking with regard to my spiritual walk.

I'd spent most of my life looking for "spiritual solutions," so to speak—quick, easy, and efficient ways to come to God. I'd tried *Our Daily Bread*, the Daily Audio Bible, the Daily Bible Online E-mail, *The One Year Bible*, *My Utmost for His Highest*, and dozens of other books and study guides. All these things are good, of course, but I had come to rely on "daily devotions" as my means to the Father.

Nothing has changed in three hundred years, apparently, because Brother Lawrence talks about the same thing in his day: "Men invent means and methods of coming at God's love, they learn rules and set up devices to remind them of that love, and it seems like a world of trouble to bring oneself into the consciousness of God's presence. Yet it might be so simple. Is it not quicker and easier just to do our common business wholly for the love of him?"

Lawrence's writings helped me put things into perspective. "Devotions are only means to attain to the end; so when by this exercise of the presence of God we are with Him who is our end, it is then useless to return to the means."

It's not about "doing devotions"—it's about being with God.

Lawrence laid out his argument quite plainly: "How can we pray to Him without being with Him? How can we be with Him but in thinking of Him often? And how can we often think of Him, but by a holy habit which we should form of it?"

So the question is, how can I form that habit? Lawrence says,

This is the best and easiest method I know; and as I use no other, I advise all the world to it. We must know before we can love. In order to know God, we must often think of Him; and when we come to love Him, we shall then also think of Him often, for our heart will be with our treasure. This is an argument which well deserves your consideration.

Indeed.

Lawrence "resolved to make the love of God the end of all his actions." Whenever he failed at this resolution, he confessed by praying a rather honest prayer: "I shall never do otherwise, if You leave me to myself; 'tis You must hinder my falling, and mend what is amiss."

In order to stay focused in prayer times, Lawrence developed a tactic that is incredibly simple, but easily overlooked: "One way to re-collect the mind easily in the time of prayer, and preserve it more in tranquility, is *not to let it wander too far at other times.*" It's easier to be close to God during prayer time when you're close to God all the time.

Father Joseph de Beaufort wrote that Lawrence's prayer was "nothing else but a sense of the presence of God." Lawrence himself describes it as "an habitual, silent, and secret conversation of the soul with God."

I like the idea of having a secret conversation with God. Even as I write these words, I try to picture my Father hovering over me, plucking at keys—like a piano instructor with a new student, or in my case, letters on a keyboard. When I pray for salvation for people far from God, I imagine I'm bowing beside Jesus, and together we're presenting each precious name to the Father. If there's an empty seat at any table where I enjoy a meal, I try to imagine Christ in the empty seat.

Over the past three centuries, *The Practice of the Presence of God* has been translated into at least thirteen languages. The book has never been out of print, and well over twenty million copies have been sold in English alone. The book has touched the lives of Thomas Kelly, John Wesley, and A. W. Tozer, among thousands of other leaders. Almost every modern pastor has preached a sermon about "practicing God's presence." It's conceivable that Brother Lawrence's little book has influenced the spiritual journey of hundreds of millions of people.

But the man himself has simply disappeared.

No monument has been erected in Lawrence's honor, and no gravestone marks his resting place. No one even knows where he is buried, and the location of his kitchen is a total mystery.

How has no one discovered his home in all this time? How has Christendom not erected a shrine in his honor, or at least a simple retreat center for silent prayer and meditation?

I decided to go hunting.

"Think often on God, by day, by night, in your business, and even in your diversions. He is always near you and with you; leave Him not alone." BROTHER LAWRENCE

I knew from reading his little book that Lawrence lived at a Discalced Carmelite monastery somewhere in Paris around 1640. I tried contacting the Order of Discalced Carmelites, but they never got back to me. I reached out to various Carmelite orders, but none of them got back to me either. I tried calling multiple numbers, but my lack of French ended conversations quickly.

After several false starts, I finally caught the trail through a Swedish retiree I met online. His website pointed me to a former Carmelite convent at the corner of Rue de Vaugirard and Rue d'Assas in Paris. He mentioned that a few of the original buildings remained, including the Saint-Joseph-des-Carmes Church. We exchanged twenty e-mails over the course of eight months, and I searched satellite images to home in on the spot. Just a few blocks northeast of the Luxembourg Gardens there's a small patch of green in a sea of brick and concrete—a garden. I discovered that the garden formed part of the convent, founded in Paris less than twenty years after John of the Cross's death.

In 1610, Pope Paul V asked Marie de Medici[3] to help the Discalced Carmelites establish a community in Paris. She met two monks in a large field on Rue de Vaugirard, where they established their convent in a house on May 22, 1611. The convent quickly outgrew the building, so Madame Medici used her connections to construct a church on what was then the southern edge of Paris. She laid the first stone on July 20, 1613, and the work was completed by 1620. The contrast was tangible—the extreme poverty of the Discalced Carmelites mixed with the lavish wealth of the Medici dynasty.

The monastery folded sometime around 1841–1845, and the property became the Institut Catholique de Paris in 1875.

All roads led to the Catholic University of Paris.

The more I researched, the more I was convinced—the Catholic University of Paris had to be the home of Brother Lawrence. The church was still active, and I wanted to get inside. I e-mailed almost a dozen staffers at the Catholic University, but none of them got back to me. No one returned my phone calls. The university website made no mention of Lawrence. The church website made no mention of Lawrence.

I knew I had to get on the ground to find out for myself.

"Converting our unceasing thinking into unceasing prayer moves us from a self-centered monologue to a God-centered dialogue." HENRI NOUWEN

Michelle and I flew from Spain to France. We stayed with some friends in a garden shed in the west suburbs of Paris, and I learned that the church ran a free tour of the chapel on Saturdays.

---

[3] She was the wife of King Henry IV and heiress of the Medici banking family of Florence, who got sinfully rich by creating a loophole that allowed them to charge interest, despite its being forbidden by the Bible. We've been exploiting it ever since.

Michelle and I eagerly joined the next day. The cathedral was Medici built, and it showed. The walls and alcoves were covered with gorgeous paintings, including a depiction of an angel stabbing Teresa of Ávila in the heart with a fiery arrow. John of the Cross lurked in another corner.

The tour was two hours long, and the program was entirely in French. Thus, it was immensely boring and in no way helpful to my search. The highlight was when a two-year-old girl slammed her father's finger in the door of a confessional.

The university itself is a rather beautiful yellow and red brick-and-stone affair with giant wooden doors. I found two signs on the outside of the compound, but neither mentioned Brother Lawrence.

Michelle and I walked quickly past the security guards, hoping we looked like busy students running late for class. It worked. We explored the courtyard, surrounded by gorgeous stone walls rising five stories into the sky. We located the garden. It wasn't huge, but it was a lovely respite from the bustling city noise. We walked the pebble path and stopped to inspect the flower beds and water fountain. We looked back at the former monastery. I knew I had found the spot. After being lost for more than three centuries, I, *Jay Brock*, had personally discovered a significant Christian site.

I was ecstatic.

We left the garden and rounded the building. I spotted a sign. "Séminaire des Carmes." I peered through the front window and saw someone inside. I excitedly knocked on the door. A kindly man in his late fifties unlocked the door.

"*Bonjour*," he said. "*Puis-je vous aider?*"

"Hi!" I beamed. "I'm Jay, from Canada."

"I am Father Jean-Louis," he said in broken English. "Nice to meet you."

"Do you work here?" I asked.

He grinned and nodded. "I am the Superior of the Seminary of the Carmelites."

"Excellent!" I said. "Do you have a moment?"

"I am actually in quite a hurry," he said. "I am so sorry, but I have a meeting. But how can I help you?"

"I know this is a random question," I said. "Have you ever heard of Brother Lawrence?"

"Yes, of course." He nodded.

"Well," I said, "did you know that this is the *very place* where he lived?"

He nodded again. "Yes, of course," he responded matter-of-factly.

I was stunned. *So much for uncovering an ancient mystery.*

"Do you know where his kitchen was located?" I asked.

"I think so," he said. "Follow me."

We returned to the garden, and he pointed to a window. I peered inside. It was a big commercial kitchen with white walls and stainless steel appliances.

"This obviously isn't Frère Laurent's kitchen, of course—there have been many renovations over the centuries. But it's likely the spot. Kitchens rarely move."

After that, Father Jean-Louis kindly excused himself, and I spent a few minutes in silence. I thanked God for allowing me to *re*discover the spot, taking a moment to practice His presence on the same ground where Brother Lawrence had once cooked his unsavory French recipes.

While I hadn't made the groundbreaking discovery I'd thought I had, it didn't ruin the moment whatsoever. There, on that very ground, a man encountered God and lived in His presence for decades. It was a fantastic moment.

Next, Michelle and I visited the basement below the kitchen, which now serves as a crypt. It was dingy and cold. The walls were lined with headstones, and a collection of skulls was encased behind iron bars. I learned that the basement had been the burial ground for the monks since the founding of the convent—meaning that potentially thousands of bodies have been placed there over the centuries. It's highly likely that somewhere, a few layers of bodies below the concrete floor, lies our dear Brother Lawrence.

No headstone marks his place.[4] Like Enoch, Brother Lawrence simply "walked faithfully with God; then he was no more." He practiced God's presence, and now he stands in God's presence. I think it's more than enough.

Michelle and I returned to our car and set our GPS in the direction of Taizé. We needed to fulfill our promise to Gustav.

"Maintain inner silence in all things so as to dwell in Christ."
BROTHER ROGER

As He did with Francis and Ignatius and Lawrence, God used a physical ailment, in this case a battle with tuberculosis, to call Brother Roger into a life of monasticism. Born Roger Louis Schütz-Marsauche, Brother Roger was the youngest of nine children born to a Protestant pastor in Switzerland.[5]

At the age of twenty-five, Brother Roger thought Switzerland was too comfortable a place to be during World War II, so he got on a bicycle and rode one hundred miles northwest. He stopped at a tiny, nearly abandoned village on a hilltop in France called Taizé. An old woman offered him a meal and encouraged him to stay. "We are lonely," she said. He never left.

Brother Roger started sheltering Jewish fugitives and refugees, and later he helped German prisoners of war. Whenever he got the

---

4 Why did Brother Lawrence simply disappear? No one knows for sure, but I've got a theory. While Brother Lawrence's monastery is, unquestionably, a significant historical spot, what if a far more newsworthy event took place on the exact same spot? As it turns out, this is the case. In 1792, France was in the middle of the French Revolution. Most of the men were off at war, and it was assumed that those who remained might accost defenseless women and children. This included the monks at the Carmelite monastery in Paris. The monks were arrested, and the chapel was turned into their prison. On September 2, 1792, a military mob stormed the church and brutally massacred 114 Carmelite brothers. I've stood on the spot where they piled the bodies. A small sign reads, *"Hic Ceciderunt"*—"here they fell." It's just a few yards from Lawrence's kitchen.
5 Like my ancestors, his mother was a Huguenot from France.

chance, he would escape to sing prayers in the woods. By 1949 seven other men had joined Roger, and on Easter that year they decided to make a lifelong commitment to monasticism.

Crowds of young people began to visit Taizé in the 1960s, and today around one hundred thousand young people visit each year. The community has never advertised itself, but as many as five thousand teens show up each week over the summer months. Guests stay for a week and have the option to spend their time in silence.

After spending months immersed in Judaism, Greek Orthodoxy, and Catholicism, I wanted to ease back into Protestantism. Taizé fit the bill perfectly—as an international ecumenical gathering, it's one of the few places on earth where thousands of Catholic, Protestant, and Orthodox Christians pray together in peace and unity, regardless of whether they speak the same language.

The Taizé community consists of approximately one hundred brothers, gathered from thirty nations and dozens of denominations. Brother Roger, who died in 2005, had friends across the faith spectrum, including Mother Teresa and two popes. He was awarded the UNESCO Prize for Peace Education and the Templeton Prize.[6]

Though Brother Roger was a Protestant from Switzerland, he appointed Brother Alois—a Roman Catholic from Germany—as the prior in his place. It's rare that a church leader gets to rub shoulders with the Catholic church's pope, the Orthodox patriarch, and the archbishop of Canterbury, but Brother Alois manages to do so.

I wanted to meet him.

"With a childlike trust, we let Christ pray silently within us."
BROTHER ROGER

When we arrived at Taizé, Michelle and I made our way to the registration office. "It doesn't cost anything to stay here," a volunteer

---

6 He gave away the one-million-dollar award.

explained. "But visitors are encouraged to offer a donation based on a grid—the older you are, and the wealthier your home country, the more you pay. The idea is that when a wealthy individual gives more, it makes up for the person who is coming from a further distance or from a poorer nation."

Since we were "old" and visiting from a wealthy nation, I expected to get hit with a large number. "Based on the chart," the volunteer said, "we would suggest a payment of around twelve dollars per person per night, which includes three meals and teatime." I looked at Michelle, laughed, and promptly overpaid the man.

We were given an info sheet and told to come back in an hour for a meeting. Our first stop was the gift shop. Everywhere we travel, Michelle collects a tea mug. I had originally suggested stamps or postcards, because they're smaller and easier to transport, but my wife presented compelling arguments about the importance of her daily tea ritual and how it serves as a bonding experience with friends.

I purchased a copy of the Rule of Taizé, the small white book that guides the common life of the community. I joined my wife in the pottery section. "Can I please buy ten of everything?" she asked.

I grinned. "You can buy as many items as you can fit in your bag." She purchased a single mug.

The Taizé brothers don't accept donations of any kind, and any inheritance they receive is given away. As their Rule states, "The pooling of possessions is total." Their only income is derived from the work of their hands—the creation of books, mugs, plates, jewelry, and so forth. "Daring to use for the best all that is available today, not laying up capital and without fear of possible poverty, gives an inestimable strength." No wonder the monks at Taizé pray so much.

We left the shop and walked to our room. Because it was "off season" and because we are married, Michelle and I got our own room. With bunk beds.

We dropped our stuff and walked to the pond, which was fed by a lovely little spring. I had never been to the headwaters of a river before. St. Stephen's Spring probably counts as the shortest river in the world, maybe thirty feet in total. Rolling up my pants, I kicked off my shoes and waded in, stooping down to drink at the source.

We joined the meeting shortly before it started. Surrounded by a sea of teenagers, I felt my age, even though I hadn't yet reached the ripe old age of thirty. Spotting a fellow "elder," a man in his sixties, I asked, "How many times have you been here?"

"Thirty-four," he replied curtly, in a thick Irish accent.

"Oh really? Wow!" I said. "For a whole week each time?"

"Yep." He nodded sternly.

He moved to the other side of the room and never spoke to us again.

A cheery brother addressed the group. "Welcome to Taizé! We're so happy to have you here. We hope that your time with us will be a blessing to you and that you will hear from God." He outlined the schedule for the week, which looked like this:

8:15 — morning prayer, then breakfast
10:00 — meetings
12:20 — midday prayer and lunch
2:00 — song practice
5:15 — snack
5:45 — workshops
7:00 — supper
8:30 — evening prayer

"I hope you will join us for song practice," he said earnestly. "We've found that when we practice beforehand, the prayer services sound much better!"

The audience laughed.

"I want you to make a commitment this week," he said. "Promise me that you'll sit beside someone new at every meal and every class and every service. You'll meet a lot of wonderful people, and some of you will even form lifelong friendships."

Everyone except Irish McCrabbypants, of course.

"You'll also have the opportunity to go deeper with a small group of people your own age," he explained. "You'll spend one hour per day together for the whole week." As he broke us into small groups, the Irish Rover wandered out of the room, never to be seen again.

After chatting with our small groups for a while, I approached the young brother in charge of the meeting, and we shook hands.

"Is it difficult to share a common life?" I asked.

"We are here for our whole lives," he said, smiling. "So we have a long time to learn to live together."

"The first step is to establish silence in oneself, so as to be ready to listen to one's Lord." BROTHER ROGER

Unlike on Athos, meals were served at long wooden tables in a room that looked more like a mess hall than a monastery. A German teenager sat down beside me and smiled.

"First time in Taizé?" I asked.

"No." She shook her head. "Third time! You?"

"First time," I said.

"You are going to love this place," she said. "When I come here, I feel so connected to God."

We heard a loud commotion at the next table. A group of young boys were goofing off.

"Not everyone who comes here is seeking God," she told me. "Most of the German kids are Lutheran. One week at Taizé counts as half a year of confirmation classes."

I laughed in dismay. "That's a pretty good deal!" I said.

"But some of them get touched by God," she said. "The prayer times here are pretty powerful."

You simply cannot miss a prayer service at Taizé. It's not that you are commanded to go, it's just that there are bells that ring for ten straight minutes, and they're so deafening that the only place you can find refuge is inside the sanctuary itself.

The sanctuary is called the "Church of Reconciliation." The exterior of the giant chapel is paneled with wood, with a small tower on top that looks like the Katholikons on Athos. The interior is not unlike an airport hangar, but with a strip of stained-glass windows along the roofline. There are traffic patterns on the floor to tell you where to sit and where to walk. At the front of the room is a stage, lit by an array of candles on geometric "shelves" in front of billowing fabric in fiery colors. It's breathtaking.

Everyone entered the room in silence. The bells rang faintly in the background.

The brothers entered in all-white robes. They seemed almost angelic. Many of the monks were in their thirties, and not one single brother had a beard.

I counted 59 brothers plus around 140 volunteers and visitors, at least 80 percent of whom were teenagers.

The brothers took their seats in the middle of the sanctuary, with two strips of green foliage to separate them from the guests. Visitors sat on their left and right, facing the brothers. The brothers sat facing forward, pointed toward the cross on the stage, one that looked remarkably similar to Francis's talking cross in Assisi.

The floor was strewn with little stools that alleviate ankle pressure for those who choose a kneeling position for the service. I chose a wall seat—both for the view and as a backrest for my aching spine.

The space felt sacred, but also very free—solemn without seeming "religious." People were sitting, standing, kneeling, lying down, reading their Bibles. Everything was well planned—at least two dozen microphones allowed different brothers to take turns leading each song or prayer or reading.

One of the brothers played "classical guitar" on an electric keyboard while the other brothers joined him in four-part harmony. The room filled with a sound so beautiful that Michelle and I turned to each other in awe. Practice made perfect.

They sang three songs. Each one was a simple prayer—one or two lines, at most, repeated several times. The main hymnbook contained about one hundred prayers in fourteen languages.

A brother read a passage of Scripture, and then we entered into a time of silence to let the Word of God sink in. It was a deep silence, broken only occasionally by a sneeze or a cough. It was so beautiful to share prolonged silence with hundreds of brothers and sisters. In a world that competes for attention, that always has an agenda to push and a point to prove, it was incredible to share a moment of silence with a large group of people. For a small moment, we weren't talkers and speakers. We were transformed into listeners and hearers.

But I'll be honest. It's hard to stay focused on God. Knowing this, Brother Roger mentioned it in the Rule of Taizé: "If your attention wanders, return to prayer as soon as you notice your distraction, without lamenting over it. If you experience your weakness while actually praying, do not forget that the essential has already been accomplished in you." The essence of prayer is a desire for relationship. Brother Roger encouraged people to see every distraction as a call back to prayer, every distraction as a call back to Christ.

After the time of silence, which lasted about eight minutes, three brothers read prayers of petition. The audience responded to each by singing *Kyrie eleison*. It was the same Greek phrase I had chanted on Mount Athos.[7]

---

[7] I later discovered that the "Kyrie eleison" prayer is over 1,500 years old—a fourth-century nun from northwestern Spain recorded that Christians chanted the phrase during lamp-lighting services in Jerusalem.

Kyrie eleison. What did it mean?

I searched through the songbook until I found the English translation.

Lord, have mercy.

Like the Jesus Prayer and the metanie and my "dark night of the soul" prayer, I was brought back to mercy. I thought about Hosea 6:6 and how it's such a hard verse for me to swallow: "I desire mercy, not sacrifice, and acknowledgment of God rather than burnt offerings." God doesn't want me to just help people; He wants me to love them. He wants far more than my time and talent and treasure; He wants my heart.

We concluded with the Lord's Prayer. The brothers stood, formed a line, and filed out of the room. The audience slowly trickled out as they felt led. In total, the service lasted just forty minutes, but the music and the silence and the candles and the readings joined together to create an intoxicating experience that seemed to last far longer. It was easily the most beautiful prayer meeting Michelle and I had ever attended.

As we exited the chapel, the truth of one of Taizé's core principles became so clearly evident to me: *Inner stillness is the key to outer strength.* Their prayer fueled their work.

"For your prayer to be real, you need to be at grips with the demands of work. . . . Your prayer becomes complete when it is one with your work." BROTHER ROGER

In the afternoon I had a long chat with two friendly volunteers—one Catholic, one Protestant.

"There are about fifty of us here right now," the Catholic said. "Half guys, half girls."

"In the summer," the Protestant added, "that number is like two hundred or more."

"Tell me about your week," I said.

"We work four to five hours per day," the Catholic answered. "Seven days per week."

"We are busy, but blessed!" the Protestant interjected. "Sharing a common life is a wonderful experience."

Despite working seven days a week, the volunteers felt it was a sustainable rhythm.

To be honest, I haven't met a lot of Christian volunteers or leaders who've served at a life-giving pace. Myself included. Many years ago, I used to be a youth pastor. I can attest to the reality of church ministry burnout. I worked for a church with a massive "back door"—the turnover of attendees and volunteers was staggering. My evenings and weekends were nonexistent. The pressure to "perform" (read: increase attendance) always hovered over me. I felt alone. By the time I was fired by the distrustful senior pastor,[8] I was pretty much toast. It took years to recover, and I still haven't ventured back into "vocational ministry."

Yet somehow Taizé seemed different.

"We never work alone," the Protestant continued. "And there's no pressure to meet a quota or anything. The focus is on God."

"There's an inner peace and silence that you get from praying three times per day," said the Catholic. "I feel the Holy Spirit here."

"Do you ever get tired of going to church so often?" I joked.

"Yes, sometimes." The Catholic nodded. "But it's important to still go, to show God you are willing."

I had read about this in the Rule of Taizé: "There are days when the common prayer becomes a burden to you. Then just offer your body; your simple presence signifies your desire, momentarily unrealizable, to praise your Lord."

Sometimes you just need to show up.

---

[8] I was the third youth pastor fired at the end of their third year.

"Prayer is an aspiration of the heart, it is a simple glance directed to heaven, it is a cry of gratitude and love in the midst of trial as well as joy; finally, it is something great, supernatural, which expands my soul and unites me to Jesus." ST. THÉRÈSE OF LISIEUX

All we did at Taizé was eat, pray, work, and sleep, and our time flew by.

Every guest worked one to two hours per day. On our first day, I volunteered, alongside a hilarious Australian dude, to clean fifteen toilets. We laughed and shared travel stories and had a great time. Work is easy when it's full of meaning and shared with others.

After chores, Michelle and I wandered to the Taizé store for a soda. Among other things, the shop sold 100 percent–recycled paper notebooks, fair-trade chocolate, and six kinds of cigarettes. Only in France.

Over the course of our time there, I did everything in my power to deliver Gustav's letter to Brother Matthew. I made a total of three trips to the front office, placing a total of fifteen phone calls. I (kindly) harassed dozens of people in an attempt to make good on my promise, yet Matthew didn't seem to exist. I prayed that an opportunity would present itself.

During our final supper in France, we met a young woman named Carrie. She was about our age, and she had been to Taizé over twenty times. As we finished our supper, the conversation turned serious.

"I actually worked here for two years," she said.

She bit her lip.

"I was in the room on the night Brother Roger was murdered."

"Inner silence requires first the forgetting of self, so as to quieten conflicting voices and master obsessive anxiety, constantly beginning again as a person who is never discouraged because always forgiven." BROTHER ROGER

"She had purchased the knife in a neighboring town," Carrie said. "Just one day before coming here."

I had heard the story and read some reports; a young woman with a serious mental illness had heard inner voices and felt she needed to kill the founder of Taizé.

"How old was Brother Roger at the time?" I asked.

"He was ninety," Carrie replied. "He was so sweet and so beautiful." She shook her head. "It was during the evening prayer meeting," she continued. "He was sitting in his usual place at the back of the room. There were over two thousand people in the sanctuary, but no one was behind him."

She paused and took a deep breath. "No one saw it coming."

The young woman had entered through a side door, walked directly to Brother Roger, and stabbed him three times in the back and throat.

"Did everyone panic?" I asked. "Did anyone scream?"

"I don't know. I think so." She shook her head. "Everyone was very confused. Some brothers disarmed the girl, and some others quickly carried Brother Roger out. He was bleeding very badly.

"For a few seconds, evil was present," she said. "But God quickly took over.

"New brothers are taught that prayer must always continue," she explained. "I don't remember who, but one of the brothers led a song. It was '*Laudate Omnes Gentes*,'[9] number 23 in the songbook, I think."

It was. *Sing praises, all you peoples, sing praises to the Lord.*

"So what happened next?" I leaned forward.

"Brother Alois was in Cologne for World Youth Day. Brother Roger had already decided that Alois would replace him when he died," she explained. "Brother Alois drove all night and was in Brother Roger's place for morning prayer."

The prayers never stopped.

"I'll never forget the prayer Brother Alois prayed at the funeral[10]

---

9 Google "Taizé Laudate Omnes Gentes." Turn up the volume.
10 A Catholic cardinal presided over the funeral, and the president of Germany and the future president of France, among thousands of others, were in attendance. Both the pope and the archbishop of Canterbury issued statements.

a few days later," she said. "'Together with Christ on the cross we pray, "Father forgive her, for she did not know what she was doing.'"

"Life on the hill continued," she said. "A brother would start a song and then break down with grief, and another brother would immediately step in to continue. The phrase 'How are you?' took on a whole new meaning."

She paused to wipe a tear from her eye. "We carried each other."

Such is the strength of sharing a common life. It's something I'm trying to cultivate in my own life, fighting back against "busyness" for the sake of developing real relationships. I'd love to be part of a community like Taizé back home. It's a dream Michelle and I share with a few close friends. We're praying for a big piece of land where we can raise our families together while intentionally helping those in desperate need. We'd love to be a safe haven for sex-trafficking victims. The first home for refugee families. A permanent home for orphans and single moms. A place where young people can learn life skills like woodworking while being trained in the ways of Christ. A place where the elderly can live out their final years with community and dignity and purpose. Like Taizé and the Ignatius Centre in Ontario, we'd like to be a place of spiritual retreat, for prayer and meditation. We'd love to build some cottages for burned-out pastors and missionaries on furlough. Michelle's best friend died when she was nineteen, so we'd love to have cabins for mourners—a place where people can cry and pray and find healing. Basically, we want to build a village of hope. We want to build a city of prayer.

Obviously, we can't just pray for a piece of land—we have to work toward it as well. In preparation, Michelle and I have volunteered at ecovillages and intentional communities. We've visited places like Taizé. We've started a charity to fight sex trafficking. We've simplified our lives so we have a margin of time and money to give. We pray and work, work and pray, pray and work, and hope to bring the spirit of Taizé to Canada someday.

"But who is not daunted by this silence, preferring to be distracted when it is time for work, fleeing prayer to wear himself out at useless tasks, forgetful of his neighbour and himself?" BROTHER ROGER

It was our final morning at Taizé, and I decided to approach Brother Alois after the prayer service. He still sits at the back of the room—but he's flanked by four brothers, and there's a red panic button on the floor by his side.

"Brother Alois," I said. "Thank you for opening your home to us this week."

He bowed slightly. He was on the small side and very handsome. He was maybe fifty, but seemed youthful.[11] He radiated warmth and was full of joy. His mouth curved upward, like he was perpetually on the edge of laughter. He had warm eyes and was fully present.

"What does prayer mean to you?" I asked.

"To pray is to achieve inner silence in all things," he said. "So as to dwell in Christ."

"Ah, good man!" I said. "I see you believe the motto of Taizé!" We laughed.

"So the question really is, how do you achieve inner silence in all things so as to dwell in Christ?"

"Yes, that is the question," he said. "You achieve inner silence by remembering His presence."

I felt like I was talking to a modern-day Brother Lawrence. "How do I do that?" I asked.

"Well," he replied with a grin, "praying three times a day helps!"

It certainly had. "How do you hear from God, Brother Alois?" I asked.

He said, "Well, I read the Bible. If anything sticks out more than the rest, if one word stands out from all the others, that's the word for today. We all want Moses' burning bush or Paul's bright light, but

---

11 It turned out he was almost sixty when we met, which further proves my point.

they could have been misinterpreted too. Paul could have said, 'I need a break; I have been arresting too many Christians.' Moses could have said, 'Ah, I'm getting too hot here in the desert.' Be simple. If a verse sticks out, do what it says."

I had read about this practice in the Rule of Taizé. "In your life of prayer and meditation, seek the word which God addresses to you and put it into practice at once. So read little, but dwell on it." I'd never been to a church that advocated reading *less* Scripture.

"So, Brother Alois," I said, "what is your prayer for the world?"

He closed his eyes. "Peace, peace, peace," he said. "A few days ago I met a Carmelite sister from Syria." He trailed off as he thought of her dangerous mission field. "So I pray for peace."

Peace again. Everything kept coming back to shalom.

"You know," he added, "we are not prayer experts here at Taizé. We are babies! We are talking to God like children."

This was a disconcerting thought. If the Taizé brothers are babies, what am I? If these men who have committed their entire lives to prayer and service are children, then what sort of malformed creature have I become? How can I have what they have? How can I dwell with Christ? I knew it started with maintaining inner silence in all things.

We shook hands and I thanked him. "Father Alois, one more thing," I said. "Can you please give this letter to Brother Matthew?"

He promised he would.

CHAPTER 8

Eastern USA

AFTER LEAVING TAIZÉ, I wanted to further explore the idea of silence. It had never occurred to me that a large part of my prayer life should be spent *not* talking, but after my time in Europe, I craved a deep silence. I had heard there was a particular strain of Christians who actually spent their entire church services in silence, and I wanted to check them out.

So I headed to Maryland to meet some Quakers.

Officially called the Religious Society of Friends, Quakerism was founded by farmers and tradesmen in the mid-seventeenth century. They were led by a twenty-two-year-old English shoemaker named George Fox,[1] who believed that the institutional church of the day was leading people away from the core aims of Christianity. This

---

[1] Among his supporters was William Penn the founder of Pennsylvania and Philadelphia and the man whose face many associate with Quaker Oats cereal boxes.

belief majorly upset the status quo, and Fox was arrested over sixty times and jailed at least nine times for his efforts. More than thirteen thousand Quakers were imprisoned—over three hundred died, and almost two hundred were sold into slavery.

After Fox told one of the judges to "tremble at the word of the Lord," the judge laughed and called Fox's followers "Quakers." The name stuck, though Quakers usually refer to themselves as "Friends."

The early Friends believed God didn't dwell in church buildings—He lived in their hearts. They truly believed in the "priesthood of all believers." They ignored rituals and focused instead on an indwelling of the Holy Spirit. They focused on simplicity and truthfulness and tried to follow Jesus' example more closely.

Today there are more than eighty thousand Friends in America, and fewer than four hundred thousand worldwide. While many Quaker meetinghouses now use programmed services, some still adhere to the original style of unprogrammed worship. They call it "waiting worship."

Silence.

"If we read the biographies of the great and wise, we shall find they were people of long silences and deep ponderings. . . . Their roots struck deep into the soil of spiritual silence." BRIDGID HERMAN

The Third Haven Meetinghouse is located in Easton, Maryland, just twelve miles from the birthplace of Frederick Douglass and about thirty miles from the birthplace of Harriet Tubman. It was built on three acres of land purchased from John Edmundson in 1682, and the meetinghouse was completed in 1684. In keeping with tradition, Michelle's "first time" experience would continue to be the best—Third Haven is the oldest frame house of worship in the United States.

Quakers have long been known as pacifists, but they've also been quite active in fighting for all sorts of reforms. In their 367-year history, Quakers have freed slaves, helped patients with mental illnesses, harbored refugees, cared for war casualties and the elderly, and started all sorts of charities. Who would have thought that worshiping in silence could lead to so much practical action?[2]

I e-mailed the meetinghouse to let them know we'd be attending their Wednesday night service. In keeping with their spiritual DNA, they invited us to arrive early so we could tell them about our sex-trafficking abolitionist work.

We drove down the long, tree-lined lane tucked between two properties. I parked the car and met Chris, the kind Quaker with whom we'd be staying that evening. He gave me a quick tour of the property. "That's the old meetinghouse." He pointed to a Cape Cod–style house with white siding and green shutters.

"There's a cemetery in the backyard," he said. "We've identified 177 graves so far. Of course, the Friends didn't use gravestones for the first hundred years, so there are probably thousands of bodies buried out there."

We went into the meetinghouse. I sniffed the air. I love the smell of cedar benches.

"No furnace or plumbing in this place," Chris said. "Just the way it used to be."

I looked down at the foot-wide floorboards.

"Pine boards." Chris stomped on the floor. "Split trunk, too. I can't say they weren't milled by slaves."

The room was full of benches, set roughly in a square. A set of guillotine-style sliding wood panels ran down the center of the room, previously used to wall off the women from the men. The room was dusty and abandoned. Piles of building supplies lay stacked on the rear benches.

It was quiet. *Really* quiet. I sat on a bench and entered into the silence experienced by generations of those who had prayed in that

---

[2] Mother Teresa, that's who. She once said that "the fruit of silence is prayer. The fruit of prayer is faith. The fruit of faith is love. The fruit of love is service. The fruit of service is peace."

place, a silence that seemed to echo through the ages. I thought about Fox and the early dissenters: young people attempting to get back to a relationship with the Holy Spirit, no matter the personal sacrifice. I sat in their silence.

"Silence is the tribute that we pay to holiness; we slip off words when we enter a sacred place, just as we slip off shoes." PICO IYER

After visiting the fellowship hall, we made our way to the "new" brick meetinghouse. Built in 1880 in the late Greek-revival style, it had heat and power, but only four-inch hardwood boards.

Two words were written on the door: *Cell phone.* Since Quaker gatherings involve total silence for the duration of the service, pop ringtones would be particularly disruptive.

We took our seats. In total, seventeen people attended the service. We sat in pews in a square, facing a central table that held the Bible and a Quaker book titled *Faith and Practice*. The silence was unbroken, except for the few seconds when my watch alarm went off. After the service, we returned to the fellowship hall.

Michelle and I sat at a table with four Quakers, and I opened my notebook. A kind man named Jim gave me the backstory on the meetinghouse. Third Haven had around 150 members, including eight committees and an average Sunday attendance of around sixty-five to eighty people. They didn't take an offering, but everyone was expected to chip in, both financially and by serving.

"That's awesome," I said. "So how do you define prayer?"

"Sitting in waitful expectancy," Jim said. "Centering your connection with God."

"So how do you pray for people?" I asked.

"We hold them in the light," a sweet lady named Peggy answered.

"And how does that work?" I asked.

"To hold someone in the light is to picture that person in the light of God's grace," she said. "We try not to say anything or add our agenda. Just by holding people in the light, God can do whatever He needs to do in their lives."

While I hadn't ever described it that way, I had definitely held people in the light before. Sometimes I've felt burdened to pray for someone but couldn't find the words to say. I've often just pictured the person's face and tried to present that picture to God, asking Him to do His will.

And now, after my visit to Third Haven, I've made "holding in the light" a regular part of my prayer life. It's had a profound impact on the way I view certain people—particularly those I dislike. There's a quote by Dorothy Day that I love to paraphrase: "I love God as much as the person I love the least." This idea has really convicted me. I started holding my "enemies" in the light, and now I love them. I don't want to hate anyone. I don't want to harbor bitterness. I want to "let go and let God."

I started with an old boss I used to have. She was the meanest person I've ever met. I started holding her in the light, praying, "God, help me to see her as You see her. Help me to love her as You love her." And you know what? Now, when I pray for her, I get kind of giddy. I'm excited for what God is going to do in her life. There's no more hatred or animosity. Only love—unconditional love that I could never muster or conjure up on my own. I feel God's love toward a former enemy. I feel what Christ felt on the cross.

"So why do you sit in silence twice a week?" I asked my Quaker hosts.

"Each Friend is a seeker of the truth," a middle-aged woman named Judy said. "We're trying to live thoughtfully, consciously, and intentionally. We're trying to find something of God in our daily lives, and silence really helps."

I resonated with Judy's answer. Michelle and I had been trying to live consciously and intentionally for the past few years. We agree with Andy Crouch that a life without meditation leads to exploitation. Silence helps determine action.

"Okay, next question," I said. "It was really quiet in there today. I've heard that people talk sometimes. Is that true?"

An elderly woman named Joyce nodded her head. "Yes, that's called vocal ministry," she said. "During an average Sunday service, maybe two or three people will share a word from God. It's rarely silent the whole time."

A younger woman named Claire took over. "If you sense that you have a word from God, you have to ask yourself three questions. Number one, is this from God? Number two, is this for me or for everyone? And number three, is this for now? If you decide to share, you try to keep it brief."

I had read in *Faith and Practice* about the Quaker definition of "brief": "It should be delivered with as few words as possible, yet as many as necessary."

"We are helping each other discover our message," Claire said.

"So what is that message?" I asked. "What do Quakers believe?"

"SPICES!" Joyce said. The group laughed.

"Spices?" I asked.

"S-P-I-C-E-S," Joyce spelled. "Simplicity, Peace, Integrity, Community, Equality, and Stewardship."

Jim said, "Those are our six values, but they aren't set in stone. Matter of fact, they rewrite *Faith and Practice* every five or six years, I think."

"Interesting," I said. "So what beliefs or values *are* set in stone?"

Jim shook his head. "None."

My eyes widened. "*None?*" I asked.

"Quakers recognize all major faiths as paths to spiritual fulfillment," he explained. "Many of us follow the Bible, but it's not the only holy book. We don't believe in heaven or hell or sin or the Trinity. We don't worry about the afterlife. We live in the here and now."

I was shocked, to be honest. I hadn't realized how far removed from its roots the Quaker faith had become.

"So what do you think about Jesus?" I asked.

"Jesus was a good man," Jim said. "But it doesn't mean He didn't sin!"

I—and the Bible—had to disagree with him there.

"In that case, who is God to you? *What* is God to you?" I asked.

They all generally agreed that the best description of God is "light." In the following hour, I learned there is no such thing as an "average Quaker." Because they don't regularly read the Bible or teach theology, very few are on the same page theologically. What unites them is a general sense of "truth" and "light." They have no definitive answers for questions about sin and absolute truth.

It was hard to swallow. I suspect George Fox and the early Quakers were real Bible-believing, Jesus-following Christians. Today, the Friends might be considered an early chapter in an ever-changing manuscript.

"All the troubles of life come upon us because we refuse to sit quietly for a while each day in our rooms." BLAISE PASCAL

As I reflected on my time at Third Haven, I was filled with sadness. While the global church has a lot to learn about silence, we also need to guard our theology like it's our life. We need to shut our mouths and listen to Christ, but we also need to open our mouths so we can sharpen each other. We must always return to the Word of God, our primary source of freshwater. The church, together as a community, needs to be "rightly dividing the word of truth."

That said, I think the church needs to start having conversations about silence. I know I rarely shut up. Even when I'm not talking, my brain is constantly thinking. Day and night, my brain is always *on.* I remember my dreams almost every single night. I can control many of them too. Neither my mind nor my ears spend much time in silence. I'm not still. I'm not listening. And I'm not the only one. It's probably city life—and selfishness, laziness, workaholism, and all the other addictions and vices that we use to distract ourselves from dealing with heart work.

In his book *The Hour That Changes the World*, Dick Eastman shares the prayer practice of an elderly lady: "I pray until I can't pray any more. Then I take my Bible and read until I can't read any more. After that, I take my hymnbook from the shelf and I sing until I can't sing any more. Then I just sit quietly and let God love me."

In silence, we commune with Christ.

God didn't speak to Elijah in the wind, the earthquake, or the fire. He spoke to him in a "still small voice," what one commentary calls "a voice of gentle silence."

If two people sat down for dinner and both of them talked the entire time, how much would they hear of the other person's point of view? Silence is a gift that allows us to turn a monologue into a dialogue. Without silence, there is no conversation. Without silence, we miss a large part of what God has to say to us.

Christians don't practice silence like Buddhists. We're not striving for emptiness and nothingness. On the contrary, we practice silence so we can hear from an ever-speaking God. Our stillness leads to action.

"Right prayer demands a quieting of the whole being," writes Dr. A. E. Day. "The truest prayer begins when we pass beyond words into deep silence; when lips are hushed; when racing thoughts are stilled; when emotions are placid as the dawning over the waveless ocean."

Like Brother Roger, we maintain inner silence in all things so as to dwell in Christ.

*"At the same time spake the Lord by Isaiah the son of Amoz, saying,
Go and loose the sackcloth from off thy loins. . . . And he did so,
walking naked and barefoot."*   ISAIAH 20:2, KJV

The Old Testament prophets, by contrast, were rarely silent. They were actors, proclaiming and performing the drama of God before the people. They were godly dudes who did all sorts of weird stuff in order to lead the people back to God. Hosea married a prostituted woman. Ezekiel slept on his left side for 390 days, then on his right side for forty days, and then he baked his bread using cow dung for fuel.[3] Isaiah walked around barefoot and stripped naked for three whole years—the text specifically mentions the phrase "buttocks bared," which is uncomfortable to type.

As uncomfortable as that is to type, nudity itself has never been much of a problem for me. As a toddler I ran around naked all the time. As a teenager I practiced the sport of mooning. As a young adult I went skinny-dipping almost every summer. Boys like to be naked. This is a fact of life. Our friends Cat and Cody have three young boys.[4] In an effort to keep their offspring clothed in public, they schedule a daily allotment of nakedness called "naked nudie time."

Many famous people were nudists. Benjamin Franklin used to take "air baths." Walt Whitman was a big fan of skinny-dipping. Charles Richter, who invented the Richter scale, was also known to experiment in the buff.

Michelle and I actually live in a nudist resort—a *former* nudist resort, that is. Last year, in an attempt to simplify our lives and increase our margin of time and money, we purchased a 1975 Airstream and moved it into a trailer park. The park was originally a Canadian nudist camp called Four Seasons. Today, clothes are mandatory, but we still have some eighty-year-old resisters.

---

[3] Ezekiel was first ordered to bake bread using "human excrement for fuel." (This is the last time that I will ever use the phrase *human excrement* in a book.) But Ezekiel was eventually permitted to cook his food over cow dung instead of human excrement. Dang it, I did it again!

[4] Their oldest son, Oakley, prays for me almost every night. My favorite prayer ever: "Dear Jesus, I pray for Uncle Jay, Auntie Michelle, and Buzz Lightyear."

Interestingly enough, I had to get naked in order to ask for my wife's hand in marriage. Michelle comes from a Finnish family, and her father insisted that I ask his permission in the sauna.

Michelle and my future mother-in-law begged him to let me ask "like everyone else," but he was adamant. "If he wants to marry my daughter, he has to ask like a man!"

So I requested to marry his daughter, buck naked, in a blazing hot Finnish sauna. He would ask a question and then throw water on the rocks. Talk about a trial by fire.

After our time in Maryland, Michelle and I took a detour to a little town called Ivor, home of the only nudist resort in all of Virginia. Founded in 1984, the camp has about forty permanent residents and over six hundred community members. Located off Tucker Swamp Road, it's roughly in the vicinity of the first peanut plantation in America. The resort itself was of little interest to me. I was interested in a small white building on the property that had recently made national news for being, well, weird.

I was on my way to visit a nudist church.

"Is not life more than food, and the body more than clothes?"
MATTHEW 6:25

"White Tail Chapel." Michelle read the sign out loud. "That sounds about right."

We arrived at the front gate, which was actually a fort-like fence. No Peeping Toms allowed. I pressed the buzzer. "Hi there," I said into the microphone. "I'm here to see Pastor Allen."

The big wooden fence swung open and we drove in. We parked

at the main building and went hunting for Allen, being careful not to peer into the houses as we walked. We eventually found his place, and I knocked on the door.

"You're early!" Allen said. "Pastor John and I were just about to sit down to pray about our meeting."

It's important to mention that we visited White Tail for purely anthropological reasons. It was not an exploratory trip to determine whether we should become nudists. We purposely visited on a weekday in hopes of mitigating our chances of seeing, well, white tail.

John and Allen walked us to the chapel. Both were bearded, but their beards were much shorter than the manes on Athos. Allen was fifty-three years old, weighed at least 280 pounds, and was a Baptist. John was sixty-two, easily 350 pounds, and was a Pentecostal. Allen worked in construction, but John was retired. "Special ops," he said. "If I told you, I'd have to kill you!"

"And they'd never find the body," Allen added. "One of the many benefits of living in a swamp!"

Awkward laughs all around.

We arrived at the chapel. It was a tiny building with white siding and a white steeple and cross on top. It reminded me of the miniature chapels in Ouranoupolis.

The interior was (dare I say?) bare—there was a crucifix and a golden angel on the wall, as well as a single stained-glass window. The chapel had theater-quality seating for thirty-six.

"Nice chairs!" I tapped on the padded reclining seats.

"Yep, we got those from a local cinema," Allen said. "We used to have metal seats, but that was awful in wintertime."

We sat at the front of the church on a makeshift stage. There was bug spray behind the pulpit.

"Get comfortable," Allen said. "Take your jacket off. If it gets too hot, I'll be stripping everything off!"

Michelle laughed uneasily.

The men were both relaxed, quite friendly, and, mercifully, clothed. I launched right into my questions.

"Okay, first question," I said. "When did you both become nudists?"

John started. "I was born naked, actually."

I laughed.

"I started stripping at age three," Allen said. "Clothes don't fit me." He pointed at his waistline. "Does this look like the body of a model to you?"

No one said anything.

"It was harder for our wives at first, but now they'd never let us leave," Allen continued as he looked at Michelle. "Women usually come to the park kicking and screaming, and they leave the same way."

John joked, "The only difference between nudists and other folks is that after a big meal, we don't have to loosen our belts."

"Okay, let's talk about the church!" I said.

"The fellowship has been active since 1985," Allen said. "And the chapel was rebuilt in 2006. We have about ten to fifteen attendees in the winter and up to forty in the summer months. We're very multidenominational. We have Methodists, Baptists, Pentecostals, Catholics, and Jews. We met a Muslim nudist once, but he didn't come to church. We're born-again Christians, after all."

"We run a Sunday Bible study at 9:30 a.m.," John explained. "And a 10:30 worship service. People love it."

Allen added, "Nudism is a great equalizer. There's a camaraderie and fellowship to it. Where else can a garbageman and a banker eat lunch together and be best friends?"

"It's a little piece of heaven on earth," John declared. "A slice of Eden, surrounded by thistles." I thought about St. Benedict. He would have fit right in.

"The man and his wife were both naked and were not ashamed."
GENESIS 2:25, ESV

"So how can you be a Christian and a nudist?" I asked.

"There are forty-six mentions of nakedness in Scripture, give or take," said Allen. "Noah was naked, but it was Ham who got in trouble for walking in on him."

"Solomon was naked," John added. "And Isaiah was naked for three years."

Allen said, "God didn't clothe Adam and Eve. He just gave them *protection*."

"And then, of course, there's Jesus Himself," Allen continued.

"Wait, what?" Michelle blurted. "How was Jesus a nudist?"

Allen said, "Jesus was in the garden after His resurrection." John nodded along. "The Bible says His clothes were in the tomb, and the text says He was mistaken as the gardener. In those days gardeners often worked naked."

I looked at Michelle. We both thought it was a stretch.

"You need to remember—we have a code of conduct that's stricter than most conservative churches," Allen said.

I doubted that.

"The park does background checks on every visitor, and we check the sex offender registry too. We also have inter-resort communication, so we can refuse anyone who isn't respectful."

"But what about lust?" I asked.

"It doesn't happen," Allen said and shook his head.

"What!" I howled. "Come on!"

"It doesn't happen," he repeated. "It's not a sexually infused environment."

I was confused. How was a park full of naked people not a sexually infused environment?

"It's like going to your doctor," Allen explained. "There are lots of forms of nudity that aren't sexual in any way."

Allen was right, of course. There is nothing sexy about childbirth. There's nothing sexy about changing a baby's soiled nappy.

"But still," I protested, "why run that risk?"

"Nudism is actually the best cure for sexual addiction," Allen declared. "It allows you to see people's true beauty and real humanity. When you first become a nudist, it's *all* eye contact. You start to connect on a level you've never connected on before."

"Nudism is also a great healer for people who have been abused," John added. "Body acceptance is the goal, and acceptance into community. No one judges what you look like; no one judges what has happened to you. Even women with mastectomies—they fit in. There's no judging or comparing here."

I didn't know what to think. Both men were faithfully married. Allen had been married for twenty-nine years, and John had been married for thirty-seven years. "Nudists run 20 percent *under* the national average for divorce," John said.

I haven't been able to confirm or refute this figure—doing the research proved to be a little . . . dicey.

"Beauty when unadorned is adorned the most." ST. JEROME

"Nudism isn't about sex. It's about being naked. Free. Unfettered. It's about being open," John explained.

"If you really want to be close to God, go home and strip naked," Allen suggested. "That's what I did. Wait until no one's home. Lock the doors, shut the blinds, and take off your clothes. Get in your closet and sit in silence. Say, 'Okay, God, I'm here. Let's talk. I have nothing to hide from you. I can't hide my shame. I'm completely exposed before you.' Then let Christ's glory cover you. It's a beautiful thing. It's a return to the celebration of David."

Allen was passionate on this point. "This is all about Jesus," he said. "We've already had a few salvations and baptisms in the hot tub. Our mission for the chapel is the great commission. We were told to go to Jerusalem, Judea, and the uttermost parts of the earth."

I shuddered when he said "uttermost parts."

"Nudist resorts are in great need of churches," John said. "Christians tend to avoid places like White Tail."

"In fact, over half the people in our congregation are wounded former churchgoers," Allen informed us. "Who is ministering to nudists?"

It was a great question, and it raised a whole series of further questions in my mind. Who *was* reaching nudists? Who was reaching porn stars? Who was reaching prostituted women? Who was reaching human traffickers? Who was reaching Wall Street bankers?

Paul tells us he has "become all things to all people so that by all possible means [he] might save some," and elsewhere encourages others to "follow my example, as I follow the example of Christ." Obviously this doesn't mean we start sinning in order to win people to Christ. But how *do* we win these people to Christ?

As Michelle and I stood to leave, we learned it was Allen's birthday. Michelle attempted a "birthday suit" joke, but no one caught it. We said good-bye and continued on our journey.

"Well, that was something!" Michelle said. "I'm glad we went there. Now I can strike it off my list of things that scare me. It's weird, but I get it."

That evening I received a follow-up e-mail from Allen. He wanted to add a couple of important things we hadn't had time to discuss. "We are Christians working in a nudist environment with nudists," he wrote. "We are not Christians trying to convince other Christians to become nudists. Our mission is from God. . . . I know I was sent to this location and placed in this work. My grandmother, although she never saw me at a nudist resort, saw me as a pastor when I was only five years old."

I appreciated his sincerity.

"Maybe one time when you come through, you two will come over for dinner," he ended the letter. "Maybe even some hot tub or pool in the evening."

I teased Michelle with the kindly invitation.

"Over my dead body!" she howled.

Later, when we got home, I did as Allen suggested. I prayed naked. I got mikvah naked—no socks, no glasses, no hair conditioner. I stood in front of the mirror and stared at all 222 pounds of hairy me. It was a sight for sore eyes. Thankfully, I wasn't wearing glasses. I prayed, but it didn't do much for me. I was worried the whole time that a spider might crawl up my thigh.

Nude church was definitely weird. Michelle and I have decided to pass on it—it's not worth the risk—but there's something about the body acceptance and openness before God that I'd like to continue exploring. At home. By myself. With the shades drawn.

Even the author of Hebrews is in favor of some form of spiritual nudity. The first verses of chapter 12 say, "Since we are surrounded by such a great cloud of witnesses, let us throw off everything that hinders and the sin that so easily entangles. And let us run with perseverance the race marked out for us, fixing our eyes on Jesus, the pioneer and perfecter of faith."

According to Craig Groeschel, it's very likely that this passage refers to the Isthmian Games, one of the four Panhellenic Games held in ancient Greece. With the exception of chariot racing, all events were held in the nude.[5] Simply put, you can run faster when you're naked.

I think this makes a good point. I have a large stock of prayer hindrances. If prayer is about running toward Jesus, then it's wise to get spiritually naked. I want a prayer life that's free and unfettered. I want a communion with Christ that's not held back by anything. I want to win this race.

---

[5] This included wrestling, long jump, and javelin throwing. *Shudder.*

"The only time my prayers are never answered is on the golf course."

BILLY GRAHAM

I've wanted to meet Billy Graham ever since I read a kid's version of his biography when I was eleven years old. A paragraph in that biography almost killed me eight years later.

Shortly after Prohibition ended, Billy Graham's father went to the liquor store and purchased two twenty-four packs of beer. Billy was eight at the time. Billy's father sat his kids at the table and told them to drink a bottle. And then another, and another, and another, until all four kids puked their guts out. None of them ever drank again.[6]

I read that story as a highly impressionable eleven-year-old and tucked it in the back of my brain. Eight years later I turned nineteen, the legal drinking age in Canada. I respected Billy Graham, and I wanted to be a godly young man who never struggled with drunkenness. So I went to a liquor store and purchased an eight-ounce bottle of Jack Daniel's whiskey and an eight-ounce bottle of Smirnoff vodka.

No one had ever told me about blood alcohol limits. Or about the danger of mixing drinks. Or about alcohol poisoning. All I knew was that it worked for Billy Graham, and that was good enough for me.

I was all alone when I chugged both bottles.

Three seconds later, I felt ill. *Very* ill. I grabbed a garbage can, and like Billy Graham before me, I puked my guts out. I started to choke. I couldn't breathe. I prayed, *God, save me!* Ten seconds later, it stopped. I passed out.

Gratefully, I didn't die. I awoke sixteen hours later and felt great. To this day, I've never been drunk. If I smell hard liquor, I feel like puking.

And for that I can thank Billy Graham's father.

---

[6] I later discovered the actual facts: Billy was fifteen at the time. Only one sister was forced to drink with him. And I have no idea how much beer Mr. Graham actually purchased.

"Prayer is simply a two-way conversation between you and God."

BILLY GRAHAM

North Carolina's Favorite Son has spoken live to over 215 million people in more than 185 countries—more than any other man in history. Including media, his message has reached more than 2.2 *billion* people. According to his staff, more than three million people have received Christ as their Savior through his ministry. Billy Graham has appeared on Gallup's "Ten Most Admired Men in the World" more than fifty times—more than any other man. He has received the Presidential Medal of Freedom, the Horatio Alger Award, and the Templeton Prize.

I don't think my generation fully realizes how truly massive Billy Graham's influence is. Dubbed "America's Pastor," Graham has advised twelve US presidents. *A dozen commanders in chief.* He urged Truman to fight Communism in North Korea. He helped Eisenhower receive assurance of his salvation. He drove around in JFK's white Lincoln convertible. He spent at least twenty nights with Johnson. He read the Bible to Nixon. Ford shared his friendship. Carter chaired a Billy Graham film crusade. Graham knew Reagan when he was a Democrat, and he was with Bush Sr. the night the Gulf War began. As a twelve-year-old boy, Clinton was deeply inspired when Graham refused to racially segregate the crowds at his Little Rock crusade. Graham supposedly helped Bush Jr. recommit his heart to Jesus. He prayed with Obama in 2010.

At the time of this writing, Billy Graham is still alive. At ninety-five, it's possible that he'll have passed away by the time this book goes to print. To meet Billy Graham, at this point in his life, is, to say the least, one of the most unlikely scenarios. It is far easier to meet the pope.

I pursued avenue after avenue, connection after connection, but every road was blocked by a web of bureaucracy. If I was to be granted the honor of meeting Billy Graham, it would be one stop short of a miracle, and only by the total favor of God and man.

I decided to knock on his front door.

"Go after a dream that is destined to fail without divine intervention."
MARK BATTERSON

I arrived in North Carolina the night before my unscheduled visit to Billy's house. His address is unlisted, but I had found his house using skills from my former career as a Realtor. When I was nineteen, I got my license, sold a bunch of houses, and flipped a fourplex. I just wanted to get rich. Then God changed my priorities. I got tired of selling, especially things people didn't need. These days I have little interest in getting wealthy. But every once in a while, those real estate skills prove helpful.

Billy lives just outside the small town of Montreat in North Carolina. Montreat is a Presbyterian community originally purchased and developed in 1907. The name is a mash-up of "mountain" and "retreat." Montreat is home to a Presbyterian college, a Presbyterian conference center, and two Presbyterian churches. Billy Graham and his family moved to Montreat around 1945 and have been there ever since.

This, of course, raises the question: Why would the world's most famous Southern Baptist minister live in a Presbyterian commune? The answer is found in three small but powerful words: Ruth Bell Graham.

Mrs. Billy Graham was the daughter of two Presbyterian medical missionaries. She began high school in Pyongyang, Korea, but finished in Montreat while her parents were home on furlough. She met Billy at Wheaton College. Ruth decided that if Billy was going to traipse around the world for crusades and meetings with presidents, she was going to live near her friends and family. Mrs. Graham remained a Presbyterian her whole life.

Montreat sounds like something out of a romantic novel. It is a stunning community, wooden cottages and stone lodges set in a forest surrounded by mountains. A river runs through it, and you can hear trains off in the distance. A coffee shop sits perched on the edge of a waterfall above a small lake. It is absolutely idyllic.

Each house has a little sign with the name of the resident family—Joneses, Smiths, Bells, Wilsons. But no Grahams that I could find.

I looked for the road that would take me to Billy's house. I knew at the end of it stood a log cabin made from locally sourced wood and stone. It has been the Graham family home for more than sixty years.

I had heard "the house that Ruth built" was well protected and that dogs roamed the hills at night. I had heard there was even a sign that warned all visitors: "Trespassers will be eaten."

The road to Billy's house was so steep, I couldn't get my car out of first gear. I arrived at a wooden gate with stone sides. The gate was open. *Is it really going to be this easy?* I thought. I passed through the gate and continued up the single-lane road. I was high in the mountains by that point, well above Montreat. I was surrounded by trees, and not another house was in sight. I rolled down my window and smelled the fresh forest air. I was so excited to finally have a chance to meet the man God had used to change a generation for Jesus. I rounded a bend in the road and hit my brakes.

It wasn't going to be that easy.

In front of me was a large fence and double gate, topped with electrified barbed wire. I parked my car and got out. The property was surrounded by forest, and a tiny stream passed in front of the gate. Beyond the gate, the land continued to climb, and I couldn't even see the house from the driveway.

I had expected there to be some sort of guard shack, but there wasn't. I looked for a doorbell or an intercom system. I surveyed the area and eventually found one—about six feet on the *other* side of the gate. I scratched my head. How was I going to let them know I was here? I thought about yelling but decided that would make a bad first impression. I was tempted to climb over or under a non-electrified section of the fence, but I had committed to *not* trespassing.

I stood in front of the gate for a moment. There was no one in sight. I was at a loss. I turned and walked back to my car. As I opened the door, I heard a voice in the woods.

"Can I help you?"

"It is not the body's posture, but the heart's attitude that counts when we pray." BILLY GRAHAM

I ran back to the gate. I looked around but couldn't figure out where the voice had come from. I spotted a video camera mounted to a tree. I waved at the camera.

"Hello?" I said. "Can you hear me?"

"Um, yes," the voice replied. "Who is this?"

"My name is Jared Brock," I explained. "I'd like to meet Mr. Graham."

I explained that I was a Christian on a prayer pilgrimage around the world and that I wanted to shake Billy's hand and ask him a few questions about prayer.

"I'll be right down," the voice answered.

A few minutes later, a giant oil truck came barreling down the hill, followed by a black Cadillac sedan, followed by a large pickup truck.

I stood at the gate and waited. The truck stood on the other side of the gate and waited. It was an old-fashioned Mexican standoff. I backed away from the fence, suspecting they were worried I would make a mad dash inside when they opened the gate. Sure enough, the gate opened once I had achieved sufficient distance.

The oil truck squeezed past my car, and then the Cadillac drove by slowly. I braced for bullets. I could see the silhouette of someone staring at me through the tinted glass. *That's some serious Franklin Graham mafia*, I thought.

The gate closed and the pickup truck rolled to a stop. A mustachioed man in a puff jacket hopped out of the cabin and nervously walked toward me.

"Hello, my name is John," he said with a twitch. "Can I help you?"

I pointed at the video camera and reminded him I was the guy on the prayer pilgrimage who wanted to meet Billy Graham.

Jumpy John interrogated me for a few minutes and quickly eased up once he realized I was neither a stalker nor a serial killer. We talked for about thirty minutes in the cool mountain air. He went on and on about Billy's ministry and influence, all of which I had previously heard. He was stalling me, and I knew it. He eventually filled me in on Billy's condition.

"It's not great," John said. "You know, Mr. Graham always prayed for one last evangelistic crusade. He couldn't travel, so we shot it from home. We'd do ten minutes of video here, and ten minutes of video there. We did the crusade via television and the Internet, a worldwide crusade, to celebrate Mr. Graham's ninety-fifth birthday.

"Then Mr. Graham went into a sharp decline," he said. "Right after the crusade, right after we celebrated his ninety-fifth birthday. It was almost like his ministry was over. It was almost like God said to Mr. Graham, 'Billy, you're done. Well done, good and faithful servant.'"

John explained that Billy was very weak and was only seeing family. He described how he spent much of his time in bed and often forgot who was who. John clearly loved him and wanted to protect him. I respected that.

"John, would you do me a favor?" I asked. "I've written a letter to Mr. Graham. Do you think you could give it to him?"

"No problem," he said. "I'll give this to his secretary. She comes up three days per week to read him his mail, so I'll give it to her."

"That's great," I said. "All I want is a chance to say hello. All I want is an opportunity. If Mr. Graham says no, you'll never see me again."

We shook hands, and he followed me back down the mountain.

"All of us love miracles. We just don't like being in situations where we need one." MARK BATTERSON

I had exhausted all avenues and had done all I could possibly do to meet Billy Graham. It rested in God's hands. Michelle and I spent a week with her grandparents in another state, and my prayers about Billy became almost constant, inexplicably desperate. He was on my mind day and night, even in my dreams. I didn't know why I needed to meet Billy so badly; I just knew I had to meet him. And I knew only God could unlock that electric gate at the end of the road.

At some point during the week, I was reminded of the story of fearful Gideon and the soaking fleece. Gideon wanted assurance he was supposed to lead the Israelite army against Midian, so he asked for a sign, and God made it quite clear. Christians have been setting out fleeces ever since, and this practice has always fascinated me.

Michelle has an amazing fleece story. One summer during university, she worked the night shift at a brake-pad factory. One night, while on her midnight "lunch break," she felt she was supposed to give her personal Bible to a certain coworker and that she had to give it to him that night. At first she didn't want to give it to him—she had owned the Bible for many years, and it was full of underlined verses, highlighted passages, and personal notes. Also, her coworker was a Muslim, and she didn't want to offend him.

Michelle prayed about it and set out a fleece. "God," she prayed, "if You want me to give him my Bible tonight, make him say, 'Muhammad is Allah's prophet.'"

Over the remainder of her shift, that coworker came up to her on three occasions, entirely unprovoked, to inform her that Muhammad was Allah's prophet. At the end of her shift, Michelle gave the Bible to her coworker. He was fired that night, and she never saw him again.

My friend Steve also has a pretty incredible fleece story. As a teenager, Steve was far from God. Drinking, drugs, sex—you name it, he did it. Yet for some reason, he still regularly attended youth group. Steve came from a Christian home, and he knew he was far from God. One night he arrived late to youth group, having just finished a shift at his job. He sat in the church parking lot and wrestled with God. "God, I know I should be living for You," he prayed. "Please give me a sign tonight. If I hear the phrase 'pink teddy bears,' I'll know I'm supposed to follow You."

My dad was the youth pastor at that church, and Steve is still a friend of mine. Steve told me what happened that night: "I walked into the youth room, and your dad was already sharing the message. I don't remember a word your dad said. All I remember is that at some point in his talk, he stopped talking. Then he said, 'Pink teddy bears, pink teddy bears, pink teddy bears.' It had nothing to do with what he was talking about. He said it three times! And then he continued with his sermon."

Steve committed his life to Christ that night and has walked with God ever since.

Now, obviously, God doesn't respond to every fleece. If He did, we'd rely on His gift instead of His Word. We'd develop a crack-like dependence on determining the will of God by using trinkets instead of the Bible, Christian community, and Holy Spirit wisdom and revelation.

I had never set out a fleece before, so I decided to lay one out for Billy Graham. I thought long and hard about the situation, and then I prayed. "God, this is my fleece: I'm going to drive back to Montreat and knock on that gate. If Billy read my letter and his answer is yes, awesome. If his answer is no, then I'll see it as a sign it's not meant to be. Your will be done. Amen."

And then we drove eleven hours back to Montreat.

"You will have it, or you will know one day why you don't have it, and you will be made content not to have it." CHARLES SPURGEON

My station wagon climbed Billy's road at eight o'clock the next morning. This time, the wooden gate was closed. I got out of my car and searched for a tree-mounted video camera.

I found it and waved. Fifteen minutes passed.

Evidently the security guard had monitors at home, because I heard a truck rushing up the hill from the city, not down the hill from the house. It was Jumpy John again. He got out in a bit of a panic but then realized it was me. His look said it all: *Oh, you again.*

"Good morning, John!" I said. "Have you had a good week?"

"Good morning," he said. "What brings you back here today?"

"Same thing as last time," I said. "What did Mr. Graham say?"

John proceeded to tell me about Billy Graham's ministry and influence. He told me about how Billy had wanted to do one last crusade and about how they taped it from his house. He told me about Billy's ninety-fifth birthday and about how he was seeing only family.

"John, can I just ask you one question?" I finally interrupted. "Did Mr. Graham's secretary read him the letter?"

"Well, um." He shook his head.

"I understand," I said.

I didn't even get a shot. I was heartbroken.

Did my fleece fail? I thought. *Did it even have a chance to be answered?*

I was sad. Mad. Frustrated. Angry. So disappointed. As Michelle and I drove, I thought long and hard about the situation. I couldn't figure out why God had burdened me so heavily with the desire to meet Billy and then left my prayer unanswered. Was God not listening? Was *I* not listening?

"The secret of all failure is our failure in secret prayer."
ALBERT ERNEST RICHARDSON

Prior to my year of living prayerfully, whenever one of my prayer requests wasn't answered, I instinctively asked two questions.

The first question was, "Does prayer really work?" It took me many months to reach the conclusion that prayer works every single time—but only if you understand that prayer is a *conversation.* If your definition of prayer is "asking for things," then prayer will be intermittently disappointing and delightful, but ultimately confounding and frustrating. It won't "work" every time, and it will drive you absolutely nuts. Trust me.

The second question I asked was, "How can I be more effective in prayer?" Basically, I just wanted to increase my shooting percentage.

I've come to understand that not all prayers get answered, and that's a *very* good thing. Even Jesus didn't get all His prayers answered—"Let this cup pass from me. . . ." If God had answered that prayer, we wouldn't have a Savior. Thank God for "unanswered" prayer.

That said, if a prayer doesn't get answered, it might just mean that God is trying to get my attention. Albert Ernest Richardson said that "every unanswered prayer is a clarion call to search the heart to see what is wrong there." Maybe God is waiting for my heart to realign with His. I called a friend to ask his advice, and he had wise words on the situation. "If you don't see breakthrough right away, let it drive you into the secret place with God."

He added that maybe unanswered prayers are calls to persevere. "Remember the man who was blind? Even Jesus had to pray for him twice, so we owe everyone at least two prayers!"

As Michelle and I drove, I came to a small spiritual crossroads. I determined to trust God in spite of receiving an outcome I definitely did not want. I didn't lose faith in Christ. If anything, my faith grew because of the experience. I realized God could most definitely have opened the gate. He could have blown it off its hinges. But He didn't. He allowed Jumpy John to protect his aging boss. In Billy's frail condition, it was probably for the best.

I would have to postpone my meeting until the other side.

"Prayer is the greatest use of my words." RICK WARREN

While we're on the subject of "the other side," have you noticed that "back from the dead" is a big genre in Christian publishing these days? With mega-bestsellers like Todd Burpo's *Heaven Is for Real* and Eben Alexander's *Proof of Heaven*, there's a whole industry that has sprung up in recent years, and there are millions of dollars to be made.[7] I'm thinking my next book will be called *There and Back Again: A Heaven's Tale.*

I wasn't particularly interested in meeting a Wesleyan minister from Nebraska whose son had a near-death experience or a nonpracticing neurosurgeon with at least five malpractice lawsuits to his credit. I wanted to meet a legitimate, active doctor who could set the record straight on miraculous healing. Since healing is intimately connected to prayer—and raising the dead even more so—I wanted to settle the issue in my mind. Because let's be honest: while I truly believe Jesus Christ raised people from the dead, it's hard to believe that mere mortals today are given the same power—especially if they're turning that gift into a highly lucrative business venture.

Dr. Chauncey W. Crandall IV is an eleventh-generation American. The first seven generations were ministers. He is director of preventive cardiology and clinical medicine at the world-renowned Palm Beach Cardiovascular Clinic in Jupiter, Florida. He's also on staff at two other hospitals. Over the past few decades, Dr. Crandall has

---

7 *Heaven Is for Real* made over $100 million at the box office. For real. *90 Minutes in Heaven*, by Don Piper with Cecil Murphey, sold over six million copies. *23 Minutes in Hell?* Multiweek *New York Times* bestseller. *To Heaven and Back*, by Mary C. Neal, debuted as a *New York Times* bestseller. While I won't go so far as Tim Challies, who said, "It's pure junk, fiction in the guise of biography, paganism in the guise of Christianity," I definitely think he's on to something.

quietly been healing bodies behind the scenes, performing over forty thousand heart procedures in his career.

He has also raised the dead.

A number of years ago, my Finnish-Pentecostal mother-in-law gave me a book called *Raising the Dead: A Doctor Encounters the Miraculous*. I confess that I didn't read it and donated it to charity three weeks later. But as I researched possible candidates for an interview for this book, the author's name came to mind.

I met Dr. Crandall at the Good Samaritan Medical Center in West Palm Beach. I passed by more SUVs and superyachts than I had ever seen in my life. The hospital was located on the water, surrounded by palm trees. It was *swanky*. The parking lot was filled with Bentleys, Audis, Jaguars, Rolls-Royces, BMWs, Lexuses, and Mercedes-Benzes. I had never seen valet parking at a hospital before.

So this is how the one percent live.

I parked my car and walked to reception. The lobby had a glass waterfall and a grand piano. The receptionist printed me my own photo badge, and I took a seat. Dr. Crandall arrived a few minutes later.

He told me I had thirty minutes, but he ended up (very generously) giving me over seventy-five minutes of his time. I later learned that an invasive cardiologist in Florida in the seventy-fifth percentile earns $461,343 per year. Chauncey was *not* a lowly 75th-percenter— he serves scores of wealthy and famous people around the world, including a number of billionaires.

I probably owed Chauncey at least a thousand bucks for my interview.

Like a great surgeon, he got right down to business. "Long story short, I was nineteen years old when I got radically saved in a prostitute's den in Togo," he began. "But then I came home and spent the next twenty-five years as an average, lukewarm Christian. I got married, became a doctor, had kids. And then one day my eleven-year-old son got leukemia."

"Heaven is full of answers to prayers for which no one ever bothered to ask." BILLY GRAHAM

"They gave him months to live," Chauncey said. "Yale, Harvard, Duke—your credentials don't help when your son is dying. I was desperate, and I didn't know how to pray. I had no one to walk with me. I started knocking on church doors. Churches didn't pray or believe in healing and miracles and deliverance. I had no one to stand with me. I needed someone to elevate my faith to believe that healing could happen. I started staying up until four in the morning, searching the Word on healing. I started fasting and praying. I was really *hungry*.

"Next thing you know, I end up flying to Mexico to spend two weeks with a faith healer," he continued. "I witnessed all sorts of miraculous healings. It was insane. I was freaking out. I'm a doctor, a sane person, and I couldn't believe what was happening! But he elevated my faith.

"I came home and truly believed God would heal my son. Three months turned into four years. When my son eventually died, I prayed for two hours that he would be raised from the dead. When I realized God wanted my son more than I did, I cried out to God, 'God, I'm either going to let this drive me away from You, or I'm going to run to You. If I run to You, I want to share my son's story with one million souls.' My son's life was the planted seed of an immense harvest."

"Tell me about Jeff Markin," I said.

"One day I was in my office, and I got a call from the ER," he said. "You never want to get that call—it means something's wrong. I go to the operating room, and there's a guy on the table. The doctors tell me he's been dead for about thirty minutes. They've tried to shock him a bunch of times, but he doesn't have a pulse."

Dr. Crandall held up his hands. "Oh my gosh, his hands were black," he said. "His feet were black. And his face was totally black. No oxygen. The room is full of nurses and doctors. I look around and say, 'So why exactly am I here?' They tell me to pronounce him dead. I check the vitals one last time and make the call. The doctors leave, the nurses leave, and one nurse stays behind to sponge down the body for the morgue."

I shifted forward in my seat.

"I turn to leave the room, and bam! God stops me at the door," Dr. Crandall said. "He says, 'Turn around and pray for that man.' I'm in doctor mode, and I'm thinking this is ridiculous. The man's dead. But I couldn't quit the feeling that I was supposed to pray for him.

"I walked back to the dead body and looked at the nurse. I felt stupid. I looked down at this dead guy. 'In the name of Jesus, spirit of death, I rebuke you. Be healed!' I said. The nurse almost fainted. Nothing happened. I called a doctor back in. 'Shock him one more time,' I said. The doc protested, but I said, 'What are we going to do, kill the guy? What's the worst that could happen?'"

The doctor shocked Jeff Markin one last time. A pulse beeped on the monitor, and the body started breathing. "I was in total shock. His black fingers and toes were wiggling," Dr. Crandall said. "I had never seen anything like it in my entire medical career. God had raised this guy from the dead. I just thought it was sad he was going to be brain dead. Black head, no oxygen. No chance. But what do you know? He woke up on Monday morning!"

Jeff Markin eventually walked out of that hospital, but not before Dr. Chauncey led him to Jesus.

"Prayer strikes the winning blow; service is simply picking up the pieces." S. D. GORDON

I caught up with Jeff Markin on the phone later to corroborate the story.

"I was fifty-three, and I had no signs of heart problems," he told me. "I was on my way to work. The last thing I remember was leaving the house that morning. I don't remember driving or making phone calls, but apparently I called my boss. He thought I sounded terrible, and he encouraged me to go to the hospital.

"I could have gone to work or caused a car crash," Jeff continued. "Any other scenario would have killed me. I parked at the Palm Beach Gardens Medical Center and walked up the front steps. I opened my wallet to show the guard my ID and had a massive heart attack." Jeff went on to describe the events as Dr. Crandall had told me.

"Incredible," I said. "Do you remember anything?"

"I don't remember anything from the hospital," Jeff replied. "But I did have a so-called out-of-body experience. I don't know how it all works. I didn't have any brain activity!"

"So what did you see?" I asked.

"I was wrapped up in plastic, and they threw me out in the trash," he said. "And then I remember standing in the back of an empty funeral home. It was for me—I had died. I felt a presence behind me on my right side, a shadowy figure. But then it was gone. The room went from dark to light, and I was staring at swirling white lights. Someone walked toward me. It was a nondescript person, not like a fancy angel. He had opaque skin, large eyes, and no hair. He said he was there to look over me. He went away and then came up and said everything was going to be fine."

"So what happened after you came back to life?" I asked.

"They did a quadruple bypass two or three days later," Jeff said. "And I woke up in my daughter's arms on the fourth day."

"Amazing!" I said. "The not-being-brain-dead part is the biggest piece for me."

"Definitely," Jeff said. "Ten or twelve days after the heart attack, I was in cardiac recovery, and Crandall explained to me what happened. He asked if I believed in God. I always knew God was real, but He was on the sideline of my life. I knew He was there and I needed Him, but I wasn't a practicing Christian. Crandall said, 'Do you want to accept Jesus Christ as your Lord and Savior?' I opened up and started crying. We prayed together at the side of the bed that day. I've had many prayer sessions with Crandall since."

Jeff was discharged almost a month after his heart attack. When I interviewed him, he was sixty-one years old and in good health. He had a fully functioning brain and no organ problems, and he worked full-time in the hydraulic retail business.

Jeff committed the next few years to growing in his faith. He was discipled by a colleague at work, and he started attending church and Bible studies. Dr. Crandall baptized him. Today he's actively involved in a men's group, attends Bible study, and serves on the youth and parking teams at his church.

"Some people think I should have all the answers, but I just have more questions!" Jeff said. "I definitely believe God has a purpose for me. I've been able to share my testimony with a lot of people, but I'm trying to strengthen my Christian walk. I want to honor the Holy Spirit. I want God to awaken people through me, and I don't want to cheapen it. I was born again physically and born again in the Holy Spirit. I have no fear of death. I'm humbled to share my story."

"So what does your prayer life look like?" I asked.

"I thank God every morning for the gift of life," Jeff said. "Look, I'm just a regular guy—a layman. My prayers aren't fancy. They're mostly short prayers. God and I have a conversation all day, and He helps me weather the storms of life. He's my anchor. I'm just trying to let the Holy Spirit lead me."

"Do people think you're crazy?" I asked.

"People are naturally skeptical of resurrection," Jeff replied with a laugh. "But they don't have to believe me. My own doctor couldn't believe it until it happened! I just share my testimony, and hopefully it plants the seed that gets people to at least give God a chance. I hope it shakes some people. Hopefully they come to the Lord before they die."

Obviously, people can read Markin's story and write it off as luck, lies, or a lack of scientific understanding. I agree with Albert Einstein when he said, "There are only two ways to live your life. One is as though nothing is a miracle. The other is as though everything is a miracle." Jeff Markin died, and one way or another, he came back to life—first physically, and then (and more important) spiritually. This is the greatest miracle of all, and it will echo for generations. And it started with prayer.

"The Christian on his knees sees more than the philosopher on tiptoe. God sends no one away empty except those who are full of themselves."
D. L. MOODY

Back in Dr. Crandall's office, our conversation continued.

"So how many people have you reached with the gospel since your son died?" I asked.

"Well over a million people!" Chauncey laughed. "Thousands of salvations. It's funny, I'm at the point now where I want to move on to the next story, like a doctor with his next patient. But God keeps bringing me back to this one."

"Have you had any other miracles since Jeff?" I asked.

"Of course, all the time!" he said. "Salvation is the biggest miracle of all, of course. I pray with patients every day—watching people recover from surgery is an amazing answer to prayer. And God still does crazy things too. I had a woman who'd flatlined; I couldn't get her heart going, and I started speaking in tongues in the operating room. The nurse screamed, but the woman's heartbeat came back. About two years ago, I had a guy who was brain dead, but he walked out just fine."

"So what's the secret?" I asked. "What's the trick?"

"No trick. You've just got to believe the Word of God, regardless of the outcome," he said. "I always pray in the name of Jesus, and I always pray boldly and out loud."

"Do people ever think you're crazy?" I asked.

"Oh sure, but you don't have to be kooky or weird about it." He laughed. "Some people have stopped referring patients to me, and I've been shunned by many, but that's fine. It takes boldness to stand in front of fellow scientists and academics and lay your hands on someone in prayer. It makes you appear vulnerable and weak."

But why *not* pray? Your options are medicine, or medicine + prayer. What do you possibly have to lose? Only a fool would reject the possibility of a miracle. The man who prays receives more answers than the man who never bothers. As Mark Batterson writes, "The greatest tragedy in life is the prayers that go unanswered because they go unasked." And "100 percent of the prayers we don't pray won't get answered."

Earlier this year, I saw a photograph of Pope Francis with a man named Vinicio Riva. In the photo, the pope has his hand on the man's bowed head, and he is praying earnestly for the man. Mr. Riva is covered from head to toe with massive tumors, a truly ghastly sight. It's a rare genetic disorder called neurofibromatosis.[8] I'm reminded of the photograph almost every single day. It says one thing to me: this is why I must believe in healing. If not for me, I must believe in healing for those who so desperately need a touch from God that they're willing to believe that God can do whatever He wants to do. I am compelled to believe in healing.

"Prayer works," Dr. Crandall said. "Prayer changes the atmosphere of the operating room from death to life."

These days, Dr. Crandall has quietly become the personal physician for many of the world's leading Christian ministers.

"So who all comes to see you?" I asked excitedly.

"I can't tell you that. Patient confidentiality!" he said. "Here's how I see it. These guys are 'generals' on the front lines of an intense battle. They've got injuries. We bring them in, heal them up, and get them back on the battlefield.

---

[8] To learn more, visit the Children's Tumor Foundation at www.ctf.org.

"You know, there's a funny thing about our office," he said. "Very few of our patients die."

"Last question, Doctor," I said. "Any advice for a guy whose grandpa and great-grandpa died in their early sixties from heart disease?"

He grinned. "Walk one hour per day, eat right, and keep doing what you're doing."

I admit that I had visited Dr. Crandall's office intending to debunk a pseudoscientific quack. I ended up eating my words, humbled that we serve a God who still heals people. From the moment I arrived at his office, it was obvious he wasn't in it for the money—Dr. Crandall only stood to lose clients and tarnish his reputation by admitting his reliance on God. But what he lost in income, he gained in relationships and miracles. I vowed to pray more for the healing of those around me. I still have questions, obviously—how do we balance an honest belief in God's healing with the recognition that miracles are rare? I don't know. I guess that's where faith comes in.

But not all prayer experiences inspire faith, as I was soon to find out.

CHAPTER 9

The Outer Limits

IN MY YEAR OF living prayerfully, I experienced some things I wouldn't have expected. I danced with Hasidic Jews, I burned my socks in a hurricane at the end of the world, I visited a nudist church, and I met the pope. But in some ways, these experiences were all normal. Tame. I wanted to experience the outer limits of Judeo-Christian prayer.

We Christians often refer to other Christians as "brothers and sisters"—a family term. We sing, "I'm so glad I'm a part of the family of God" perhaps a little more often than we should. But what would any family be without some crazy uncles to liven up the family reunions?

The truth is, there are a lot of people who claim the name of Christ and have some seriously questionable beliefs and practices. And I wanted to find out what they had to say about prayer.

So while most of my journey so far has been organized around geography, these stops in my year of living prayerfully are arranged around a quirky state of mind. They're a little off the beaten path and of questionable spiritual value. In any case, they certainly are strange.

"The person with the Spirit makes judgments about all things, but such a person is not subject to merely human judgments." 1 CORINTHIANS 2:15

When I think of strange spiritual stories, I remember one particular fellow I knew growing up, whom I shall call Nelson.

A flamboyant actor, Nelson had a flair for the dramatic. One day, while flirting with a girl at school, he pretended to fall over. Unfortunately, he made his move on the edge of a staircase and tumbled down a flight of concrete steps. He smashed his knee in the process.

A few weeks later, a few of us from the youth group attended a special Pentecostal event. It was held in one of those open-air gospel tents, led by a booming choir and a charismatic preacher. I don't remember what the traveling minister talked about, but I do remember that he shouted the whole time.

After his lengthy sermon, the preacher informed the audience that God wanted to heal everybody. He invited people to come forward for prayer. A few people came forward. He smacked them on the forehead, and they fell to the floor. I was shocked. I had never seen anything like this before. The preacher continued to smash people in the face, something he called "slaying in the Spirit." I wasn't sure which spirit, exactly, wanted to "slay" people.

Eventually the line stopped. The preacher was surrounded by fallen bodies, the aftermath of a zombie-style prayer apocalypse. He looked around the room. "Somebody in here has a headache!" he boomed. "Come forward and be healed!"

A woman came forward, and he smacked her in the head. *Little good* that *will do*, I thought.

"Somebody here has a backache!" the preacher yelled. "Come forward and receive a healing touch from God!"

An elderly gentleman went forward, and he, too, was laid flat on his back.

"Somebody here has knee pain!" the preacher hollered. I turned to Nelson. *The preacher must have seen him hobble in*, I thought. Nelson stood and stoically limped to the front of the tent.

The preacher put his hand on Nelson's shoulder. "Are you going to sue me?" he asked.

"Pardon?" Nelson said.

"I said, 'Are you going to *suuuuuue* me, brother?'" he yelled.

Nelson shook his head.

"Then in the name of Jesus," he screamed, "be healed!"

The preacher wound up and kicked Nelson in the knee as hard as he could. Nelson dropped with a shriek of pain. I choked. *Oh my word. He has no idea what happened to Nelson's knee!*

Suddenly, much to my surprise, Nelson hopped to his feet. "I'm healed!" he yelled. The audience erupted into cheers of approval. Nelson danced a little jig to prove the "miracle."

A few weeks later, a surgeon was tasked with repairing Nelson's knee joint.

I'm not against the so-called "sign gifts"—not by any stretch. God can do whatever He wants to do, and He can use whatever person or method He so chooses. My mother-in-law prays in other languages during her private prayer times. My grandfather-in-law was miraculously healed from cancer after receiving prayer from people around the world.

I had never received the gift of tongues personally, but Nelson was always pressuring me to get it. He told me some people received it by making something up to start and eventually the Holy Spirit would take over. He suggested I start with the phrase "Gotta-buy-a-Honda-not-a-Hyundai."

As the years went by, Nelson's affinity for the sign gifts grew. Soon he was speaking in tongues, passing out on restaurant floors, barking in the Spirit, and puking black "demons." He could shoot "spiritual fireballs," and he claimed Jesus once appeared to him in a hotel closet.

Then Nelson started drinking heavily. He spent tons of money on clothes and jewelry, and he quickly developed a reputation for sleeping around.

I was so confused, and not just by Nelson. I looked at the leaders of the Pentecostal movement. Many of them were embroiled in affairs, and many more had been caught in some sort of financial impropriety. These pastors had private jets, sprawling mansions, fancy cars, huge salaries, and pending investigations with the IRS, which they all called "attacks of the enemy."

Nelson particularly loved Benny Hinn, one of the more charismatic members of the "Holy Spirit Movement." He showed me videotapes of Hinn knocking people out, much like a UFC fighter or the knee-snapping tent preacher.

When Hinn became embroiled in a financial scandal of his own, I asked Nelson what he thought. "He is a *man of God*," he shot back. "How dare you speak out against God's anointed one! Do you want to grieve the Holy Spirit?"

Nelson's blind allegiance and sinful lifestyle were what grieved me most.

Over time I distanced myself from Nelson, but I always felt like I needed to revisit the charismatic movement in the future. I wanted to give Benny Hinn another chance.

I also wanted to get healed myself. To be honest, I wanted God to embarrass me. Sure, I had preconceived notions about Hinn, but I wanted healing even more. As I mentioned earlier, my body doesn't heal. Much of my body is in constant pain. I've seen specialists, gotten tests, and tried all the treatments in the book. Nothing has ever worked.

And now I had nothing to lose. I wanted God to use Benny Hinn to heal me so I'd have to eat my words. My pain outweighed my pride.

"Nothing is so inconsistent with the life of any Christian as overindulgence." ST. BENEDICT OF NURSIA

Benny Hinn, whose real name is Toufik Benedictus Hinn, was born to an Armenian mother and Greek father. Though raised in an Eastern Orthodox household, Hinn was educated in Israel by Franciscan nuns.[1] Soon after the Six-Day War, Hinn's family moved to Canada.

Once his "Miracle Crusade" brand exploded, Hinn rewarded himself with a multimillion-dollar ocean-view mansion, a handful of luxury cars, fancy jewelry, and $3,000-per-night hotel suites. He owns a private jet named "Dove One," which, according to his website, "meets minimum standards of need."

Benny Hinn once said, "I'd be a fool to be in this for the money." For what it's worth, in the world of megarich pastors, Hinn barely gets a seat at the adult table. In the circles in which Hinn rolls, private jets and giant homes are par for the course—Joel Osteen, Creflo Dollar, and Kenneth Copeland have each spent more than $10 million on houses and planes. "Bishop" David Oyedepo has a net worth of $150 million and has *four* private jets. Jan Crouch has a $100,000 air-conditioned mobile home for her dogs. Pastor Chris Oyakhilome makes over $2 million *per month*. It's reported that T. D. Jakes has a net worth of over $150 million. Pat Robertson reportedly owned rights to a *diamond mine*.[2]

Surprisingly, it wasn't difficult to convince Michelle to attend a healing service with me. It turned out I wasn't the only one who

---

[1] He did not maintain their vows of poverty and chastity.

[2] Don't get me wrong, I'm not against diamond mines and private jets. I'd love to encrust my future plane with rubies and emeralds for Christmas and then stuff it full of air-conditioned dog homes. I'm just against using God to get all those things. As one blogger put it, a lot of preachers are "flying high on the widow's mite."

wanted to set the record straight on Benny Hinn. Michelle told me she had already been to a Benny Hinn event as a kid.

"There are two things I remember from the experience," she said. "The first was that I felt scared by so many yelling people and felt guilty that I wasn't yelling too. But I also recall having the thought, *If I ever get really sick and doctors can't heal me, I am going to come see Benny Hinn.* It was a comforting thought for a ten-year-old."

Both Michelle and I were willing to give Benny Hinn another chance.

"I know me, and those close to me know me. But sadly, the outside world thinks I'm some kind of a crook." BENNY HINN

I looked on Hinn's website but couldn't find any events happening in North America in the near future. Most of his listed events were happening in India or elsewhere, with the exception of one night in London, England. Since the UK was already on our prayer stopover list, we added a night with Benny to our schedule.

We got off the Underground at the Elephant and Castle station. The street was covered in litter, and the run-down buildings were covered in graffiti. We quickly walked up the street and came to a small sign that read "Night of Miracles with Benny Hinn."

We hurried past the huge merchandise tables and made our way into the auditorium. An eerie green light filled the room. We arrived at five o'clock, well before the seven o'clock start time. A long line of people surged toward the front section of the sanctuary. Ushers tried to hold the crowds back, but people kept pushing. A man on the PA system desperately tried to calm the crowd. "Please stop pushing," he said. "People are getting hurt." No one listened, and he had to repeat his announcement seven times.

It was frantic. Everyone wanted a front-row seat. "This is crazy," Michelle said. "And dangerous."

The man beside me had a very different opinion. "It's like the crowds waiting to see Jesus!" he proclaimed.

We eventually found seats and settled in. I looked around. The venue wasn't huge, maybe three thousand seats. "I don't get it," I said to Michelle. "Three thousand seats, on a Monday night, in a rough part of town, in England of all places—why is Benny Hinn here? It seems a bit beneath him."

I hadn't followed Hinn's work in almost a decade, and it all made sense when I researched the matter further. It turned out Hinn was still trying to clear his name after being photographed while holding hands with a female televangelist.[3]

The auditorium was full by 6:10, so they started fifty minutes early. A choir and song leader mounted the stage, and the band started to play. I definitely felt out of place at first, not unlike being lactose intolerant in Wisconsin. But eventually Michelle and I got into it—we sang and danced along with the rest of the crowd. There was so much joy in the room.

After two hours of singing, a pastor got up and gave the warm-up sermon. He talked for about twenty minutes. He mentioned they would be taking an offering, and then he introduced Benny Hinn. Up to this point, Hinn hadn't been visible. Suddenly, the camera panned to his place in the front row. The place erupted. People went berserk. I'd never seen anything like it, not even at a rock concert.

Hinn appeared to be a little out of sorts. His face was flushed, his hair was tousled, and only his top jacket button was actually buttoned up. He was wearing a dark blue jacket with a row of unbuttoned gold studs all the way up the front. It looked like a colonial soldier's uniform. He wore an Anglican-style collar, a giant wedding ring, and, oddly, a golden-calf belt buckle.

---

[3] To his credit, after the supposed relationship, Hinn remarried his wife at the Holy Land Experience theme park in Orlando, Florida. The park is owned by the same woman who owns the $100,000 doggy home.

It was a sign of things to come.

Within seconds of mounting the stage, the crowd gave him a standing ovation. He quieted everyone down, which took some doing. When everyone had been seated, Hinn opened his Bible and leaned over the pulpit.

"We need to talk about prosperity," he said.

"Prayer is always in danger of degenerating into a glorified gold rush."
A. W. TOZER

Benny Hinn launched into a lengthy sermon on wealth and how to get it. He explained how God wanted every Christian to be rich, and Hinn proved it too. He said that Abraham and Isaac and Solomon were rich, although he forgot to mention Jesus or Paul or any of the apostles or the Acts 2 church. He flipped from text to text, pasting together a patchwork theology in defense of earthly accumulation.

After two hours of talking about wealth, he offered an altar call.

"If anyone would like to give one thousand British pounds," Hinn said, "please come to the front."

I couldn't believe it at first. "An altar call for an offering collection?" Michelle whispered in my ear. "Is he serious?"

I felt ill. "I think so," I whispered back.

"If anyone would like to give one thousand British pounds," Hinn repeated, "please come to the front now and receive your blessing." After a good number of people came to the front, he prayed for them. Then he looked back at the audience. "If there is anyone who would like to give one hundred pounds or more, please come to the front and receive your blessing."

More people came forward.

The crowd at the front was decent, but it wasn't huge. Hinn switched into high gear.

"Let me tell you something. I've had a word from the Lord," he said. "Here it is. Are you ready? If you give to God tonight—it doesn't matter what the amount—if you give *tonight*, God will give it back to you tenfold within three years' time."

The crowd went wild.

"Did you hear that?" he said. "You will have a *tenfold* increase if you sow your seed tonight!"

The crowd reached a fever pitch.

"You'll be on top, not the bottom!" he screamed. "You will be the head, not the tail! You will have employees working for *you*!"

The people around us went ballistic. The young man beside me screamed, "Amen, amen, *amen*!"

Streams of people made their way to the front of the auditorium.

My soul freaked out.

I looked around the room. The crowd was overwhelmingly composed of ethnic minorities and people who didn't seem like they could afford the amounts Hinn was requesting. I saw moms with their little kids, like Michelle as a child. I saw a sickly old man, stooped at the waist, make his way toward the front. He was stopped by two burly security guards. He was in desperate need of a touch from God, for physical healing. They directed him back to his seat.

I witnessed the emotional manipulation as the pianist played classic gospel hymns like "Draw Me Nearer" and "The Old Rugged Cross" to draw people to the altar.

"Hold your offerings high in the air!" Hinn shouted. "Wave your offerings before the Lord!"

Thousands of people waved their checks in the air.

My stomach was churning. Was this the Holy Spirit? Mental illness? Mass hysteria?

I watched as Hinn preyed on desperation. "Come forward now!" he said. "God will heal you every time!"

I looked at my watch. We had been there for almost five hours, and it was the first time Hinn had mentioned healing.

"We need to go," I said to Michelle. "We won't be home until one o'clock."

I didn't have to ask her twice.

"God, pity us that after years of writing, using mountains of paper and rivers of ink, . . . we are still faced with gross corruption in every nation, as well as with the most prayerless church age since Pentecost."
LEONARD RAVENHILL

We rode home in silence.

Michelle finally whispered, "You know, I'm not denying that God might have used Benny in the past. But when you turn it into a business . . ." She trailed off.

There's a big question we should be asking constantly in Christian circles, and especially ones where lots of money changes hands: Who profits from this? If televangelists lived like Shane Claiborne and gave away their donations, they would be far easier to believe. But their lives often don't back up their message. Or, sadly, their message *precisely* backs up their lifestyle.

I had hoped the rumors were false and God would use Hinn to heal my body. When the outcome proved drastically otherwise, I hesitated to even write about it. Because from what I've seen, ten years after my conversation with Nelson, nothing has changed in hard-core charismatic circles—you still can't question "the man of God."

Where did this belief come from? It certainly isn't found in the Bible. First John 4:1 tells us to "test the spirits to see whether they are from God, because many false prophets have gone out into the world." I was taught as a child to never trust any human who tells you to blindly trust him or her.

But of course, as many followers are quick to inform you, you should never question these self-appointed "anointed ones." Again, who profits from this belief? Hinn himself said, "Because we are continually growing in the Lord, preachers and lay people alike must be open to the Lord's correction."

One thing was sure—Michelle was at peace. She realized her childhood self wasn't crazy.

Michelle and I have continued to ask God for wisdom and understanding regarding healing and other spiritual gifts. We would love to see supernatural "signs and wonders," but they would have to be paired with the gospel of salvation for the glory of God alone.

I later chatted with a teenager who has the gift of healing. He has pretty much kept it a secret as he learns to best steward his gift for God's glory. I asked him what he thought about the idea of someone turning healing into a moneymaking venture. "I think there's an even bigger question here," he said. "What I wonder is, has God anointed *anyone* to be able to heal people every single time?"

"Well, that was the promise given at the service!" I said.

"Think about it for a minute, really think about it," he said. "Imagine if there was a person on earth who could heal *every single time*. I don't think any human could handle it. They'd be overrun by people. The immense wealth and colossal power would totally destroy them."

It's also worth mentioning that charismatics don't have a monopoly on healing power. When we attended his event, Benny Hinn even admitted that more people are healed during Catholic communion than in Pentecostal healing services. No wonder they call it "the meal that heals." Who knows anything anymore?

Despite what happened in the Benny Hinn service and what I've observed about some high-profile Pentecostals, I'm ultimately hopeful for the future of the Pentecostal church for four big reasons. First is their sheer passion. In an age of complacency toward spiritual matters—yet still with a massive passion for iPhones, football, and video games—Pentecostal denominations lead the church in straight-up excitement. Dancing in church? Awesome. Singing at the top of your lungs? Fantastic. Responding to good preaching? I love it. Rolling in the prophetic? Let's do it. Healing people? I'm in—as long as God gets the glory.

Second, many charismatics I've encountered are the most Scripture-steeped Christians I've ever met. There's a high value placed on God's Word in many Pentecostal churches, and it shows.

Third, you won't meet a more generous group of people. Whether rich or poor, there's a huge value on giving generously and sacrificially within the charismatic community.

Fourth is their embrace of multiculturalism. I've had the privilege of speaking in a number of Pentecostal churches, and each time I'm struck again by the fact that there remains a united group of people gathered from every tribe and tongue and nation under the sun.

I think the Pentecostal movement has an enormous opportunity to become a world leader in the Christian church, but they need to root out the selfishness of prosperity theology in order to get there. Purge the profiteering televangelists. No more health-and-wealth theology—it's time for a deep commitment to real gospel truth. If Pentecostal churches make *selflessness* one of their core values, there's no telling what God could do.

Here's what I know for sure: God can do whatever He wants. He can forgive our sins, heal our bodies, and make us rich—as long as He gets all the glory, honor, and praise. God can use anybody He chooses. A faithful prayer warrior. A Sunday school teacher. A Catholic priest during communion. Maybe even you or me.

"Whatever happens, take responsibility." TONY ROBBINS

People say Christians are crazy, but I would like to submit another group of people for consideration: fire walkers.

Some people say fire-walking is dangerous, and those people are correct. Two-thousand-degree coals will typically burn your feet.

Walking on fiery coals is a path only fools would dare to tread. And I was about to become one of those fools.

The reigning master guru of fire-walking is Tony Robbins. Robbins claims to be a Christian, and he has successfully taught tons of people how to safely walk across red-hot coals.[4]

Born Anthony J. Mahavorick, Robbins was raised by his mother in Azusa, California. Over the past thirty-seven years he has reached over fifty million people across one hundred countries, including four million at live events. Talk about an overcomer—he also beat a brain tumor in the process. Trained by Jim Rohn, Robbins uses neurolinguistic programming and other methods to help people treat anything from stress to colds to depression to phobias to learning disabilities.

I wondered if prayer had anything to do with his method, so I sent an e-mail to his legion of assistants and asked if Michelle and I could attend an upcoming event. I was informed by a kind lady that someone would be in touch, and that "participating of this event together will allligned many things in your life."

Gratefully, my assigned agent wrote and spoke better English. Tom was relentlessly positive, and we chatted for almost an hour. It turned out he was originally a golf pro, and he had taught Tony how to golf. Given the size of Tony's arms, we can safely assume he regularly hits five-hundred-yard drives. Not only was Tom good friends with Tony Robbins, but he had another claim to fame—his great-uncle invented polling, the method by which politicians judge the success of whatever they're currently telling the public they believe.

Tom is a Christian, and he is from Finland, so we had lots to talk about. He told me there are tons of Christians on Tony's staff and they pray before every event. There are almost four hundred on staff

---

[4] One report kept surfacing that twenty-one people in San Jose had suffered from second- and third-degree burns after a Tony Robbins fire-walking event, but it turned out the story was actually Fox News fiction.

at Tony's organization, plus around three hundred volunteers who pay their way to each event.

The event I would attend was a multiday conference, and it promised total life transformation. By practicing Tony's habits, attendees were promised they could unleash power from within themselves. That sounded interesting, although admittedly a bit hucksterish.

Michelle and I stayed with family about thirty-five minutes away from the convention center and left with plenty of time. We didn't have any problems until the final mile. Suddenly, we were stopped dead in bumper-to-bumper gridlock—for over two hours. I noticed our car was stuck between three BMWs and an Audi. I eventually found a parking spot, and then we had to walk over two miles in the hot sun. I burned my feet, and I hadn't even fire-walked yet.

We registered for the event, and a volunteer named Thor took us to the very back of a giant room. We had missed the first forty-five minutes, my feet were aching, and I was sweating profusely.

The room was packed with almost six thousand people, seven screens, and one giant person on stage. Literally—Robbins towers to a height of six feet seven inches.

A Tony Robbins conference defies explanation. It's part dance club, part healing service, part rock concert, part sales conference, part New Age summit, and part tent revival. I looked around the room. It was full of highly groomed males with rippling muscles and overtanned yoga chicks with Botox treatments. Everyone had stars in their eyes—they were about to witness miracles, receive revelation, and connect with a deeper power.

Tony was hilarious. His presentation was the first time I had ever heard anyone turn "many are called but few are chosen" into a dating metaphor.

Tony was an absolute force of nature, totally indefatigable, with more energy than any other fifty-four-year-old in history. A Tony

Robbins event puts even a hard-core Pentecostal church service to programming shame. Tony spoke for *eleven* straight hours. There were no breaks for him or the audience—not for lunch, dinner, or a bedtime snack. What a machine.

Robbins is both brilliant and earnest, and I would love to be his friend. But what he was selling was far more than the audience could handle.

As I looked around the massive room, I realized that everyone there was desperate for a touch from God. From *anything*. People were there in search of purpose and mission and real meaning. It hit Michelle, too. People can get this—community, a sense of mission and purpose, healing from their hurt—in church. For free. Over the course of the event Robbins taught people to believe in themselves, to "unleash the power within." Instead of hymns, the crowds swayed to the theme songs from *Titanic* and *Gladiator* and *Chariots of Fire*.

By the time the night was over, people were lying prostrate on the floor, moaning and crying and laughing uncontrollably. They were "worshiping," but there was no one on the receiving end. It was total madness, crazier than any Benny Hinn service.

Of course, the biggest difference between a Benny Hinn service and a Tony Robbins event is that at the end of a Tony Robbins event you get to walk on fire.

"I prayed for freedom for twenty years, but received no answer until I prayed with my legs." FREDERICK DOUGLASS

My mother-in-law is a wonderful woman—she's kind, patient, generous, funny, and mostly understanding of her nut job son-in-law. But she was dead set against the idea of me walking across a bed of hot coals. She had sent me an amazingly cryptic Bible passage earlier that morning, and it had been rattling around in my head all day:

> Listen, my son, accept what I say, and the years of your life will be many. I instruct you in the way of wisdom and lead you along straight paths. When you walk, your steps will not be hampered; when you run, you will not stumble. Hold on to instruction, do not let it go; guard it well, for it is your life.

It was almost midnight by the time Tony finished speaking, and we made our way (in bare feet) to an abandoned parking lot behind the convention center. Hundreds of volunteers repeatedly chanted, "Yes, yes, yes, yes."

Gawkers on the street lined the fence, intrigued and possibly horrified by what was about to happen. I prayed I wouldn't get a foot infection from the slimy pavement.

I learned that no prayer is necessary to walk across hot coals. There is nothing spiritual about it at all, in fact. Tony had taught us a very simple neurolinguistic programming technique. We were instructed to "make a move," some sort of repetitive physical action that would pump our bodies full of testosterone. I went with a manly combination—a Hulk-style chest flex paired with a front double bicep curl. We were told to reach the front of the line, get in the zone, "make our move," and then calmly walk across the coals while focusing on the phrase "cool moss."

The line started moving, and people walked across hot coals. I panicked. *God, what have I gotten myself into?* I looked at Michelle. "What have you gotten yourself into?" she mouthed, grinning.

I got to the front of the line and stared down at the glowing embers, two thousand degrees of heat ready to bake my bones. I started to get into the zone. "It's your turn!" a volunteer yelled. "Head up and go!" He shoved me onto the coals.

I wasn't in the zone.

I hadn't made my move.

I hadn't even prayed.

My first step—my right foot caught a hot coal right between my big toe and the ball of my foot. It was *hot*. The ball of my left foot landed on an equally fiery chunk of flaming wood.

There was no "cool moss" for me.

I chanted, "Oh-shoot-oh-shoot-oh-shoot-oh-shoot-oh-shoot"[5] as I stormed across the fiery chasm. I walked so quickly that two volunteers had to grab me at the end and spray cold water on my feet.

And then it was over. I hadn't died or burned my feet off. I exhaled with relief.

My wife was equally relieved. "Mom will be happy," she said. "Can we go home now?"

On our two-mile walk back to the car, I watched Michelle's video playback of my firewalk. For some inexplicable reason, I had unconsciously decided to high-step march and beat a pair of imaginary drums as I walked. No wonder I singed my soles.

The next morning I had two fat blisters where the first two coals had landed. I wore the marks for months. Every time my feet hurt in the week that followed, I thanked the Father for putting up with a ridiculous son like me.

A lot of people, myself included, are guilty of treating God like a self-help guru. Prayer is our mantra, a way to bolster our confidence and psych ourselves up for whatever challenges lie ahead. To some extent it works. But prayer isn't a mind game; it's not a pseudoscientific technique for achieving success in life. It's a deeply intimate form of communication with the Lover of our souls. Prayer isn't about self-improvement. We don't "gain confidence"; we enter God's. We don't "become a better person"; God conforms us to the

---

5 Except I didn't say "shoot."

image of His Son. We don't "attain perfection"; we're covered by the spotless Lamb. Prayer can get us through the fiery seasons of life, but it's not the prayer that gets us through—it's the God who's willing to carry us across that bed of burning hot coals.

Attending a Benny Hinn healing service had been a strange experience, and Tony Robbins's event had been stranger still, but I was about to top both experiences with my next stop—a visit to the most hated family in America. I wanted to find out what on earth they possibly prayed about.

"We're not angry; we're zealous. You have been lied to all your life."
SHIRLEY PHELPS-ROPER

"Are you kidding me?" I yelled. "You've got to be joking."

It was seven thirty on a Sunday morning when a police officer pulled me over somewhere in Kansas. It was a trap. The speed limit had dropped from 45 to 30, and the cop had been waiting just ten feet past the sign.

The police officer walked toward my vehicle, and I reluctantly rolled down the window. "I've got you doing 47 in a 30," he said. "License and registration, please."

I handed him my papers and rolled up the window. He returned to his car to process my ticket. I hadn't had a speeding infraction in many years, and of all the possible mornings to get pulled over, he'd picked a fine day. We had woken up at two thirty that morning, driven all night, and were on a tight schedule.

"What's taking him so long?" I groaned in frustration. "Tickets *never* take this long to process!"

He appeared at my window a few minutes later. "Step out of the vehicle," he instructed. "I'm going to need to see your passport."

"My passport?" I asked. "What does my Canadian passport have to do with an American driving infraction?"

He laughed as he inspected my passport. "I'm not going to give you a ticket, but there seems to be an irregularity with your information," he confided. "My station ran your license, and it seems someone by the name of Jared Brook may be traveling on a stolen passport."

"Well, good news, officer!" I joked. "My name isn't Jared *Brook*. As you can see, that's my own name on my passport there. B-R-O-C-K."

He looked up and grinned. "You didn't steal a passport, did you?"

"Nope!" I replied.

"Promise?" he asked.

"Promise." I nodded. "I'm actually on my way to church."

As soon as the words left my mouth, I freaked out. *Dear God*, I prayed, *please do* not *let him ask me where we're going to church!*

Gratefully, he didn't ask. We drove away quickly, but under the speed limit.

We were on our way to Westboro Baptist Church.

"It's a sin to pray for America."   FRED PHELPS SR.

Westboro "Baptist" "Church" is a small gathering of people in Topeka, Kansas. They are self-proclaimed "Primitive Baptists," which I assume means they haven't yet learned to get along with others. They are a "church" in the sense that they call themselves a church but operate more like a hate cult.

I had checked out their website in advance. Their stats are impressive, if not concerning:

6,801: soldiers that God has killed in Iraq and Afghanistan

52,285: pickets conducted by WBC

919: cities that have been visited by WBC

1,185: weeks that WBC has held daily pickets on the mean streets of doomed America

10,431: people whom God has cast into hell since you loaded this page

218,400,000+: gallons of oil that God poured in the Gulf

$17.5 trillion+: national debt of doomed America

8: people that God saved in the flood

16,000,000,000: people that God killed in the flood

144,000: Jews that will be saved in these last days

0: nanoseconds of sleep that WBC members lose over your opinions and feeeeelllllliiiiiings[6]

For more information about WBC, feel free to attend one of our weekly church meetings . . . Regular service time is on Sunday at 12:00 p.m.

The Westboro website shares links to a handful of "sister sites," including GodHatesIslam.com and GodHatesTheWorld.com, as well as GodHatesTheMedia.com—though I can't imagine where Westboro would be without all the free publicity.

Their online statement of faith says they believe in the Five Points of Calvinism, one of which is "Irresistible Grace," but it's obvious from the rest of their website that they prefer to focus on "Total Depravity"— that man is totally and utterly evil. They're also massive fans of predestination, which they define as God choosing whom He will save and damning the rest—even if they wanted to be saved. One of founder Fred Phelps Sr.'s estranged sons, Nate, puts it this way: "The heart of Calvinism is the doctrine of absolute predestination. . . . My father has simply refined Calvin's doctrine to the point where the vast majority of us are going to hell."

"It is against the law to read the Bible in Canada." FRED PHELPS SR.

Westboro Baptist Church was founded by Fred Phelps, a cantankerous "minister" with a perpetual hate for America, and especially gay people.

---

6 A few clarifications, if I may: It was actually BP that leaked the oil, soldiers die because that's what happens when countries go to war, there definitely weren't sixteen billion people on earth in Noah's day, and I'm not entirely sure why the national debt made the list.

The church has been around since 1955, but they didn't rise to national fame until 1998, when they picketed the funeral of Matthew Shepard, a young college student who was beaten to death for being gay.

Since then, picketing has really become their modus operandi. With signs like "God Hates Fags," "Thank God for Dead Soldiers," and "Thank God for 9/11," they've managed to stay in the headlines ever since.

Westboro planned to picket the Sandy Hook Elementary School shooting funerals, but the Internet activist group Anonymous hacked their website and publicly released the personal information of church members. On the day of the funeral, a group of police officers, fire-fighters, and bikers from New York drove down to create a human wall to shield mourners from the protesters. WBC never showed up.

The church has around seventy regular attendees, most of whom are members of the Phelps family. Fred Waldron Phelps Sr. had thir-teen children, many of whom have spawned similarly large troops of offspring. One of Fred's more outspoken daughters, Shirley, has eleven children.

To give you some perspective on how hateful Westboro has be-come, even the KKK has held counterprotests against WBC.

Westboro attempted to picket a funeral in Canada in 2008, but the government banned them from entering the country. The United Kingdom quickly followed suit. They've fared far better in America—despite Westboro's being sued for $10.9 million, the Supreme Court ruled in their favor and awarded them $16,000 for legal fees. They ruled that picketing fell under constitutionally protected free speech and noted that WBC was "entitled to 'special protection' under the First Amendment." Despite a boatload of criminal charges, no Westboro congregant has ever served time.[7]

There's a good reason why the Phelpses have never been successfully

---

[7] Except the current leader, Steve Drain, who spent a night in prison for breaking the nose of a fifteen-year-old boy who flirted with one of his kids. He then went home and beat his daughter, she alleges.

prosecuted—they're a family of lawyers. Many of the aunts and uncles are lawyers in a family law firm, and Fred Sr. was himself a disbarred lawyer.

The Westboro church-family spends upwards of $250,000 per year on protests. Among other things, Westboro hates Baptist churches, movie theaters, Katy Perry, Mister Rogers, Comic-Con, the Kansas City Chiefs, Desmond Tutu, Princess Diana, and the NBA. They planned to picket at Steve Jobs's funeral,[8] but they never ended up making the trip. They've picketed the funerals of dead soldiers, decried Lady Antebellum concerts, and even protested a hardware store that sold Swedish vacuum cleaners.

I watched a birthday statement in which Fred Sr. shared choice words for Billy Graham, calling him a "hell-bound false prophet," a "lying, money-grubbing Arminian heretic." He assured the listeners that Graham was indeed doomed for eternal punishment. "At 88, Graham will soon die and split hell wide open. And Westboro Baptist Church will picket your funeral. Amen."[9]

"There is only one way of victory over the bitterness and rage that comes naturally to us—to will what God wills brings peace."
AMY CARMICHAEL

I arrived at the address on my GPS: 3701 SW 12th St, Topeka, Kansas, USA, 66604. *Of all the possible numbers to begin a zip code . . . ,* I thought.

We drove past the church and then parked around the block. "I don't want to go anywhere near that cult!" Michelle said. She napped in the car.

I walked to the church. It wasn't so much a church as it was a large white-and-brown Tudor-style house. I had heard that Fred Sr. lived in the back half of the second story. The sign on the corner read,

---

[8] They tweeted the announcement from an iPhone.
[9] Graham is ninety-five at the time of writing this, so I think we can rule "will soon die" as a false prophecy.

"President's Day Is Idolatry!" An upside-down rainbow American flag waved on the flagpole. A white banner with red letters was draped across the building: "godhatesamerica.com."

I went to the front door of the church and tried to open it. It was locked. I checked my watch. Service was due to start at noon, but I was five minutes early.

I waited five minutes, but no one showed up. I rang the doorbell, repeatedly. I knocked on the door, repeatedly. I tried the side door, but no one answered.

You cowards, I seethed. *How dare you talk a big game but then refuse to show your face when someone actually comes to your turf to talk!*

I was so mad. Westboro was willing to force their way into the faces of millions of people but wasn't willing to have one rational conversation with someone who truly wanted to understand what they were thinking.

I went for a walk to stomp off my anger.

As I circled the block, I realized most of the houses had brand-new fences. The houses also had surveillance cameras mounted to their walls. Every house's shades were drawn. I peered between two fence boards. There were no fences in between the houses. They were all connected into one giant backyard. It all made sense—Westboro families had purchased all the houses on the block and turned it into one giant compound.

I saw someone sprint between two houses. *Signs of life!* I thought. I started knocking on doors. If a house had a video camera on it, I pounded on the front door. I knocked on seven doors before circling back to the church. I rang the doorbell and knocked some more.

I was about to give up my search when a rather shifty fellow scurried out of the church building. I pounced like a cat. "Hey there!" I waved. He froze.

"Hi!" I said. "My name is Jared, and I'm here for church. What's your name?"

"Uh, church is over. Did you ring the doorbell?" he stammered in a British accent. "I'm Matt from England."

"Hello, Matt from England!" I said. "Yes, I rang the doorbell. You know I rang the doorbell, because you were inside."

He unconvincingly pretended that the doorbell didn't work.

"Did you try knocking?" he asked.

"Yes, I did," I said. "You know I knocked on the door, because you were inside."

"Did you e-mail ahead of time?" he asked.

"Yes, I did," I said, nodding. "But I never heard back."

"Oh," he said. "Sorry about that."

"Right," I said. "So what brings you here? Are you visiting?"

"No," he said. "I've been going here for a few years."

"Really?" I asked in shock. "What brought you here?"

"I came here for the good theology," he said. "I like that they practice what they preach."

"I see," I said. "Did Fred Phelps preach today?"

"Uh, no, one of the elders did," he said. "We haven't seen Fred in a while."

I later learned that Phelps had reportedly been excommunicated a few months earlier in an elder-led coup, although the church is silent on membership details.

"So," I said, "can I at least get a tour?"

Matt from England rang the doorbell and a voice answered immediately. He asked if I could have permission to enter but was flatly denied.

I've since seen pictures and video of the facility. They meet in the basement, presumably for protection from drive-by shootings. The room has walls covered with 1960s faux wood paneling, reddish-orange padded pews, and aging pinkish carpet. They even have their own sign workshop.

Matt and I stood in silence for a moment. He was in his early thirties.

"So you guys protest at concerts and stuff all over the world, but you also picket locally, right?" I asked.

"Oh yes," Matt answered. "We regularly protest the Episcopalian church up the road."

"And why's that?" I asked.

"I forget," he said. "They said something bad about us back in the day. It was before my time."

As we chatted, four different cars drove by—the people in each one glared and shook their heads in disgust.

One vehicle circled twice, carrying two guys in a truck. I prayed no shotgun would emerge. I wanted to scream, "Don't shoot! I am *not* one of them!"

The church door opened and a young Asian man walked out. He was immediately followed by an even younger woman in a bonnet, but she ran away quickly.

"Hi, my name's Jared!" I said. "I came here for church!"

"Hi, I'm Jack," he replied. "Church is over."

"Yes, I realize—"

"Did you try ringing the doorbell?"

He repeated the whole process, almost verbatim. I kept eyeing Matt from England. He was twitching nervously, anxious to move on.

"Sorry again about church," he said.

"Yeah, it's a real shame." I nodded. "I woke up at 2:15 this morning to drive here."

As a concession, he offered me a copy of the sermon notes. It was a ten-page document.

The sermon started with a map of the ancient world, followed by a section about graven images, which apparently includes the Sistine Chapel, Jesus fish bumper stickers, and WWJD bracelets.

The next section was something about Syria, followed by a few paragraphs about abortion, and then some notes about NPR and Afghanistan. There was an excellent tirade against "sorceries like the abuse of pharmaceuticals," with specific mentions of Justin Bieber and the legalization of marijuana in Colorado. The document ended with a piece on stealing and included the story of a man who stole $200 worth of ice cream, as well as a person who stole a ring off a dead woman in a Wichita fast food restaurant. The sermon ended with the words "I love you all. Amen."

Needless to say, there wasn't a lot of focus to the message—just an overwhelming sense of negativity toward humanity in general.

Matt from England and Jack from Asia ran away as an older couple approached.

"God, grant me the serenity to accept the things I cannot change, the courage to change the things I can, and the wisdom to know the difference." "THE SERENITY PRAYER"

I was approached by a couple in their early forties. The woman was tall and gaunt; the man was clean cut and wore a pair of dark sunglasses.

"Can I help you?" the man asked sternly.

"Hi, I'm . . ." I was confused. "Where, exactly, did you come from?"

"We saw you on our home monitor," the woman said curtly. "Is that your wife in the car parked around the corner?"

I was *so* creeped out.

"Um, yeah. My name is Jared," I said. "I drove nine hours to come to church today, but you wouldn't answer the door. I rang and knocked and sent an e-mail ahead of time."

"Yeah, we saw you on the church monitors," the man replied. "I'm Charles, and this is my wife, Rachel."

At least this guy is honest, I thought.

Charles scanned the street furtively. "Why don't you come inside where we can talk?" he invited.

Charles F. Hockenbarger was a relatively polite man with an intense gaze and fairly steady eye contact. Rachel I. Phelps-Hockenbarger, daughter of Fred Sr., had inherited her father's bitter contempt for humanity, and you could not pay her to make eye contact. The family resemblance was uncanny, and a little unsettling.

Both the husband and wife texted on cell phones. I wasn't quite sure where to begin.

"So—um, let's start at the beginning, I guess," I said. "What's the most important thing I need to know about Westboro and what you believe?"

"That God loves everyone," Rachel snapped. "That's the greatest lie ever told. God loves everyone. Oh, *please!*" She rolled her eyes.

I had read about this belief on their website. The page mentioned that the word *hate* appears in the NIV Bible eighty times, and it listed the eighteen times it appears in connection with God. They neglected to mention that the word *love* is mentioned 551 times.

As we chatted, Rachel pecked away on an iPhone, and Charles filled out a contract for a National Geographic documentary.

"Why do they want our Social Security numbers?" he cried. "I'm not giving them my social insurance number!"

Given their antigovernment survivalist mentality, I was surprised they even had Social Security numbers.

"Why would they ask for that?" he continued to complain. "It's not like we're accepting payment."

"Wait, they don't pay you?" I asked.

"We don't accept payment for anything," he said. "Or donations."

I doubted they'd qualify as a legal charity anyhow.

"Why don't you accept donations?" I asked.

"Because we don't want anyone to get the wrong impression," he said. "We wouldn't want someone to think they're going to heaven because they supported us."

The group spends upwards of $250,000 per year on traveling to protests, all of it gleaned from personal savings. Rachel followed in her father's footsteps and works as a juvenile lawyer. Charles owns his own business, though I can't imagine who knowingly does business with any of the Westboro folks.

"All of our surplus goes to protests," Charles explained. "We're committed to the mission."

"So you're going on National Geographic, eh?" I said. "That seems like an odd choice for them. What's the strangest show you've ever been offered?"

"We were offered a wife-swap TV show one time," Rachel said. "But we don't have time for that. Besides, they probably would have sent over some kind of whore. We're too busy with protests."

I cringed. I couldn't get used to their harsh language—and it got far, far worse. I can't print many of the words they said again and again. At one point, after Rachel said a certain obscenity repeatedly, I tried to get her to stop.

"I'm sorry; I know it might seem normal to you," I said, "but I'm pretty sure that word is considered hate speech in Canada."

Rachel rolled her eyes. "Oh, please," she said. "Canada is a nation full of [more obscenities]."

I winced. "Do you guys really think that picketing is the best way to effectively communicate your message?"

"What do you mean by *effective*?" Charles asked. "Our goal is *not* to win souls. That's not the point. Salvation belongs to the Lord—it's our job to spread the message. My job is to plant the seed, not to make people like me."

"Okay, I know this might sound like a weird question, but do you guys ever pray?" I asked.

"Oh yes, all the time!" Rachel answered. "Our goal is to pray without ceasing. We prayerfully discern where to picket and when to picket, and we pray about what to write on every sign."

Every sign. Signs like "AIDS Is God's Gift." "Fags Die God

Laughs." "Pray for More Dead Soldiers." "Planes Crash God Laughs." "Billy in Hell."

"We don't hold a regular prayer meeting, if that's what you're asking," Charles added. "Because we don't find it in Scripture."

I hadn't seen any mention of picketing, either.

"But we pray twice during our Sunday service, and every once in a while we get together to pray if we need discernment on something," Charles said.

"I read and pray with the kids every morning and night," Rachel added. "I use the Lord's Prayer as a model."

"So what's your prayer for the nation?" I asked.

"I pray for the last sheep," Charles said. "That the final sheep would be found."

Rachel added the finishing touch: "That God would return and destroy the wicked."

I was stunned.

"Okay, here's an even more random question," I said. "Around one in four Americans claims to be a Christian. Out of the roughly seventy-five million Christians in the United States, how many do you think are *actually* Christians?"

Rachel looked at her husband. "What are we up to now?" she asked. "Forty-three members?"

"Wait, wait, wait, wait!" I said. "Are you saying the *only* Christians in America are the ones who go to Westboro Baptist Church?"

"You know, we pray about this all the time," Charles said. "Elijah thought he was the only one, but God revealed that there were seven thousand who had not bowed to Baal. We pray that God will reveal them to us. If we find them, it's not outside our thought that we might move to join them. The whole church should be together."

"What about Terry Jones?" I asked. "Have you ever heard of that guy who burned those Korans in Florida?"

"Ha!" Rachel snorted. "We've burned Korans in front of the church before."

"We don't associate with him," Charles informed me. "He's a kook."

He likened the folks at Westboro to the prophet Jonah but failed to see the irony in how the story ends.

"Well, hey, I need to run," I said. "Shall we pray together?"

Charles looked at Rachel. "It's up to you, dear!" she said.

"What, are you serious?" I asked. "You won't *pray* with me?"

"Um, no, actually." Charles shook his head. "I don't know you. I wouldn't want you to think that I condone or approve of what you're doing."

"I see," I said. "Well, tell you what, then. I'm going to pray for you, and you can pray for me. How does that sound?"

"I suppose we could do that," he said.

"Hey, Rachel," I asked. "How's your father?"

She glared. "Fine."

I didn't press the subject.

Fred Phelps died exactly thirty-one days later, survived by a small cult and/or a large family.

And Billy Graham.

"In the Gospel of Jesus Christ, grace is the most predominant attribute of God." CHARLES SPURGEON

When I left Westboro, I was mad. Angry. Furious. How could these people call themselves Christians? How dare they claim to love Jesus? I was *fuming.*

Then it dawned on me.

I was filled with the same hatred that filled Westboro.

Dang it.

When I realized I was no different from the Phelps family— broken, sinful, bankrupt—I was again reminded of my paraphrase of

Dorothy Day: "We love God as much as the person we love the least." I made it personal so it would hit me harder: "I love God as much as the person I love the least." How convicting is that? It stabbed me in the heart like a knife. *I love God as much as the person I love the least.* At that moment, it was Westboro. I immediately started holding them in the light.

I was a grieving mess when I left Westboro. They truly believe God hates people. They believe only those predestined for heaven will be saved and that everyone else will burn in hell immediately. I saw no love at Westboro. They do not care about winning souls to Christ. The backlash of hatred they receive fuels their belief that they are on the right track.

From where I stand, much of their problem rests with the way they read the Bible. They read every single word literally—just like the Pharisees did in Jesus' day. And because they focus so heavily on the Old Testament, it ends up overflowing in vitriolic hatred for humanity.

But more than that, Westboro is missing real prayer. I didn't see any evidence of a healthy relationship with Jesus Christ. Sure, they had memorized great swaths of Scripture, but there was no sense that they communed with Christ, who died for the unjust. They didn't have any of the love that compelled Jesus to say, "Let any one of you who is without sin be the first to throw a stone."

It's not enough to pray over a sign and assume God must have inspired you to write hateful phrases. Prayer is about steeping in the Spirit of a God so loving that He totally changes you. Jesus never leaves us the same. True prayer conforms Christians to the image of Christ.

We need to pray for the Phelps family and the folks at Westboro Baptist Church. Matthew 12:37 says, "By your words you will be acquitted, and by your words you will be condemned." We need to pray that their hate speech will turn into love.

We especially need to pray for the children at Westboro. The kids go to school, but they don't have any friends there. The older girls have all but given up hope of ever getting married. I watched a documentary on the Phelps family, and I almost cried as I watched children as young as seven carry hateful signs to protests. They didn't even know what their signs meant. The Phelps parents are breeding their children to hate.

During the documentary, a car drove by and pelted a dear seven-year-old boy in the face with a large, high-speed Sonic soda. I almost wept again. The poor boy held his little face while his mother mopped his soaking clothes and a sibling went in search of his glasses. Their own children are the victims.

I pray for Westboro and the Phelps family every single day. I'm praying that a spirit of grace and love will fall on them. I'm praying that spiritual bonds will be broken. I'm praying that local churches will love them to Jesus.

Not only do we need to pray for Westboro and the Phelps family, but we need to pray for our own families and churches. We need to pray that the Holy Spirit will help us to guard our theology and "rightly [divide] the word of truth."

We all need Jesus to save us from ourselves.

CHAPTER 10

Korea

LOOKING AT A MAP as I planned my visit to the world's largest church in Seoul, South Korea, I realized that Seoul is just a few miles south of the North Korean border.

I had seen North Korea in the news a lot that week, and I found it fascinating. North Korea is officially called the Democratic People's Republic of Korea (DPRK), but don't let them fool you—a democracy it is not. It's an old-fashioned hereditary dictatorship started by Grandpa Kim Il-sung, a hardy fellow who "outlived Joseph Stalin by four decades, Mao Zedong by two, and remained in power during the terms of office of six South Korean presidents, seven Soviet leaders, ten U.S. presidents, fourteen UK Prime Ministers, twenty-one Japanese prime ministers, five popes."

North Korea is slightly smaller than the state of Mississippi and has a population of about twenty-five million—over half of which require food aid. Millions of people have starved to death since the Kim dynasty took charge, and there are around nine million people in the military. Technically the USA and the DPRK have been at war since 1953, as neither country has signed a formal peace treaty.

Kim Il-sung was succeeded by his son Kim Jong-il, who later passed power to his youngest son, Kim Jong-un, the current leader. He has already executed hundreds of people, including members of his own family.

The so-called "Hermit Kingdom" is one of the most closed countries in the world. There are over two hundred thousand prisoners in gulag-style concentration camps—some are there just for listening to a South Korean song. *Christianity Today* has named North Korea the hardest place in the world to be a Christian—there are at least fifty thousand Christians in work camps. In the past sixty years, over four hundred thousand people have died in these concentration camps.

I wanted to pray in the most dangerous place on earth for Christians. I wanted to spark a small light in a dark, dark place.

I learned online that it was fairly easy for Canadians to visit North Korea. Not many people do, of course, but it was theoretically possible. All foreign tour companies must be approved by the domestic state-run tour agencies. I learned that the tour agencies were accepting applications for a special New Year's trip to North Korea, and I was hooked on the idea. I e-mailed eight government-sanctioned tour operators and asked for information. I eventually applied to one of the tour companies but was rejected because they thought I was a journalist.

So I applied with another company. It was the same tour company that first brought Dennis Rodman to North Korea. I figured if they could take care of a flamboyant power forward, they could take care of one Jew-ish prayer pilgrim. The company's instructions were clear: "At least two months prior to the date of travel, submit your DPRK visa application." I applied with only fifteen days' notice. I booked my nonrefundable flight from Vancouver to Beijing and prayed I hadn't just wasted thousands of dollars. I was approved with one day to spare.

I stocked up on Canadian flags, and Michelle dropped me off at the Victoria Ferry Terminal. We said good-bye. It was the hardest, most real good-bye we had ever said. We prayed and lingered as long as possible. We didn't know if we would see each other again.

"Prayer is our declaration of dependence upon the Lord." PHILIP YANCEY

I flew from Vancouver to Beijing, and then from Beijing to Pyongyang. The flight to Beijing was full of Chinese people, which really shouldn't have surprised me. Every single person had an IPhone or a BlackBerry, as part of China's "minimum one cell phone policy." I heard one woman fret over how she was going to sneak maple syrup through Beijing security.

I entered the plane and instantly regretted purchasing cheap seats. Not that I'd ever purchased non cheap seats, but this would have been the flight to do it for. I passed by rows of sleeping pods cov ered with sumptuous leather, widescreen TVs with premium sound systems, and little cupboards filled with caviar and champagne and baby unicorns.

I put my seat in the upright position lest I put too much weight on the back end and flip the plane during takeoff.

The in-flight dinner was served with a side of turbulence, fol- lowed almost immediately by a giant rush to the bathroom. I joined the long line, and we passed over Alaska by the time I reached the front.

I wasn't looking forward to the repulsive experience known as airplane bathrooms. To my surprise, the man ahead of me in line emerged from the tiny compartment carrying a bar of soap, a bottle of shampoo, and a third item, which I assumed was a loofah. The man had just joined the mile-high-shower club. The floor was positively swampy, but the scent of Dove soap was welcome. There was a sign on the toilet seat: "No Throwing Wine Bottles Down the Toilet." The golden age of flight has ended.

I arrived at the Beijing airport and caught a cab that wove through the congested streets at breakneck speed. The driver turned on two radios and sang along to whichever song he preferred.

I checked into my hotel and went out for dinner with the people who would be visiting North Korea with me. It wasn't a big group— just an Irish national and an Australian. The joke basically wrote itself.

Within minutes I realized this was a truly unique group—the Irishman was a beer-drinking sailor, the Australian was a gluten-free, lactose-intolerant, hypochondriac vegetarian, and the tour host was Korean American with strong North Korean sympathies.

The Irishman had actually been to North Korea a number of times, and his purpose for revisiting was to see some friends.[1] The Australian lady was some sort of human rights consultant but spent most of her time asking what ingredients were in each dish. The American host was in the process of forging backdoor partnerships between North Korea and Korean American businesses, which I'm pretty sure is illegal.

We started the next morning with a "Western breakfast," which consisted of eggs, donuts, and a salad bar. It was the last decent meal I ate for days.

We received our bright-blue DPRK tourist visas at the airport, complete with official passport photos—mine, I'm proud to say, was a selfie. We were given a little booklet titled "Useful Korean Phrases." Word number one was "hello." The Korean word for "hello" is *annyonghassimnigga*. I skimmed down the list. "Waitress!" was spelled

---

[1] I later learned that he had fallen in love with a Korean tour guide. He spent close to $10,000 each year just to spend a few fleeting moments with his forbidden love.

chopdaewondongmu. "I am British" and "I don't eat meat" didn't apply, and the rest of the words were unpronounceable to me. I stuffed the booklet in my bag and never looked at it again.

We boarded the plane and said good-bye to modern civilization.

"Here is the world. Beautiful and terrible things will happen. Don't be afraid." FREDERICK BUECHNER

I was handed a list of rules provided by the state-sanctioned tour agency. "State-sanctioned" was another word for "heavily censored."

> Visitors must: Respect the nation's current and former leaders at all times. When taking photos of their statues, they must be sure to capture the entire statue. Do not take photographs of military, construction sites or impoverished areas. These photographs may be deleted. Do not bring anything written in Korean. Not walk around unaccompanied by your North Korean tour guide.[2]

We arrived at Pyongyang International Airport, which looked a lot like a landing strip in a cow field. We walked from the plane to the terminal, which had a gorgeous, ornate ceiling and a dirty concrete floor. "You'll see that a lot in North Korea," the Irishman whispered. "They're always trying to distract you."

The airport was freezing cold. "You'll find that a lot too," he said. "They only heat one room at a time."

There was a large line to pass through customs, but we got special treatment. We were quickly whisked to the front counter. The customs officer took my passport and visa.

He asked me a question in Korean. I didn't say anything back. He asked me another question in Korean, but I remained silent. He asked me a third question.

"I'm here for pleasure?" I shrugged and laughed.

---

2 So basically, to "not walk around" without a guide means that the *guide* is actually a *guard*, right?

"USA?" he asked.

"No," I pointed at my passport. "Canada."

He stamped my passport and uttered the only "Canadian" phrase he knew.

"Bon voyage," he said.

Our passports and visas were confiscated as soon as we got through customs. "We will look after these for you," the American guide said. "For safekeeping."

We grabbed our luggage and located our Korean guides. There were four in all—one for each of us. We shook hands. Mr. Chen was in his late fifties, and I was informed he was the man in charge of the tour agency. Mr. Lee was the bus driver. Mr. Kam was a smiley fellow in his early thirties. Ms. Kim, decked out in high heels and fur and makeup, reminded me of Elizabeth Banks's brilliantly gaudy character in *The Hunger Games*.

Mr. Kam started the indoctrination as we walked to the bus. "What is the first thing you notice?" he asked. "Fresh air!" he exclaimed, not giving me time to think.

I sniffed the air. It smelled like jet fuel and diesel fumes. I was informed that North Korea didn't have any air pollution whatsoever. Mr. Kam made no mention of the total lack of industry, but he did say that if I ever smelled pollution, it was China's fault.

We boarded the tour bus. There were only eight of us, but the bus contained eighty seats. I looked out the window. Everyone was in uniform. Soldiers wore green, and everyone else wore dark blues and grays. Mr. Lee started the bus.

"You can take pictures, maximum ten in total," Ms. Kim said. "With our permission." I looked out the window. "Barren wasteland" was the phrase that came to mind. North Korea is one of the least agriculturally cultivated places on earth, and it showed.

"What are those little piles in every field?" I asked the guides.

"Organic fertilizer for springtime," Mr. Kam answered.

"What's in it?" I asked.

"Chemicals," he explained.

"This is the first year that Western tourists have been allowed to visit the Democratic People's Republic of Korea for New Year's," Ms. Kim announced. "You should be very grateful."

We drove along the main highway from the airport to Pyongyang. No cars passed in either direction, with the exception of one wood-powered truck filled with young soldiers.

Ms. Kim hovered over me and stared at my face.

"Can I help you?" I teased.

"Korean women don't like men with beards," she said.

Nice to meet you, too, I thought. Sadly, Michelle also hates my beard. Perhaps she'll love it by the time I start to look like Moses. I looked at my reflection in the window.

I was, apparently, the ugliest man in North Korea.

"In a Pyongyang restaurant, don't ever ask for a doggie bag."
CHRISTOPHER HITCHENS

Pyongyang was once known among missionaries as the "Jerusalem of the East." In fact, Ruth Bell Graham spent her high school years in a boarding school in Pyongyang in the 1930s. Pyongyang was a historical bastion for Protestant Christianity. By the 1940s almost one in three of its citizens were church-attending Christians. But when the Korean War ended in 1953, a new power took control of the capital. Owning a Bible became an act of treason, and those who shared their faith risked being executed. More than three thousand churches and two hundred fifty thousand Christians simply disappeared. Within one generation, Pyongyang went from being the "Jerusalem of the East" to the world's top persecutor of Christians.

Pyongyang is a "showcase capital," built to impress upon visitors the sense that the nation is strong and mighty and technologically advanced. Buildings in Pyongyang are "purpose built," meaning they sit empty for most of their life span. We passed by one street that was built to host the thirteenth World Festival of Youth and Students in 1989. (Basically, the Commie Kid's Olympics.) It contained a soccer stadium, a swimming complex, and a dodgeball stadium. We saw no signs of life.

There were very few cars, even in the capital city with a population of 2.5 million people. "That's because regular citizens aren't allowed to own cars," the Irishman informed me. "Only politicians and party-faithful businessmen." We still managed to wait at one traffic light for eleven minutes. Unlike any usual metropolis, Pyongyang felt like a ghost town. There were no stores on the streets, and no ads anywhere.

We arrived at the Yanggakdo International Hotel. "It's pretty much the only hotel that Western visitors stay at," the Irishman told me. "I don't know anyone who's ever stayed anywhere else."

"You can go wherever you want," Ms. Kim directed. "Just stay within one hundred meters of the hotel."

"I've heard about a man who snuck out," the Aussie whispered. "He was shot as a spy."

I doubted the story was true, and it was unlikely anyone had ever snuck out—the hotel was built on an island for that very reason.

We were never allowed out of our guide's sight. Mr. Kam was never more than ten feet away from me. If I went to the washroom, he would either wait at the door or accompany me inside.

We checked into the Yanggakdo International Hotel, and Mr. Kam escorted me to my room. It was one of three rooms booked in the entire hotel. We arrived on the fortieth floor. The doors opened, and we stepped into a dark hallway.

"Um, Mr. Kam?" I asked. "Why are the lights out?"

"Oh, it's okay. We are saving power," he said. "Eco and friendly!"

He showed me to my room. "I think you will like very much. Five stars."

I looked around. It was a tired, Cold War–era room, complete with a giant turn-knob radio. *Three stars at best*, I thought.

I had heard rumors that the rooms in North Korea were bugged. I briefly checked the lamps, but I didn't know what I was looking for. I took a shower and was grateful to find the hotel had hot water.

The room had a sweet 1950s telephone, but I didn't attempt to place a call. Michelle was visiting some friends on Vancouver Island at the time and didn't have any way to contact me. She was afraid even to send an e-mail for fear it might (somehow) incriminate me. All she could do was pray.

That evening our group went out to a local "pub." We parked in a back alley and entered through a side door. We walked up a freezing-cold flight of stairs and into a little heated room. It was empty. Mr. Chen panicked, grabbed his cell phone, and ran out of the room. We were ushered to a table and poured a round of pints. A TV played the state-run news in the background. There were no commercials, just cuts to long clips of military footage.

A few seconds later, Mr. Chen joined us at the table.

Two minutes later, two "separate" groups of four women each appeared. They sat at nearby tables and ordered a round of pints. I had stepped into a real-life version of *The Truman Show*. Mr. Chen had ordered people to fill the pub. Everything was coordinated and planned to revolve around us.

"Then you will know the truth, and the truth will set you free."
JOHN 8:32

The North Korean–South Korean demilitarized zone (DMZ) is the most heavily militarized border on the planet.

Our tour of the DMZ started as all tours inevitably start—with a trip to the unheated gift shop. I went to the bathroom, but there was no running water.

We boarded a military bus and made our way to the international border. The narrow road was lined with giant chunks of concrete designed to block the roadway in case of invasion. I was told the surrounding fields were littered with land mines, more than almost any place on earth.

The soldiers took us to the room where the armistice was signed.

"Can I take a photo with you?" the Aussie asked the ranking officer.

The army major declined, and pointed her to a lesser-ranking soldier.

The major explained the war through a translator. He kept looking at me whenever he said the phrase "American Imperialists." I grinned and flashed my Canadian flag. The other tourists laughed, but the major didn't look happy.

He took us to the DMZ. There were three bright-blue buildings in the middle, painted the same color as my tourist visa. On the North side, an impressive array of soldiers marched and patrolled constantly, while their leaders surveilled the South with binoculars. The South side was a far more modern affair—they didn't have any soldiers at arms, just a few dozen high-tech video cameras.

We went into the middle blue building, where peace talks were negotiated, and took turns standing in two countries at the same time. The army major pointed to a Canadian flag on a list of countries that supported South Korea and the United Nations.

"See, you supported America!" he said through a translator.

"Hey, now, don't bring me into this!" I shot back. "I had nothing to do with it!"

"Yes," he replied. "But don't you think that future generations should be held responsible?"

"Absolutely not. That's absurd," I said. "Should German children pay for the war crimes of Nazis?"[3]

The room was tense. I realized that no one had probably ever had a rational disagreement with the major before. I prayed for favor.

He smiled and moved on.

At the end of the tour, despite having been reticent to be in photos beforehand, he offered to be in three photos with me. He even smiled for two of them. He shook my hand and wished me well. I wished him well, and silently prayed that the truth would set him free.

"The North Korean capital, Pyongyang, is a city consecrated to the worship of a father-son dynasty." CHRISTOPHER HITCHENS

Over the course of our time in North Korea, we didn't visit one "proper" restaurant like you'd see anywhere else in the world. Most were in private heated rooms at the end of unlit hallways, on the second or third floors of empty hotels or office buildings. Each restaurant came equipped with karaoke screens featuring war songs and war footage. The food in North Korea was not so much "food" as it was "matter." One dinner was a plate of what I am certain was sticks.

On New Year's Eve we had lunch on the third floor of an icy hotel, in a warm room with just one table. Nine bowls were already in place when we arrived, and I would describe their contents as follows: bad kimchi, raw potato, salty minnows, old tofu, seaweed wafers, beef gristle, rotten raw fish, dry sauerkraut, and some delicious little honey cakes. The picky Australian ate none of it.

---

[3] While the United Nations compares in no way to the Nazis, and their actions were justified, I needed to provide an extreme example to make my point. It worked.

We finished lunch and reboarded the bus. Four waitresses in fancy dresses waved good-bye. The bus wouldn't start. The waitresses continued to wave. The bus driver continued to rev the engine. The waitresses started to shiver in their thin dresses but stoically continued to wave. Mr. Kam rushed us back into the hotel to admire the heated floors in one of the hotel rooms. Minutes later, he rushed us back to the bus. "No problems, no problems," he said.

That evening we drove down to Kim Jong-il Square. Finding parking was easy, even for a bus on New Year's Eve. We walked to the square. The atmosphere was electric—they had actually turned the lights on. We joined a crowd of over two hundred thousand people. Kids played with balloons, but the place seemed remarkably hushed. Hundreds of openmouthed Koreans stared at the bearded foreigner—a first for many, and certainly for New Year's.

Every building sported a photo of Kim Il-sung and Kim Jong-il. The personality cult was crazy. I had been told stories about how Kim Jong-il set a world record and hit over a dozen holes in one the very first time he played golf. A teenage schoolgirl once drowned while attempting to rescue portraits of the leaders from a flood.

"Our great leader Kim Il-sung is greater than Lincoln, Washington, and Jefferson," Mr. Kam told me. "Combined!"

"Two things," I corrected. "One, he *was* greater, not *is* greater.[4] He's dead. Two, I'm Canadian, so I don't care."

Mr. Kam laughed. "Kim Il-sung is the eternal president. He is forever with us, in our hearts."

The fireworks were the best I had ever seen—no doubt the North Koreans had spent half their GDP on the impressive display. Set to military music over the Taedong River, the event was truly awe inspiring but somehow empty. It was idol worship. Everything was done to honor the images of Kim Il-sung and Kim Jong-il.

In the morning, I would be told to bow before those images.

---

4 Not that I think Kim Il-sung was greater. Lincoln had a beard.

"No Compromise is what the whole Gospel of Jesus is all about."
KEITH GREEN

I received a wake-up call from the front desk the next morning: "Hello, your time is up." It was an ominous message, and one I didn't want to hear that morning.

There is a New Year's Day tradition in North Korea that any party-faithful member is obliged to perform. Citizens visit the Kumsusan Palace of the Sun to bow before their fallen-yet-eternal leaders.

I had learned about this tradition ahead of time and had tried to avoid it at all costs. I asked if I could stay behind at the hotel, but I was told it would be seen as disrespectful. I explained to my American guide why I couldn't bow. I asked if I could stay on the bus but was told that would be seen as *very* disrespectful.

"Here's how it works," Mr. Kam told us. "Once we get inside, you must be silent. We will enter the room of the Great Leader Kim Il-sung. We will stand in groups of four and bow at his feet. Then we will bow at his left side and his right side. Then we will go into the room of the Great Comrade Kim Jong-il, and we will do the same thing. Then we will bow before a statue of the two great men together."

Seven bows in all.

I asked the Irishman what he thought I should do.

"Just bow, mate," he said. "If your heart's not in it, it's not a big deal."

But it *was* a big deal for me. I wouldn't have bowed to Babylon's golden image had I been with Shadrach, Meshach, and Abednego, and I wouldn't have bowed to a statue of Hitler. I certainly wasn't about to bow to the Kim family, especially since they are holding at least fifty thousand members of my spiritual family in concentration camps right now and since they've killed more than a million people over the course of their reign.

I felt sick.

We arrived at the palace and joined the massive throng. There were tens of thousands of people in line, and almost everyone was in full military uniform, with medals from shoulder to waist. Many of the older men had actually fought alongside Kim Il-sung in the 1950s.

We walked through a giant blow-dryer.

"To clean the dust off," the Irishman whispered as he patted down his hair.

Following the lead of Lenin, Stalin, and Mao Zedong, North Korea has preserved Kim Il-sung's body and placed it on display in a glass coffin, surrounded by a red rope. Hundreds of soldiers were in line ahead of us, and I watched as they approached in groups of four. Their bows were not simple head nods. They were full Korean bows—ninety degrees at the waist. I looked around the dark, silent room as we entered. As a Caucasian, I already stood out among the all-Korean crowd.

I knew that if I didn't bow, there was the outside potential of some angry army officer simply shooting me on sight, but I wasn't really worried about getting killed. I was far more worried about getting detained or thrown into a concentration camp. In times like these, there's only one thing to do: pray for God's best, prepare for Satan's worst. I had pored over maps ahead of time, inspecting the coastline and rivers, planning my escape route in case of imprisonment. When Michelle and I had said good-bye, it kinda-sorta was a real good-bye. We had lingered as long as possible, choked by tears. We didn't know what would happen.

Our group of eight went up in two sets of four. I was part of the first set. With my heart pounding, I managed to stay upright, refusing to even nod my head, as everyone else bowed. I didn't shake. I didn't sweat. I didn't cry. Instead, I was filled with brokenness for North Korea and with an overwhelming sense that God was in control.

Instead of bowing, I prayed the Lord's Prayer. First I whispered it at Kim Il-sung's feet. Then I prayed it at his left side, and then at his right. I prayed it again at the feet of Kim Jong-il. And then at his left side, and then at his right. For good measure, I prayed the Lord's Prayer once more—in front of the statue of the two men together.

I like to say that I planted seven prayer bombs in the very heart of North Korea. But seriously, what other prayer could be more powerful than the prayer of Jesus Himself? This is the prayer of my heart—His Kingdom come, His will be done. No one hungry, everyone forgiven.

I honestly didn't mean it as a sign of disrespect toward the fallen leaders. I feared their power greatly, but I simply had more respect for a far greater Leader. Like the rest of us, the Kims were sinful men in need of a Lord and Savior. I know, so deeply, that God is going to sort out North Korea. And America, and Canada, and the rest of the world, and me. He'll make everything right and just and true. The battle belongs to the Lord, and we already know that He wins the war.

We left the hallowed halls of the giant palace. As we made our way back to the bus, my American guide was clearly angry. I didn't care. I couldn't morally, politically, or spiritually bow to those men. Thankfully, I wasn't arrested.

Even in the best of times, I have trouble living completely for God. But at least I know now that, on some very small level, I'm willing to die for Him.

"It's the first effect of not believing in God that you lose your common sense." G. K. CHESTERTON

Near the center of Pyongyang, on the banks of the Taedong River across from Kim Il-sung Square, stands an absolutely magnificent monument. At 560 feet, it's the tallest granite tower in the world, a fact my guide was quick to point out.

It was modeled after the Washington Monument but built one yard taller. It's a four-sided structure with an elevator up the middle and a flickering flame on top. Constructed on the occasion of the founder's seventieth birthday, it contains exactly 25,550 blocks: one for every day of Kim Il-sung's seventy years of life (not including leap days).

Its name is the Tower of the Juche Idea. The Juche Idea is a philosophy concocted by the nation's founder, Kim Il-sung. A toxic blend of self-reliance, nationalism, and Marxism-Leninism, it's the nation's unofficial religion.

After leaving the Kumsusan Palace of the Sun, I got to ride up the tower with Mr. Kam. From the lookout I could see the entire city.

"Do you believe in God?" I asked him.

His response was immediate and emphatic: "No. I believe in *me*."

That is the Juche Idea, in a nutshell.

Mr. Kam went on to tell me he was in control of his fate and was the master of his destiny. He explained he was totally independent and didn't need to rely on anyone for anything.

The entire nation is fashioned around this idea. It's a philosophy that basically states, "We are God." It's the same idea that's been plaguing humans since the Garden of Eden, and the Juche Idea is just one of its many names. Any philosophy not founded in Christ, when taken to its extreme, will destroy more lives than it promises to save. In the casea of North Korea, ultimate self-reliance has turned into absolute state-reliance—for housing, jobs, transportation, and even food and clothing.

North Korea is not simply a country—it is a cult. Its people have never known anything different, and those who dissent are likely to disappear. Citizens worship the Kim family, but, ultimately, they worship themselves. They're just like the rest of us. Left to our own devices, we will make God in our own image.

As I stood atop the Juche Tower and looked out over Pyongyang, I was reminded once again that we are *not* fighting against flesh and blood. We're fighting against philosophies and deceptions in the spiritual realm. Pyongyang is filled with people God loves deeply, but they have exchanged the truth for a lie. Jesus died to save North Koreans, most of whom still have not heard the Good News.

While Mr. Kam smoked a cigarette, I prayed the Lord's Prayer from all four corners of the Juche Tower.

"To get nations back on their feet, we must first get down on our knees."
BILLY GRAHAM

It was my last night in North Korea, and I was broken at the thought of fifty thousand Korean Christians still in chains. I felt overwhelmed by the need to pray for the Kim family and for the twenty-five million souls whom they have oppressed. It was clear they were all in chains. If Kim Jong-un held legitimate democratic elections, the next leader would execute him in seconds. If the citizens somehow mounted a revolt, millions would perish. If everything stays the same, millions more will starve, and tens of millions will never know freedom in the flesh, nor freedom in Christ. I was wrecked. I felt powerless all over again, just as I was in the red-light district in Amsterdam.

I wanted to cry out to God for North Korea's spiritual freedom, but I couldn't find the words. So I sang a prayer instead. I sang a song by Bluetree called "God of This City." I broke open the hotel window and sang it over Pyongyang, again and again and again, "You're the God of this city, you're the King of these people. . . . And greater things are still to be done here."

Deep down, I think I was also singing the song over my own heart. A large part of me wants to be like Kim Jong-un. I want wealth and control and power. I want to play God. Part of me believes in the Juche Idea, that I'm somehow the master of my fate and the captain of my soul. But I know that God's not done working in me or through me. Greater things are still to be done in my heart.

"We are too busy to pray, and so we are too busy to have power. We have a great deal of activity, but we accomplish little; many services but few conversions; much machinery but few results." R. A. TORREY

It's easy to be cynical about prayer. It's easy to dismiss prayer and call for governmental intervention in North Korea. It's easier to cut a check or volunteer a few hours toward a cause instead of persistently praying that God would end injustice.

In doing research for this book, I came across an amazingly cynical poster on the Internet. It's designed to look like one of those Successories motivational posters, with a doctored photo, black outline, and quote at the bottom. In the image I discovered, there was a picture of praying hands and a quote that read, "Prayer—A Way of Doing Nothing That Feels like Accomplishing Something."

I almost groaned when I read that. Could the poster's creator be any more jaded? That person is missing the point of prayer. Consider it from another angle: if you ate lunch with the president every single day, you'd probably become more political. If you played golf with Bill Gates every morning, you'd probably get better at handling money. If you hung out with Steven Spielberg every afternoon, you'd probably watch more movies. What would happen if you hung out with Jesus every single day? Whoever made this poster clearly doesn't understand that prayer isn't primarily about *doing* anything—it's about *becoming* someone who does something.

Imagine that poster in another form: "Talking with Your Spouse—A Way of Doing Nothing That Feels like Accomplishing Something." That's called *being married*. "Playing with Your Kids—A Way of Doing Nothing That Feels like Accomplishing Something." That's called *parenting*. Spending time in prayer? That's called *following Jesus*. Prayer changes us because that's what relationships do.

Of course, a cynical person could claim that changing ourselves doesn't change anything significant in the world. Just because we become different people through spending time with Jesus, it doesn't mean that oppressive nations like North Korea will change as a result.

There was an interesting cover story in *Christianity Today* on the work of Protestant missionaries—specifically non-state-funded missionaries intent on converting people to Christianity. Researcher Robert Woodberry studied the correlation between Protestant religion and democracy around the world, and the evidence he found "was like an atomic bomb. The impact of missions on global democracy was *huge*." Missionaries brought about reforms, fought colonialism, taught people to read, and rallied support for struggling peoples around the world. The conclusion the article makes is striking: "Want a blossoming democracy today? The solution is simple—if you have a time machine: Send a 19th-century missionary." Changed people change nations.

As we'll see in the next chapter, many missionary movements were begun and sustained by prayer. As Oswald Chambers says, "Prayer does not equip us for greater works—prayer is the greater work."

"I pray, and I obey." DAVID YONGGI CHO

I flew from North Korea to China, and from China to South Korea. Each seat on the second flight had its own TV and video game controller. I knew I was back in the Western world when I overheard an American ask the flight attendant about lunch.

"What is it?" the American asked.

"Kimchi with fried rice," the attendant answered.

"Is it chicken?"

Compared to the barren desolation of North Korea, South Korea was a writhing mass of humanity. I stayed in the capital city of Seoul, with a population of ten million, give or take. A friend of a friend met me at the airport and brought me to a hostel in the university zone. It was nice to stay in a quiet, clean little hostel. "Little" was the key word in Seoul. The bathroom was so small that the shower was built into the sink. The bath towels were roughly half the size of my torso. My knees touched the wall whenever I sat on the toilet. But the bathroom size didn't matter. I was there to see Yoido Full Gospel Church.

Yoido Full Gospel Church is the largest church in the world, with more than one million members. Started in a living room in 1958 by Dr. David Yonggi Cho and his mother-in-law, the church has grown exponentially over the decades. Around 200,000 people attend the main campus on any given Sunday, and there are twenty-odd satellite sites around Seoul.

The church occupies an entire city block on the Han River—prime real estate in a booming metropolis like Seoul. I wanted to visit Yoido because it's a church that claims to be founded on prayer.

The service started at 9:00 a.m., and I arrived an hour early—surely a record for me. I walked the block to get a sense of the place, counting at least seven major buildings, most of them over ten stories tall. Skyscraper church.

Across the street were acres of buses. On the main thoroughfare, a big street market, selling everything from shoes to Pringles, had been constructed to take advantage of the multitudes passing by.

Once inside the church's café, I took a virtual tour of the church on a touch-screen monitor. I learned that new attendees can participate in a three-week membership course and receive a gift upon completion—Pastor Cho's Annotated Bible, a free medical checkup coupon, and a voucher for a flu shot.

As I entered the auditorium lobby, an usher pointed at a sign that said, "Foreigners." Following the sign toward a section in the gallery, I watched as streams of people poured into the auditorium—mostly pushy Korean women in their late fifties. The ceiling looked like a giant flying saucer. I took a seat about thirty minutes before the service started. The first few thousand seats were already full—one half contained solely middle-aged men in suits with yellow badges. Another section was filled with men wearing beauty queen–style sashes. A third section contained about one hundred men in Godfather-black trench coats, with Michael Jackson–style white gloves. A fourth section held men in all-white suits, seated in fives, not unlike the Backstreet Boys.[5]

The auditorium was 95 percent full by nine o'clock. By 9:07, the entire auditorium and seven overflow chapels had been filled. I doubted anyone could beat the South Koreans when it came to on-time church attendance.

A full choir mounted the stage, along with an orchestra, an organist, an opera singer, twelve backup singers, and the main worship leader. They bowed before the cross and started singing.

"'Tis So Sweet to Trust in Jesus" was sung in double time, with a karaoke-style bouncing ball to help the audience follow the lyrics on two giant screens. "Draw Me Nearer, Precious Lord" was also sung in double time. Perhaps all that fast singing allowed them to fit in more songs. The Doxology was sung at regular speed, but the Apostles' Creed was recited in double time. It was all very jubilant. The on-screen images depicted Jesus as a Caucasian. They had been trained well—everyone knows Jesus has blond hair and blue eyes.

The preacher rose from a leather La-Z-Boy and opened his Bible on the pulpit. An usher walked through our section. He held a sign that read, "No Flash During Worship Service." Each pew seat had a built-in headset with ten language options, including Russian and Mongolian. My headset didn't work. A portable replacement was rushed in. The sermon was a mixture of health-and-wealth with a big push to read and pray in the year ahead. Though bereft of personal stories, the pastor moved through his points speedily enough. Nothing really "landed" for me in this service. I hoped the English-specific service would be a better match.

---

[5] Badges, beauty queens, godfathers, and Backstreet Boys—church leadership at its finest.

"Going to church . . . doesn't make you a Christian any more than going to McDonald's makes you a hamburger!" KEITH GREEN

The morning service finished, and I made my way to the Sunday school building. At twelve stories tall, it was the largest Sunday school building I had ever seen. Twenty-one of us packed into a five-by-six elevator with a "MAX 20" sign.

I walked the hallways in search of the right room number. There were chicken-wing ads all over the walls.

"Is this where the English service meets?" I asked the usher. He said it was, and I took a seat. When the service started, the room was half full. It took almost half an hour to reach capacity.

The pastor's message was on prayer. He challenged us to pray prayers that required us to have faith. "How will the world be different if your prayers are or aren't answered?" he asked.

"Don't rely on your plans," he said. "Rely on prayer. Don't rely on strategy, rely on the Savior."

He told the story of a guy who went to the mall and sensed that God wanted him to do a handstand. He resisted, but God told him three times to do a handstand. So he did it. A college girl grabbed him and asked why he did a handstand. He explained that God had told him to do it. She told him she had been suicidal that morning and had prayed, "God, if You're real, make someone do a handstand."

I thought about pink teddy bears.

"We must be willing to look ridiculous," the pastor said.

I thought about Dr. Crandall.

The sermon was followed by my second communion of the morning, as well as a healing time. I didn't know it ahead of time, but they say a healing prayer every week. And why not? What's the worst that could happen—someone gets healed? It was the third healing service I had attended on this trip, but nothing had been healed so far. The pastor informed the crowd of all the recent healings at Yoido, which helped elevate my faith a bit. Still, I prayed God would heal my body in His time. Maybe it was cop-out prayer, but I hadn't seen much of a personal precedent for immediate healing.

"Prayer in the sense of petition, asking for things, is a small part of it; confession and penitence are its threshold, adoration its sanctuary, the presence and vision and enjoyment of God its bread and wine."
C. S. LEWIS

I visited an expat church later that afternoon. The man who greeted me soon discovered I was Canadian.

"Hey, we actually have another Canadian here," he said. "Do you know her?"

I rolled my eyes. Did he have any idea how huge Canada is? Of course I didn't know her. But then he introduced us.

"Actually, I do know you," she said. "I was in Hamilton at the premiere of your documentary on sex trafficking!"

"What are the chances?" I laughed.

The Canadian introduced me to a few other people, including a curmudgeonly fellow from Belfast who reminded me of the grumpy Irishman at Taizé. We shook hands.

"Are you a Baptist?" he asked.

"Uh, why?" I asked.

"You shake like a Baptist."

The service began, and we took our seats. I opened the bulletin and read the first paragraph.

Father, we confess that we naturally do not know how to pray. We do not know how to talk and commune with you. We heap meaningless words and phrases. We are content to babble words. We are weak and helpless, even in the simple act of crying out to you. Teach us to pray.

I had picked a good Sunday to be in Seoul.

The preacher mounted the pulpit. He assumed a wide-legged rock-star stance and appeared to be straddling the podium. His legs poked out from both sides of the wooden pulpit. He looked like a Christian cowboy.

"Please turn to First Koreans," he started.

The audience howled.

"Sorry." He blushed. "Please turn to First *Corinthians*."

His sermon was on prayer, which was fine with me. He explained how we can use prayer to hear from God.

"So often we focus on talking *to* God," he said. "But it's rare that we stop to *listen* to Him."

He challenged us to listen to God in three ways:

1. Let God tell you who He is.
2. Let God tell you who you are.
3. Let God tell you what to do.

"Listening to God is *not* easy," he said. "It takes a lifetime of struggle and hard work to be part of any healthy relationship."

"Prayer is something we need to work at," he continued. "Be willing to wrestle with God, knowing full well that He can break you."

"Contrary to popular teaching in South Korea, prayer isn't a get-rich-quick scheme," he said. "Prayer is like pregnancy—it takes labor to create life." *Labor*, I thought. *Ora et labora.* A prayerful life is full of action and exercise and hard work and labor. Prayer is the work of life.

I partook of my third communion of the day. *Not a bad way to start the New Year*, I thought.

That night I had dinner with the friend of a friend who had showed me to the hostel, and he explained why prayer is so highly valued among the churches in South Korea.

"In the New Testament, the Christians prayed together every day," he said. "So every morning, churches in Korea get together to pray. I think that is why we have so many good churches. I think that is why God has blessed the Korean church."

It was a simple yet powerful concept.

Many churches in Seoul have an early morning prayer service. Yoido Church has a five o'clock prayer meeting every weekday.

They also have a prayer mountain.

"[Jesus] went up on a mountainside by himself to pray." MATTHEW 14:23

Prayer Mountain's official name is the "Osanri Choi Ja-sil Memorial Fasting Prayer Mountain." Named after the founding pastor's mother-in-law, it's more of a small city than a prayer retreat. The eighty-one-acre campus includes 211 prayer grottoes, a convenience store, a bookstore, a restaurant, a cafeteria, two tennis courts, a running track, a cemetery, and sleeping facilities for over 10,000. The main sanctuary and thirteen chapels can seat almost 16,000 people. The facility runs a minimum of twenty-eight prayer services per week, and almost 1,500 guest ministers come to preach each year.

I had tried for weeks to book a night at Prayer Mountain but hadn't had any success. I wanted to spend twenty-four hours in prayer and fasting, but I couldn't seem to get through. Each time I called, a pastor would ask me to e-mail my request. They always promised to write back. I was given an e-mail address like RevJohn1234 or PastorFrankie90210, but not once did I receive a return message.

I started e-mailing random congregants I found online, but only one person got back to me. He was very kind, but ultimately unhelpful: "I am pretty sure that your steps of faith will introduce you to the right people chosen to accompany you through an exciting adventure loaded with surprises and revelations from the Lord."

I eventually gave up and figured I could arrange a night when I actually visited the church. On Sunday I met with a staffer and asked how I could book a room for fasting and prayer. "Oh, you don't need to worry about that," she said. "Are you going there tomorrow? It won't be busy on a Monday."

On Monday I boarded the bus from Yoido Church to Prayer Mountain. The bus ran twelve times daily, and it was free. We pulled away from the curb at exactly five minutes past the hour. The bus was about 80 percent full, at least forty people in all.

A sermon played over the sound system while the driver honked his horn and muttered at traffic. He laid on his horn at least six times in our one-hour trip. Only one honk was warranted—a garbage truck literally ran us off the road. Pounding through a dozen heavy-duty fixed road cones, we heard a sickening *thump thump thump* from the underside of the bus. The bus driver ground to a halt and got out to assess the damage. Nothing was broken, and we continued on our way to Prayer Mountain.

I had expected a rocky hilltop amid a pine forest, but Yoido's prayer mountain was a hill outside an industrial district. I made my way to the registration center.

"Hello!" I said. "I would like to book a room for prayer and fasting."

"No." The woman behind the glass shook her head.

"Um," I stammered, "I spoke with a staff member at Yoido and she said—"

"Sold out."

"What!" I said. "But she said—"

"Today is Monday," the woman explained. "Very busy. Sold out."

It was Monday, and all 1,500 beds were sold out. I almost wept. I had fasted before, but I wanted to pray and fast at *the* Prayer Mountain. I explained I had come all the way from Canada and had tried to book a room for many weeks.

"I can offer you a prayer grotto for one hour," she said.

With a key and a map, I found my way to the grottoes. They were little cells with four-foot-high metal doors. I searched for my room. It was located at the very back, in an older section. My Caucasian frame had been "upgraded" to a five-foot door.

Unlocking the cell, I saw a tiny red cross, a laminated set of instructions in Korean, a green TV tray, and a tiny red pillow. There was no room to lay down and no room to stand up—just enough space to kneel down, which I couldn't do because of my bad foot.

So I squatted.

The room smelled musty, with black mold on the ceiling and mud on the walls. The paint had been scratched away by some bored intercessor, and someone had started a little garbage pile in the corner.

I squatted there for about five minutes, trying but unable to pray. I was too disappointed.

Since trees seemed preferable to a stuffy cell, I walked the prayer path that ran atop the row of grottoes. Everyone was speaking in tongues—Korean, specifically.

Standing on the path, I closed my eyes and prayed, giving my disappointment to God. Letting the wind brush against my face, I began walking again along the prayer path, saying the Lord's Prayer. And then a texting college student ran into me.

I think most Christians would agree that the ideal prayer spot would be like the ideal writing spot: a mountain cabin in an evergreen forest by a freshwater spring. But if I waited for the perfect writing cabin, I'd never finish writing this book. While it's good to have a designated prayer spot, it's important to remember that prayer is meant to happen everywhere. After all, Daniel prayed in the lion's den. Jonah prayed in a fish's stomach. Elijah prayed in the desert. And Jesus prayed on the cross.

"Fasting as it relates to prayer is the spiritual atomic bomb that our Lord has given us to destroy the strongholds of evil." BILL BRIGHT

While I didn't have a chance to fast at Prayer Mountain, I was reminded of a previous fasting experience.

A few years ago, Michelle and I ended up completing a forty-day fast. We drank only water, fruit juice, and vegetable broth. We weren't trying to kill ourselves; we were just trying to go deeper with God.

It was one of the worst experiences of my life.

We moved in slow motion. Time stood still. The days dragged on, but nothing was accomplished. I was plunged into depression. Seeing friends lost its joy. All I wanted to do was be alone.

Fasting is an interesting Christian practice. Not many people do it, and I can see why—it's painful. Though billions around the world feel this pain on a regular basis, I understand why those of us who have the option tend to avoid it at all costs. It hurts to go to bed hungry. It hurts to wake up hungry.

So why would anyone who can afford food choose to do without? I think Andrew Murray says it best: "Fasting helps to express, to deepen, and to confirm the resolution that we are ready to sacrifice anything, to sacrifice ourselves, to attain what we seek for the king-dom of God. . . . Prayer is the reaching out after God and the unseen; fasting, the letting go of all that is seen and temporal." Essentially, we fast in order to grow closer to God.

And you don't have to fast food.[6] You could give up cable or Facebook or watching sports or texting. You could cut coffee or shop-ping or any other number of things. Next year, I'm going to give up pancakes for Lent.

As Andrew Bonar puts it, to fast is to "abstain from whatever hinders direct fellowship with God." Speaking of Andrew Bonar, my favorite line by the Scottish minister is a hard-core fasting quote: "Oh brother, pray; in spite of Satan, pray; spend hours in prayer, rather neglect friends than not pray, rather fast, and lose breakfast, dinner, tea, and supper—and sleep too—than not pray. . . . And we must not *talk about* prayer—we must pray in right earnest. The Lord is near."

---

6 Of course, we could all survive a fast food fast.

In hindsight, I realize that neither Michelle nor I was even remotely close to being spiritually prepared for a forty-day fast. We didn't think it through. Even though we started with a specific prayer focus, we lost it as the fast dragged on. I also lost forty-four pounds—a tiny bit of fat and every ounce of muscle I had ever earned at the gym. I gained all the weight back in less than two months, with a few extra pounds for good measure.

We knew nothing of this ahead of time, but Bill Bright nails it when he says that "fasting reduces the power of self so that the Holy Spirit can do a more intense work within us." I'd never felt so weak and powerless in my entire life. And while I didn't see, feel, or know it at the time, God used that fast to radically change the direction of our lives. We both had sensed that a time of change was coming, but the fast gave us the boldness to act on the opportunities that appeared.

Another good thing came out of that season of starvation—the day we broke our fast. Michelle and I shared communion, and it was one of the most precious meals of my entire life. In that moment we realized that food was a joyous blessing from God, a totally undeserved gift.

Nowadays when we bow our heads before meals, we no longer say grace—we receive it.

"Man still does not realize the spiritual power that [the Holy Spirit has] given to him." DAVID YONGGI CHO

David Cho is the South Korean Billy Graham. Cho was raised a Buddhist but gave his life to Christ at the age of seventeen while dying of tuberculosis. He was miraculously healed. He met his future mother-in-law while attending Bible college, and together, the two started the church in her home with just five people. Over the next fifteen years, it grew to about ten thousand people. Then they built Prayer Mountain. Membership reached two hundred thousand less than a decade later, and seven hundred thousand by the early nineties.

Dr. Cho apparently prays five hours per day and won't stop even if the president calls.

He didn't take *my* phone calls either.

I tried quite hard to meet with him. I worked the referral chain, tried every avenue, and called every phone number. Eventually I got through to his office, but they declined an interview. Many, many times.[7]

Eventually, the office offered me a concession: "If you have any chance to come to our office, we will give you some gift."

Sadly, I had already left Seoul, but I was curious about what was in the package. I wanted "some gift."

"If you have any chance to come to our office, we will give you our last year's conference bag with about twenty items in it."

Twenty items sounded nice.

Dr. Cho couldn't meet with me, but his secretary finally succumbed to my incessant requests and let me ask him two questions via e-mail. She sent back a curt reply:

> Dear Mr. Brock:
>
> Thank you very much for your e-mails.
>
> Dr. Cho has written a memo to give to you as follows:
>
> **1. What does prayer mean to you?**
>
> *Prayer is conversation with God Himself in serving Him.*
>
> **2. What is your prayer for the global church?**
>
> *To fulfill God's purpose.*
>
> The subject of prayer is too huge to describe in writing.
>
> So you should pray honestly and you should experience by yourself.

The Lord knew I was trying.

---

[7] I later learned he was embroiled in yet another Pentecostal financial scandal—a few months after my departure, Cho was convicted of tax evasion and the embezzlement of $12 million in church funds. His three-year jail sentence was suspended, and he was fined almost $5 million. His son—the architect of the scheme—went directly to prison.

CHAPTER 11

England

I LEFT THE KOREAS, but I wasn't finished with my Asian exploration. I had heard a story that I wanted to investigate involving a missionary to China and a conference in northern England.

Michelle and I flew to London and rented a car. I had never driven on the left side of the road before. Not only was the car on the "wrong" side of the road, but the steering wheel was on the "wrong" side of the vehicle—in front of what is usually the passenger seat. The car also had a standard transmission, so I had to learn how to shift gears with my left hand. Mercifully, the pedals were all in their proper places.

I eased my way into traffic and prayed harder than I had ever prayed in my entire life. Minus North Korea.

Keswick is a lovely town with lots of old gray stone, a market square, and more bed-and-breakfasts than you could possibly imagine. Located in the heart of the Lake District by the Skiddaw Mountains, the town draws hikers and tourists all summer long. We didn't pass a single chain hotel. We also didn't see any mountains, because it rained the whole time.

We arrived late and checked into a rather odd bed-and-breakfast—full of bicycles and ladders in the front hallway. The next morning we experienced our very first "full English breakfast," which consisted of tea, orange juice, cookies, oatmeal, granola, berries, bananas, croissants, grapes, pineapples, prunes, yogurt, five kinds of cold cereal, eggs, hash browns, back bacon, sausage, smoked salmon, tomatoes, mushrooms, beans, toast, butter, jam, jelly, and honey.

I don't know how the British do it.

"No other single agency can compare with [the Keswick Convention] in fruitfulness. . . . There is not a mission field which is not indebted to Keswick for one or more of its labourers." DR. EUGENE STOCK

The Keswick Convention was founded in 1875 by Reverend T. D. Harford-Battersby and his Quaker friend Robert Wilson. The first meeting was held in a tent, with several hundred people in attendance. The purpose was to promote personal holiness, encouraging people to go deeper in their relationship with God.

Keswick's theology was influenced by folks like John Wesley, Phoebe Palmer, and Charles Finney, and it in turn influenced major Christian leaders like A. B. Simpson, D. L. Moody, and R. A. Torrey. Stephen Olford and Henrietta Mears, both Keswickians, were instrumental in the spiritual growth of Billy Graham and Bill Bright, the founder of Campus Crusade for Christ. Billy Graham received what Keswickians would call a "second blessing"[1] over a two-day period in England and called Stephen Olford "the man who most influenced my ministry."

---

[1] Keswick promoted a "second blessing" theology where people were "saved then surrendered." Early Keswickians believed that most Christians make God their Savior and then languish in sin, and only when they later surrender and make Him Lord do they really start to become holy. Some modern theologians disagree with the overly simplistic Wesleyan perfection promoted by the convention, but that's a different discussion.

Several famous missionaries were proponents of the Keswick Convention, including Andrew Murray and Hudson Taylor. Taylor was the founder of China Inland Mission (CIM). Taylor was an early believer in "faith missions" and was famous for never asking for money. He believed that it was possible "to move man, through God, by prayer alone."

Taylor spent over five decades in China, where he founded over two hundred mission stations and recruited over eight hundred missionaries. Together they led more than 125,000 Chinese people to Christ—the generational impact is tens of millions of people won to Christ. Shortly after Taylor's death, CIM became the largest Protestant mission agency in the world.

But before much of this happened, Taylor was invited to be a guest speaker at the 1887 Keswick Convention missions tent.

It was a remarkable moment in history.

At the age of twenty, Amy Wilson Carmichael attended the 1887 Keswick Convention and heard Hudson Taylor issue an invitation to join the mission field in China. She was gripped by the call of God and dedicated her life to missions.

She applied to CIM and traveled to London for training. Because of health issues, she ended up serving in Japan before finding her lifelong vocation in India. During her ministry, Carmichael rescued over one thousand children who had been forced to work as Hindu temple prostitutes. The first girl she rescued was only seven years old.

Despite a lifelong struggle with a debilitating nerve condition, Carmichael served in India for fifty-five years without taking a single furlough. Before her death in 1951, Carmichael published thirty-five books. Her church and the mission she founded still exist to this day.[2]

---

[2] Thank God for unanswered prayer. As a child, Carmichael often prayed that her eye color would change from brown to blue. She would rush to the mirror in the morning and then cry when her prayers weren't answered. As an adult, Carmichael snuck into Hindu temples by disguising herself as an Indian woman. She wore a sari and dyed her skin with coffee grounds. While blue eyes would have been a dead giveaway, she discovered that her brown eyes helped her gain acceptance in India.

But Taylor and Carmichael weren't the only interesting people roaming around the 1887 Keswick Convention missions tent that week. Another twenty-year-old was in the crowd.

He was a young Scottish legal clerk, apprenticing for a comfortable career as an attorney-at-law. As he listened to Hudson Taylor, he, too, heard the call to China. Quitting his apprenticeship, the young man applied to CIM, receiving word of his acceptance on his twenty-first birthday.

The young Scotsman sailed to China as part of The Hundred, the first major wave of CIM missionaries to reach the shores of China. During his missionary service, he acquired land, built a church, established the first Bible seminary in the province, and was the longest-serving missionary in the region: fifty years altogether, just one year shy of Hudson Taylor's record. In the black-and-white photo of The Hundred, the young man was photo #1.

His name was John Brock, and he was my great-great-grandfather.

"Do not work so hard for Christ that you have no strength to pray, for prayer requires strength." HUDSON TAYLOR

As tends to happen in northern England, it had started raining by the time we finished breakfast. The locals seemed to shrug it off, walking their dogs and chatting happily. I decided to be stoic and join them.

Though I had done months of research, I still hadn't discovered the exact spot where my great-great-grandfather had heard the call.

Michelle and I walked to the Keswick Convention headquarters, located just a few hundred yards from our bed-and-breakfast. It was closed for an unspecified reason. I banged on the door for five minutes. No one answered.

We drove to the Town Hall Information Center. They didn't have

anything for us and informed us that the municipal archives were also closed. They didn't know why.

We stopped at a coffee shop, and I pulled out my laptop. I reread all my research, searching desperately for any clue that might lead us to the spot. After an hour of searching, I found something I hadn't seen before—Eskin Street. I didn't have an exact address, but a quick search showed it wasn't a huge street.

We got in our car and raced through the rain. The GPS led us past the Keswick Convention headquarters to the street corner nearest our bed-and-breakfast.

I went into the laundromat on the corner.

"Excuse me, sir," I asked over the hum of the dryer. "Have you ever heard of Hudson Taylor or the Keswick Convention?"

He had not. I thanked him and moved on.

I asked every person we passed on the street, even knocking on a few front doors, but no one knew anything. Then I knocked on the door of one particularly pretty bed-and-breakfast.

"Excuse me, ma'am," I said. "I know this might sound strange, but have you ever heard of Hudson Taylor or the Keswick Convention?"

"Oh, sure I have!" she said in a lovely English accent. "They used to pitch a tent on this very street."

"Where?" I said. "Do you know the exact spot?"

"Well, of course." She pointed. "It's right behind you!"

I spun around.

"Thank you!" I said. "Thank you so much!"

She waved good-bye as we crossed the street.

No historic plaque marked the site—the property had been turned into apartments for seniors—but I didn't care. I walked around it in the pouring rain. Not large, the space still would have been big enough for a revival tent. It seemed to me I was standing at Ground Zero. This was where a global move of God that had won millions to Jesus had been born. It felt like holy ground.[3]

I thanked God for giving me a strong spiritual lineage, glad that

---

[3] A few months later, I discovered that I hadn't actually found the spot where John Brock received the call. While the tent was usually erected at the Eskin location, they moved it a few streets over for the 1887 convention to accommodate the larger-than-usual crowds. At least now I have an excuse to revisit northern England, and I plan on taking my entire family next time so we can discover it together.

my great-great-grandfather had listened to the call. And as I thanked Him, I resolved to do the same.

"Prayer is where the action is." JOHN WESLEY

There was another John in England, a far more famous John, whose theology heavily influenced the Keswick Convention.

John Wesley was one of nineteen children born to Samuel and Susanna Wesley.[4] Learning Latin and Greek from his mother, he received a master's degree from Oxford.

As it turns out, John Wesley is one of the most misquoted fellows of the Great Awakening, including gems like these:

> "I set myself on fire and people come to watch me burn."
>
> "In essentials, unity; in nonessentials, liberty; and in all things, charity."
>
> "Do all the good you can, by all the means you can, in all the ways you can, in all the places you can, at all the times you can, to all the people you can, as long as ever you can."[5]

Standing just five feet four inches tall, Wesley was a man God used to fight the slave trade, grow the First Great Awakening, and spark Pentecostalism and the Holiness movement. Starting from an old cannon foundry in 1739, the Methodist enclave grew into a worldwide movement with over eighty million adherents today.

Wesley was especially known for prayer—the famous evangelist spent two hours in prayer each day, mostly in a small closet off his bedroom.

Michelle and I decided to visit his house.

---

[4] Susanna was the youngest of twenty-five children.

[5] Wesley may have said these things, but according to Kevin Watson, assistant professor of historical theology and Wesleyan studies at Seattle Pacific University and Seattle Pacific Seminary, they can't be found anywhere in his numerous diaries, journals, or sermons.

"The hinges on the door to our prayer closets have grown rusty due to underuse." MAX LUCADO

The Wesley property is a compound of yellow brick buildings, fronted by a giant statue of Wesley. The base of the statue is carved with the words "The world is my parish." Wesley's Chapel, built in 1778, was the sanctuary where Wesley preached to thousands each week.

After touring the chapel, we walked to the cemetery in the backyard. Wesley died on March 2, 1791. His last words were "The best of all is, God is with us." Like Francis of Assisi, Wesley was buried alongside his lifelong ministry companions, which I thought was beautiful. Wesley's own grave, in fact, holds the bones of many other people, including at least five ministers. One can only imagine the bickering.

Wesley's house is simple. Made of yellow brick, it is four stories high, and each floor has two rooms. Though not large, it must have been quite busy in Wesley's day, housing John, his mother, a cook, a maid, and a guest preacher. It also served as a gathering place for daily visitors, most of whom were fellow ministry leaders.

When we entered Wesley's study, I noticed two very odd chairs.

The first remarkable chair could be used either in a forward position for sitting or in a backward position for writing. A desk and reading lamp were built into the headrest, and there was an inkwell and quill drawer under the seat. Wesley would sit backward and straddle the backrest, not unlike the cowboy preacher I had encountered in South Korea.

The second chair was a spring-mounted bouncy chair.

"This was Wesley's workout chair," the guide said. "For doing assisted squats."

"Ah, I see," I said. "It would seem that Wesley liked to keep a firm backside."

The guide laughed. "Wesley rode a great distance on horseback,"

he explained. "He used the chair to stay in shape during the winter months."

"What's that contraption?" I pointed to a steampunk gadget in the corner.

"Ah, yes, that's a machine for giving people little electric shocks." The guide smiled. "It seems that Wesley was also something of a mad scientist."

We toured the kitchen, the parlor, and the guest room and then made our way to Wesley's bedroom. Off the back of his room was a small addition in which he spent time each morning listening and talking to God—his prayer closet.

Wesley kept up his regimen by going to bed at nine o'clock and waking at four o'clock, insisting that everyone in his household do the same. He would begin his day by studying the Scriptures and praying. The room that would later become known as the "Power House of Methodism" is about the size of a modern walk-in closet, perhaps six by seven feet, with hardwood floors and a large window to let in plenty of light. The walls are covered with white wainscoting and green patterned wallpaper. It has high ceilings and a small coal-burning fireplace in the corner. The room is bare except for a small hardwood desk with four drawers and a padded kneeling stool. On top of the desk were just two items—a brass candlestick and a giant Bible.

After our guide left the room, I decided to attempt a round of sortes biblicae with Wesley's Bible—just to see where his Bible would fall open. It landed on Psalm 31:19: "Oh how great is thy goodness, which thou hast laid up for them that fear thee; which thou hast wrought for them that trust in thee before the sons of men!"

I knelt on the stool and prayed the Lord's Prayer, asking God to use our generation the way He used Wesley and the early Methodists. I'm convinced the answer will be found in our prayer closets. As E. M. Bounds writes, "Prayer is not learned in a classroom but in the closet." The world is our mission field.

"Missions, after all, is simply this: Every heart with Christ is a missionary, every heart without Christ is a mission field."

COUNT ZINZENDORF

Count Nikolaus Ludwig von Zinzendorf und Pottendorf was a missionary in the truest sense of the word. Karl Barth said that Zinzendorf "was perhaps the only genuine Christocentric of the modern age." Just a few days before John Wesley's nineteenth birthday, Zinzendorf offered asylum to a group of Moravians who were fleeing from the Habsburg empire—the same ones who drove my ancestors from the Channel Islands.[6] The Moravians built a small village on the edge of Zinzendorf's property in eastern Germany. As the village grew, religious infighting reached a fever pitch. The village founder, Christian David, became a Westboro-style fanatic and declared that Zinzendorf was the Beast of the Apocalypse.

Zinzendorf called the Moravians to prayer and made them sign a contract that they would unite together in community. They adopted the motto "In essentials, unity; in nonessentials, liberty; and in all things, love." After weeks of prayer, on August 13, 1727, in what became known as the "Moravian Pentecost," twenty-four people committed to pray for one hour each day. More joined them, and they prayed twenty-four hours per day—for *over one hundred years straight.*

The village was named Herrnhut, which means "The Lord's Watch."

From a community of less than six hundred, Herrnhut sent out over two hundred missionaries to more than a dozen nations within their first sixty-five years. People literally sold themselves into slavery in order to reach African groups in the Caribbean. When news would return that one had died, two more would step forward to take that person's place.

---

6 The 640-year-old dynasty continues to this day but without its former power. The recently deceased heir went by the lengthy name of Franz Joseph Otto Robert Maria Anton Karl Max Heinrich Sixtus Xavier Felix Renatus Ludwig Gaetan Pius Ignatius von Habsburg. In a nod to Richard the Lionheart, Robert the Bruce, and John of the Cross, his body was buried in Austria, while his heart was buried in Hungary. I'd like our land back, please.

It was through the Moravians that John Wesley came to faith in Christ. He made a trip to Herrnhut and stayed for three months.

Remarkable as Herrnhut's story is, there is a little-known order of nuns in La Crosse, Wisconsin, who have been praying continuously for over 135 years. It's conceivable that these ladies might one day become the next Taizé, or perhaps they will develop into a female version of Mount Athos. With better cheese, I hope.[7]

As I neared the end of my year of living prayerfully, I wanted to learn more about prayer revivals. One name kept popping up—Pete Greig. I discovered that he lived in London, so Michelle and I met up for breakfast with the man who has popularized the modern 24/7 prayer movement.

"We weren't trying to start a movement. I just got hungry for God."
PETE GREIG

The British serve a mean full English breakfast, but we didn't want to fall asleep during our meeting with Pete Greig, so Michelle and I ordered omelets.

Pete Greig gets around. He holds down three jobs: first as the Director of Prayer for Holy Trinity Brompton (of Alpha Course fame), second as a church planter, and third as the founder of 24/7 Prayer. He rubs shoulders with the likes of Brad Lomenick, Tim Hughes, and Desmond Tutu, and he's also the author of over half a dozen books on prayer and revival.

In 1999, Pete visited Herrnhut and decided to start a 24/7 prayer meeting back home in England. The first meeting was held on September 5. Pete claims that was the day when "God sneezed," and something went viral. It was the same day that Mike Bickle started the International House of Prayer in Kansas City.

---

[7] The reigning leader for the oldest site of continuous worship goes to a monastery in St. Maurice, Switzerland. Inspired by a Greek Orthodox idea and built in AD 515, the *Akoimetoi* ("Sleepless Ones") practiced perpetual praise for nearly four hundred years.

A number of global prayer initiatives were launched in the following weeks.

Under Pete's leadership, 24/7 Prayer has started "boiler rooms" in over one hundred countries. The nonstop prayer meetings are hosted in a wide range of places, from war zones to slums to cathedrals to jungles. They even have one in a brewery in Missouri.

Pete arrived a few minutes late, and he looked so wonderfully British—decked out in a brown blazer, navy vest, and plaid collared shirt. His hair looked frazzled, as though he had intentionally stuck his finger in an electrical outlet.

Our food arrived, and Pete said grace. He was silent for a moment, but it wasn't one of those oh-shoot-we-weren't-clear-about-who-was-going-to-say-grace kind of moments.

"Jesus, we invite You to be the fourth at this table," he prayed.

I thought about Brother Lawrence and smiled. Michelle asked about Pete's work, and he asked about our journey and the book I was writing about the experience. He liked the idea.

"Most prayer books are written by introverts," he noted.

It's true—almost every prayer book I've read has been written by an introvert. As Philip Yancey says, "Most of the great books on prayer are written by 'experts'—monks, missionaries, mystics, saints. I've read scores of them, and mainly they make me feel guilty." Most prayer books I've read have focused on silence and contemplation and quiet time, and that's fine, but they miss a whole part of the demographic that can't sit still.

"I prefer kinetic prayer," Pete said. "I like to *move* when I pray."

I thought about Gustav and his mission to move the Swedish church.

"So what does that look like for you?" I asked.

"I'll read a verse and then go for a twenty-minute jog in the morning or afternoon," he said. "I'll try to focus on that verse the whole time. Then in the evening when I'm walking my dog, I try to practice examen. And I climb a mountain every year."

No big deal.

"Another active way I pray is by using a whiteboard," he said. "I write down every possible request that I can think of, and then I erase each item as I pray through it."

Michelle loved that idea.

"Do you have any other interesting prayer methods?" I asked.

"Yeah, I like to pray through the Lord's Prayer," he said. "I take the time to really pray through each section. 'Our Father'—just spend a few minutes focusing on God as our Father. 'Your will be done'—surrendering control and trusting His sovereignty. 'Give us our daily bread'—presenting our needs to God. 'Forgive us our trespasses'—confessing our sins. Notice that Jesus' prayer doesn't start with confession. It's about relationship first."

"So how do you define prayer?" I asked.

"Prayer is a living conversation, but it's more than just talking," Pete answered. "It's a conscious responsiveness to God's presence."

Pete Greig is a smart dude.

"The Bible says to pray at all times with all kinds of prayers," he continued. "But a lot of people think that prayer is just one thing. That's like going to a buffet and only ever eating one item. You'll get sick. You need a huge variety in order to stay healthy. Prayer is a menu, not a dish."

Pete Greig is a *genius.*

"I've been thinking about something lately," he said. "So much of the Christian prayer life consists of asking God for things. So what are we going to pray about when there's no more pain and sin and suffering?"

That messed me up. I think most Christians, myself in particular, see God mostly as a needs-and-wants fulfillment service. In the Garden of Eden, Adam and Eve literally had no needs. When we get to heaven, we'll have everything we need. We were created to walk and talk with God, not just ask Him to fix everything that's wrong with the world. Prayer wasn't created as a way to tell God our problems—He already knows them anyway. Humans were created simply to *be* with their Father.

"I think that every time of prayer should probably start with a time of silence," Pete said. "I have a friend whose son comes home from school and flops down on the couch in his dad's study. He never wants to talk, he just wants to sit there—to be in his dad's presence. After ten minutes they start talking, but my friend loves that his son just wants to be with him. Sure, the son eventually asks for keys to the car, and food, and money for the mall, but that's not the primary reason why he spends time with his dad."

That was it, right there. That was my prayer metaphor. Prior to this year of living prayerfully, prayer was simply asking for keys to the car and money for the mall. Now, I'm just trying to hang out with Dad.

"I think a lot of Christians pray out of guilt,"[8] Pete continued. "I remember Brennan Manning once asked me, 'When do you feel like you've prayed enough?' I told him that I never felt like I had prayed enough. He said, 'Then you must feel guilty all the time.' And he was right."

"So how did that change your prayer life?" I asked.

"I used to spend an hour just trying to get through my prayer list," Pete said. "But now I take that first hour to just connect with God in silence. Then, for the other twenty-three hours out in the world, I pray for things as they come up. But that first hour is about reconnecting with our Father."

Silence kept coming up again and again. I recalled a quote from Mother Teresa: "The more we receive in our silent prayer, the more we can give in our active life." To paraphrase a song best covered by Keith Whitley, perhaps "you pray it best when you pray nothing at all."

---

[8] Prayer shouldn't be a guilt-induced practice. I have a friend who recalls attending a retreat as a teenager, and he's never forgotten the (hilariously fundamentalist) words of his group leader: "If you are not praying, you are wasting the blood of Christ." Whew. Thank God for the grace He extends to ragamuffins like you and me.

"He is not saved yet, but he will be. How can it be otherwise... I am praying." GEORGE MÜLLER

George Müller was a prayer machine. His entire life was "work and pray, work and pray." He started 117 schools during his lifetime, which educated over 120,000 kids. He also started five orphanages in Bristol, England, where he took care of exactly 10,024 orphans. While Michelle and I weren't able to visit any places connected with Müller, his prayer life has definitely impacted my own.

Müller kept a prayer journal, and he made over fifty thousand requests in all—five thousand of which were answered on the same day he prayed them. In one instance, the orphans stood around tables set with plates, but there was no food to be found. Müller thanked God for breakfast and was interrupted by a knock at the door—a baker couldn't sleep because he was worried the boys would need some bread for breakfast. Stories like this happened time and time again.

Müller never asked for money, but God always seemed to provide just the right amount at just the right time—many millions of dollars, by today's standards. Müller prayed for hours each day, always with his Bible open, and God answered his prayers time and time again.

Müller was a generous guy too. He gave away almost 300,000 Bibles, 1.5 million New Testaments, and over 110 million gospel pamphlets. He supported other missionaries, including the then up-and-coming Hudson Taylor. More than one hundred years after his death, the organization he founded is still giving away millions of dollars each year.

In addition to being one of the founding members of the Brethren movement, Müller also became a missionary—at the age of *seventy*. He traveled to over thirty nations and reached an estimated three million people, covering more than two hundred thousand miles (without a plane) over a period of seventeen years.

On top of all this, Müller also had an amazing beard.

There's a verse in Scripture—Psalm 2:8—that continues to mess me up: "Ask me, and I will make the nations your inheritance, the ends of the earth your possession."

Müller wasn't a wealthy man, but he had a massive inheritance. Consider the following story: Müller had five friends who were far from God. He decided to pray for them every single day until they came to faith in Jesus. After a number of months, the first one came to Christ. Ten years later, two more came to faith. After twenty-five years, the fourth man had become a Christian. As for the fifth man, well, he was a real holdout. So Müller continued to pray for the man, every single day. For sixty-three years and eight months.[9]

I read this story and felt so inspired. I thought about Psalm 2:8. *Ask Me.* I'm at the point in my life where I've come to this conclusion: I don't need lots of money. Or power. Or fame. I want the lost as my inheritance. I want my friends and family who are far from God to be filled with new life in Christ. I want my non-Christ-following friends to get caught up in a story and a vision and a mission that's greater than themselves. I want their days to be filled with purpose and meaning. I want people I know who are living for themselves to come into a relationship with a God who can turn them into everything they were created to be, who can craft them into selfless servants who pray passionately, live prophetically, and love others unconditionally. That's what I really want.

So I made a deal with God.[10] I said, "God, I'm going to make You a deal. I'm going to pray for my friends who are far from You every single day—up to, *but not exceeding*, sixty-three years and eight months. If they're not saved by then, it's on You!"

I sat down and wrote out a list of people I know who are far from God. On my first go-round, I had exactly ninety-nine names. That

---

9 Müller eventually died, and before his coffin was placed in the soil, his fifth friend accepted Jesus into his life.
10 Don't make deals with God.

list has since expanded. These days, I'm praying daily for over 220 people who don't have a relationship with the Father who loves them deeply. It's not a crazy-long prayer—I just speak their names out. I've committed to not going to sleep until I've prayed for everyone on the list. And, by God's grace, I'm going to continue to pray for them every single day for sixty-three years and eight months.

For some of you who are reading this and are over forty years old, this could be a good deal for you—you could live to be over one hundred years old this way. Not bad at all. But seriously, here's your highly encouraged homework assignment: Who are your first five? Who do you love who's far from God? Who do you want to see in the family of God and the Kingdom of Heaven? Commit to pray daily until they're in a deeply committed relationship with Jesus.

It won't be easy, but it *will* be worth it. Are you up for the challenge? History will be altered if you take it.

I really mean it. History will be altered by your salvation prayers. When I was in high school, my sister started hanging out with a girl named Karyn. A few of us started praying for Karyn's salvation. Pretty soon, she came to Christ. We started praying for Karyn's brother, Kevin. Pretty soon, Kevin came to Christ. We started praying for Kevin's friend Richard. Pretty soon, Richard came to Christ. Today, Karyn is a photographer and ardent missions supporter. Kevin planted a church. Richard is a pastor-in-training. All three are married. Their kids will be raised in the way of Christ. Think about it: the prayers of a few teenagers have reset the course of entire families for generations to come. This is the power of prayer.

"He who has learned to pray, has learned the greatest Secret of a holy and happy Life." WILLIAM LAW

For our last stop in England, Michelle and I took the Underground to Elephant and Castle, the same metro stop as the Benny Hinn conference. We passed a large sign that read, "Metropolitan Tabernacle Baptist Church (Spurgeon's)."

Charles Haddon Spurgeon was born in 1834 and got saved at the age of fifteen. He started preaching at age sixteen and quickly earned the nickname "The Boy Preacher." Spurgeon became a pastor at age seventeen; his first meetinghouse was a barn. He preached over six hundred times before his twentieth birthday. He took the pulpit of New Park Street Chapel at the age of twenty and soon packed it out.

Spurgeon was a pretty lively fellow, and attendance grew to more than ten thousand people. The church rented buildings for a few years before the Metropolitan Tabernacle was built to accommodate the crowds. The congregation included members of the royal family, the prime minister of England, and Florence Nightingale, among others.

In all, Spurgeon published over two thousand sermons. His sermons were so popular that they literally sold by the ton—at one point selling more than twenty-five thousand copies per *week*. Known today as the "Prince of Preachers," Spurgeon preached to almost ten million people over the course of his life. In his early twenties, he founded Spurgeon's College, which during his lifetime trained almost nine hundred pastors. He also founded the Stockwell Orphanage for boys, offering shelter, education, and a loving environment for impoverished, fatherless boys in London. This legacy continues in the form of Spurgeons, the charity he started in 1867.

Finding an open side entrance to the church, Michelle and I went inside to the bookstore. Though I wasn't able to arrange an interview with Spurgeon (since he died years before I was born), I decided to interview him anyway, using quotes from one of his many books on prayer that lined the shelves.

Jay Brock (JB): Okay, Mr. Spurgeon, let's start with an easy question. I was at a Benny Hinn convention right down the road from your church. What do you think of all that?

Charles Spurgeon (CS): We must never let our profit interfere in any way with the glory of God.

JB: I agree. Next question—do you think that prayer really works?

CS: Prayer moves the arm that moves the world. . . . You can be omnipotent if you know how to pray, omnipotent in all things that glorify God. . . . Prayer is the slender nerve that moveth the muscles of Omnipotence.

JB: But why pray? Won't God do what He wants to do anyway? Does He really need us to ask? Hasn't He already predestined everything?

CS: Why pray? Might it not as logically be asked, Why breathe, eat, move, or do anything? . . . Our prayers are in the predestination.

JB: Oh, wow—so Christians need to pray because God's plan depends on it? I've never thought about that before. So how can we learn to pray?

CS: Prayer . . . is an art that only the Holy Spirit can teach us. He is the giver of all prayer.

JB: That doesn't exactly help me.

CS: There is a secret work of the Spirit of God going on within you that is teaching you to pray.

JB: Well, I appreciate the encouragement, especially from someone like you, Mr. Spurgeon.

CS: When the Creator gives His creature the power of thirst, it is because water exists to meet its thirst. When He creates hunger, there is food to correspond to the appetite. . . . When He inclines men to pray, it is because prayer has a corresponding blessing connected with it.

JB: That's pretty awesome, actually. So how do you define prayer, Mr. Spurgeon?

CS: True prayer is the trading of the heart with God.

JB: So when are Christians most effective in prayer?

CS: After the soul has unburdened itself of all weights of merit and self-sufficiency. . . . We are powerless in this business. . . . "He that hath made his refuge God," might serve as the title of a true believer.

JB: Any prayer tips for beginners?

CS: As a rule, keep to present need. . . . The plainest, humblest language that expresses our meaning is the best.

JB: Any other advice?

CS: Ask for great things, for you are before a great throne.

JB: So what are you praying about these days?

CS: I have now concentrated all my prayers into one, . . . that I may die to self, and live wholly to him.

JB: Wow, that's hard core. How important is prayer to the church?

CS: We shall never see much change for the better in our churches till the prayer meeting occupies a higher place in the esteem of Christians.

JB: I've heard that your Monday night prayer meetings used to be quite an event. How many people came each week?

CS: Scarcely ever numbers less than from a thousand to twelve hundred attendants.

JB: Wow, that's crazy! I'm going to go check out your prayer room.

CS: That's cool.[11]

---

11 Charles Spurgeon may have said "that's cool," but it does not appear in any of his extensive writings.

"Let the fires go out in the boiler room of the church and the place will still look smart and clean, but it will be cold." LEONARD RAVENHILL

I finished my interview with Spurgeon and left the bookstore. I found a church employee and asked if I could have a tour of the building.

"Can I take a peek into the sanctuary?" I asked.

"It's closed," he said.

"Oh," I said. "Is there any way that you could open it for me?"

"I can't," he replied.

"I really won't be more than a minute," I said.

"Come back on Sunday," he said.

"Aw, shoot, I actually won't be here on Sunday," I said. "We're leaving tomorrow."

"Sorry." He shrugged.

"Can you make an exception?" I begged. "I've come all the way from Canada."

"There's nothing I can do," he said.

As soon as the man walked away, I snuck into the sanctuary. It wasn't the same as when Spurgeon was there. A fire burned down the original Tabernacle, which I expect was far bigger than the present model.

But I wasn't at the Metropolitan Tabernacle to see the sanctuary—I was there to see the boiler room. It was in the basement that Spurgeon's true spiritual power lay hidden.

Here's how the story goes:

> Five young college students were spending a Sunday in London, so they went to hear the famed C. H. Spurgeon preach. While waiting for the doors to open, the students were greeted by a man who asked, "Gentlemen, let me show you around. Would you like to see the heating plant of this church?" They were not particularly interested, for it was a hot day in July. But they didn't want to offend the stranger, so they consented. The young men

were taken down a stairway, a door was quietly opened, and
their guide whispered, "This is our heating plant." Surprised,
the students saw 700 people bowed in prayer, seeking a
blessing on the service that was soon to begin in the auditorium
above. Softly closing the door, the gentleman then introduced
himself. It was none other than Charles Spurgeon.

Knowing that the church staff would not be inclined to assist me in
any way whatsoever, I didn't bother to ask if I could see the basement.

Gratefully, I found a staircase quickly. Michelle stood guard while
I zipped down the steps. There wasn't much to see, of course—just
a long hallway and a few empty classrooms. It didn't matter—it was
on that very ground that hundreds of people had prayed for salvation
and watched a mighty revival sweep over England. God used Charles
Spurgeon because of the spiritual power that emanated from a basement, and I was in that basement. I thanked God for the faithful
prayer warriors that stood behind every great move of God.

Spurgeon was the first of many revivalists I discovered via Pete
Greig. I flew back to North America and spent the last leg of my
travels discovering the revivals that had happened close to home.

Much closer to home than I'd expected.

CHAPTER 12

Hamilton, Ontario

AS MY YEAR OF LIVING prayerfully wound down to a close, I hit the books to learn as much as possible about prayer revivals. I ordered over sixty classics and read around the clock.

I explored the world of George Whitefield, the twenty-six-year-old man called "the most brilliant and popular preacher the modern world has ever known." But Whitefield was the opposite of a hotshot. Deeply committed to the gospel, he put the cause of Christ ahead of his own agenda.

His fearless preaching swept across Britain and transformed the American colonies—they called it the Great Awakening. Benjamin Franklin noted in his autobiography that Whitefield had a powerful voice and estimated that he was capable of reaching over thirty thousand people without the aid of amplification. By the time

Whitefield died at age fifty-five, he had preached over thirty thousand sermons.

I visited the Boston area, where Whitefield and Jonathan Edwards led the First Great Awakening in America. I stood on the very stone where Edwards preached to the masses in Northampton.[1] It was an incredible experience to picture an enormous crowd, gathered in the square, and I imagined Edwards preaching to the masses, each one clad in colonial attire. There were horns in the streets and the avenue was bustling, but I imagined the onlookers focused on the Word of God.

The First Great Awakening was a great time for higher education—Pete Greig informed me that the Presbyterians founded Princeton in 1746, the Baptists built Brown University in 1764, the Dutch Reformed started Rutgers in 1766, and the Congregationalist Eleazar Wheelock started Dartmouth in 1769. All told, revivalists founded over six hundred colleges and universities.

I learned about the Second Great Awakening, which ran from 1790 to 1840, and visited upstate New York, where a young lawyer named Charles Finney barnstormed the countryside as a traveling preacher before becoming an antislavery activist and the president of Oberlin College.

I learned about Daniel Nash, Finney's secret partner in prevailing prayer. Nash would arrive in town a few weeks before Finney and douse the area with prayer—he'd get on his knees and pray for weeks on end. Then Finney would arrive and set the place on fire. In one town they visited, someone hanged and burned effigies of Finney *and* Nash—they hated Finney's message, and they hated Nash's prayers. Nash died in 1831, and within four months Finney left his itinerant preaching ministry. Nash's tombstone reads, "Laborer with Finney, mighty in prayer."

The Second Great Awakening reached all sorts of interesting

---

[1] Edwards later published a book on prayer, whose breathy title is *An Humble Attempt to Promote Explicit Agreement and Visible Union of God's People, in Extraordinary Prayer, for the Revival of Religion and the Advancement of Christ's Kingdom on Earth.*

places. Samuel Mills started a prayer meeting on a haystack. William Tennent started a Bible college in a log cabin. An elderly pastor named J. J. Cheek "took in 1,000 new members in two months, and died of overwork."

I learned about James McGready, a frontier evangelist who was so ugly that people came to listen to him preach. *A man with a face like that must have something to say,* they thought. He convinced church members in Kentucky to pray for him at sunset on Saturday evening and sunrise Sunday morning, and during the summer of 1800 they saw over eleven thousand people come to Christ during a communion service.

I read about the formidable Evan Roberts, the twenty-six-year-old Welsh coal miner who led the 1904 Revival in Wales. After witnessing a revival in a neighboring town, Roberts returned to his home village in hopes of preaching the gospel. The minister wouldn't let him preach on Sunday or at the Monday prayer meeting, so Roberts just preached afterward. His famous prayer consisted of just three words: "Lord, bend us."

He preached night after night, with people staying past four o'clock in the morning. Over thirty thousand people were converted in the first few months, and more than one hundred thousand came to Christ in less than a year. Five years later, 80 percent of the converts were still walking with God. The social change was drastic: judges had no cases to prosecute. Police went unemployed, so they started church quartets. Illegitimate births dropped 44 percent within a year. Mining operations slowed down because coal miners stopped cursing and the horses couldn't understand their new language.

While most of these revival leaders were bold, charismatic, larger-than-life personalities, the two key figures in the Third Great Awakening were nothing of the sort. One was a quiet man in his late forties, and the other was a woman.

Their names were Jeremiah Lanphier and Phoebe Palmer.

"To clasp the hands in prayer is the beginning of an uprising against the disorder of the world." KARL BARTH

Jeremiah Calvin Lanphier was forty-nine years old when he took a position as a layman city missionary with the Old Dutch North Church on Fulton Street in New York City in July 1857. Each day he took to the streets, witnessing door-to-door at houses and shops. By noon he would return to the church exhausted and fall on his knees in prayer. Finding that the time in prayer refreshed him spiritually, he decided to host a weekly noonday prayer meeting.

Lanphier printed twenty thousand invitations and handed them out door-to-door. His first prayer meeting was on September 23, 1857. He opened the doors and took his seat at exactly noon.

Five minutes went by, but no one appeared. Lanphier paced the room, fighting fear with faith. Ten minutes passed. Fifteen. Twenty. Thirty minutes passed before the first man arrived. In total, six men prayed that first Wednesday. The next week there were fourteen to twenty people (depending on the source), and by the following Wednesday, there were twenty-three to forty intercessors.

Then the stock market crashed.

It ruined hundreds of thousands of people from New York to Philadelphia. Thousands of merchants closed their doors, and banks and railroads went bankrupt. Stockbrokers and clerks were out of work, and suicides and murders increased. By the end of October, over thirty thousand were unemployed.

People piled into Lanphier's church. He moved from a weekly prayer meeting to a daily prayer meeting, and they started an overflow service at a neighboring church. Lunchtime prayer meetings popped up all over the city. By early 1858, newspaper editor Horace Greeley sent a reporter to do a proper count. Over the lunch hour he rode a horse and buggy between the meetings as fast as he could. He counted 6,100 people across twelve prayer meetings.

By springtime, over ten thousand businessmen were gathering daily for prayer in New York. Every church and public building was filled over the lunch hour in Manhattan. Business owners confessed their sins and repaid those they had cheated. Criminals turned to the Lord. Crime drastically decreased. Wealthy people helped the poor. A ship reportedly entered New York Harbor, and a dockhand led the captain and thirty men to Christ before the ship was docked on shore.

Michelle and I visited New York and found the site of the Fulton Street Revival. It was a few hundred yards from the World Trade Center complex. Nothing remained of the church—today the corner is occupied by three run-down high-rises and a Chipotle franchise.

The Fulton Street Revival swept the nation. Two thousand gathered for prayer in Chicago, four thousand in Philadelphia, one thousand in Louisville, two thousand in Cleveland, and six thousand in Pittsburgh. Two thousand in Charleston met every night for eight straight weeks. Three thousand came to Christ in Newark, New Jersey. Washington held five services per day to accommodate the crowds. Businesses closed for lunch and posted signs that read, "Will reopen at the close of the prayer meeting." In Portland, 240 stores closed for prayer from 11:00 to 2:00 each day. By May, fifty thousand New Yorkers had come to faith.

The revival spread up the Hudson River. Baptists in Schenectady, New York, had "so many people to baptize that they went down to the river, cut a big hole in the ice, and baptized them in the cold water." And you *know* it's a real salvation when Baptists use cold water.

While many believe the Fulton Street Revival was the start of the Third Great Awakening, some historians believe the Awakening actually started a few months earlier, in a city just north of the American border.

Of all the possible places in Canada, the revival had started in the same city where I had started my prayer pilgrimage one year ago.

Hamilton.

"A single prayer [can] change the course of history."
MARK BATTERSON

Hamilton is the ninth largest city in Canada. Boasting a population of over five hundred thousand, it's an amalgamation of six former municipalities. Situated on the shores of Lake Ontario in the heart of the Golden Horseshoe, it's an hour south of the nation's largest city, Toronto, and just an hour from the US border.

Hamilton has traditionally been a smoggy blue-collar steel town, but it has recently rebranded itself as the waterfall capital of Canada. Based on the Niagara escarpment, it has one of the best views in the nation and hosts one of the largest art crawls on the continent.

Right around the time Lanphier started his prayer meeting, in September 1857, a woman and her doctor-turned-evangelist husband were delayed in Hamilton on their way home to Albany. They had been preaching to massive Canadian camp crowds all summer, and while stopped in Hamilton to catch a connecting train, their luggage was lost in the transfer.

Two local Methodist ministers convinced the couple to lead a prayer meeting, since they were stuck in town until their luggage could be located. On Thursday, October 8, 1857, Walter and Phoebe Palmer led a prayer meeting in Hamilton, which boasted a population of twenty-three thousand at the time. Only sixty-five people attended the service. Thirty agreed to fervently pray for a revival and to invite their friends to church the next night. Despite the poor turnout, Phoebe Palmer declared that something big was about to happen.

The next night, in the basement of John Street Methodist Church, twenty-one people came to faith in Christ. Twenty people got saved on Saturday, and another thirty-four were converted on Sunday. Services were held from seven o'clock in the morning until ten o'clock at night, with Mrs. Palmer leading most of them. Within ten days almost four hundred people were won to Christ, including John Moore, the city's mayor.

News of Hamilton's revival reached New York on November 5, 1857, and it fanned the flames of the Fulton Street Revival. While the American revival swept west across the frontier, Canada's revival swept east across Ontario, Quebec, Prince Edward Island, Nova Scotia, and Newfoundland. To be sure, Hamilton wasn't the "cause" of the New York revival, but it was indicative of a greater move of God that just happened to start north of the border.

It was the beginning of the Third Great Awakening.

The 1857 panic in Lanphier's New York led to a three-year depression and ultimately the start of the Civil War. Despite the immense upheaval, the Third Great Awakening that started in Hamilton would echo through the ages. The decades that followed were an amazing period where God worked throughout America and around the world.

Over one million people came to faith in Christ by the end of 1859. Andrew Murray championed the South African Revival in 1860. Charles Spurgeon's Metropolitan Tabernacle was constructed in 1861. Abraham Lincoln issued the final Emancipation Proclamation in 1863. In 1865, Hudson Taylor began the China Inland Mission, and William and Catherine Booth started the Salvation Army. George Müller built the last of his orphanages in 1870. D. L. Moody shot to prominence a few years after the Great Chicago Fire of 1871.[2] The Keswick Convention began in 1875. C. T. Studd and the Cambridge Seven sailed to China in 1885. Amy Carmichael, John Brock, and The Hundred received the call of God in 1887.

---

[2] Though never ordained, Moody pastored churches, founded a Bible college, and later helped J. Wilbur Chapman receive assurance of his salvation. Chapman's future assistant, Billy Sunday, became a preacher and started a meeting. That meeting later invited Mordecai Ham to preach, and Billy Graham got saved during the meeting. My grandfather Clarence Black, to whom this book is dedicated, came to faith after attending a Billy Graham crusade in Toronto.

"Go home. Lock yourself in your room. Kneel down in the middle of the floor, and with a piece of chalk draw a circle around yourself. There, on your knees, pray fervently and brokenly that God would start a revival within that chalk circle." RODNEY SMITH

I returned to Hamilton to visit the spot where it all began.

I found the northwest corner of John and Rebecca Streets, where the Palmer prayer meetings took place. It's now a parking lot beside a corporate building. The spot, just a few feet from Hamilton's art crawl, is one I've driven by many times. No marble memorial or bronze plaque marks the spot where the Third Great Awakening began.

Somehow that is fitting. Only God gets the glory when revival comes to town. Count von Zinzendorf exhorted Christians to "preach the gospel, die, and be forgotten." Like St. Benedict, our calling is simply to pray and work, pray and work, pray and work. And somewhere, somehow, at some unknown intersection between prayer and work, God indwells our humble offering—God indwells *us*—and turns human actions into spiritual awakenings.

As I stood on that nameless place where the Third Great Awakening began, I reflected on the incredible journey the past year had been. I had prayed more in one year than in my entire life up to that point, yet I felt like I had barely scratched the surface.

Revivals have started all over the world, but now I've come full circle to the place where I began. Prayer is all about returning to where it began for each Christian—faith in our Father. Prayer is about constantly returning to our first love. There comes a point where you need to lose your religion in order to restore your relationship. Prayer isn't about repeating rituals; it's about spending time with Dad.

One year ago, prayer was a way of asking things from God. Today it has a prized new definition for me: prayer is simply a constant communion with Christ.

After an intense year of learning about prayer from some of the best sources on earth, I don't feel like I'm further along. If anything, I feel like a first-year university student—I now know all the things I don't know—all the things I haven't yet learned, understood, or experienced. I am not, in any way, a prayer expert. I'm a failing student who's playing catch-up, at best. Rather than coming to the end of a journey, I've only just begun. And I'm okay with that.

Like parenting or marriage or a lifelong friendship, communion with God is a thing to be enjoyed over decades of intimate relationship, not mastered over a quick year of fact gathering and story chasing. Still, one year taught me a lot about prayer. Exploring Catholicism taught me some beautiful prayer traditions, especially Brother Lawrence's "practice of the presence of God." Pentecostalism challenged me to pray bolder prayers. My experiences in North Korea and not meeting Billy Graham grew my trust in God. From my time on Athos, I came to treat prayer with far greater reverence. The revivalists stoked a passion in me for reaching the lost. If I hadn't visited Taizé or the Quaker communities, I would never have realized the profound need for silence. Judaism brought me closer to Jesus, and my trip to Jerusalem reignited the Lord's Prayer in my life.

One year on the road taught me that if I want to learn to pray, I have to ask God to teach me. If I want to learn to pray, I have to get down on my knees and actually *pray*. And rather than simply seeking God's gifts, I need to seek God's heart. I have to know Him and hear Him and practice His presence. I have to constantly commune with Christ.

I feel like I've changed a lot this year, yet not at all. I suppose that strength is gathered on the journey, not granted at the outset. Francis de Sales was right when he said that "true progress quietly and persistently moves along without notice."

That said, my prayer life looks much different than it did at the start of my year of living prayerfully. I pray a lot more, which is a good thing. I also feel less guilty when I forget to pray. I just keep coming back to my first love. I try to stay focused on the relationship with God. I talk a lot less when I pray. I still haven't spoken in tongues, but sometimes I get nature to pray when I don't have the words—I let a rushing river say my prayer. I let the mountain wind be my whisper. I let the chirping birds be my song. A day in nature is never wasted.

I've come to realize that prayer is the main dish, and everything else is gravy. I am convinced that prayer can change everything. We must never take prayer lightly—every prayer has the potential to change the course of history. Every choice changes the future. Every prayer echoes for eternity.

And so I'm developing the disciplines of listening and practicing God's presence and looking for signs of God every day. Like Watchman Nee, I'm trying to see that "every need is a call to prayer." I still have fears about being a parent, and Michelle still has insecurities, but we're learning to trust God. As we pray, we are realizing it's far more about Him and far less about us.

Like my grandfather, I pray for my grandkids every single day—and I don't even have kids yet. Thanks to Grandpa, I've gotten over most of my fear of being a dad. Michelle and I still haven't taken the plunge, but that's mostly because I'd like to wait until I can afford a live-in nanny. And maybe a cook, tutor, house cleaner, driver, pilot, and bodyguard for each child. Kidding. Sort of.

I've learned a world of prayer traditions, and a few of them have stuck. I pray the Jesus Prayer, using my metanie, on a regular basis. Since discovering my newfound love for the global family of God, I pray, "God, bless Your church and make it look more like You" whenever I drive past a church building. Every time I drive past a brothel or strip club, I pray that God would shut it down. These are just a few modern-day mitzvahs—invitations to connect with God—I'm trying to work into my daily life. I'm allowing God to guard my heart and mind and give me peace by turning every anxiety into a supplication. I'm trying to see every need as a call to prayer, every face as a chance for intercession, every piece of bad news as a call to pray and work.

The Lord's Prayer has definitely become my go-to prayer. I still pray it with trepidation, but I love it nonetheless. I pray a salvation prayer for a few hundred people every night before bedtime. I hold people in the light as they come up—mostly people in need. There aren't any enemies left, which is good.[3] I pray for the folks at Westboro every single day—I'm giddy for what God is going to do in their lives. I'm praying that Christians all over the place will start to pray for them as well.

I gave up on sortes biblicae, but I'm still working on Ignatian meditation and examen. Like Brother Lawrence, I'm trying to practice the presence of God. Like Brother Roger, I'm trying to maintain inner silence in all things so as to dwell with Christ. I sing prayers, read prayers, breathe prayers.

Like Benedict, I'm committed to *ora et labora*—prayer and work. My life has become an incredible adventure—a challenge, for sure—but my days are filled with purpose. I'm trying to forget about me and focus on making my life count for something more.

At the end of the day, though, I'm just trying to be faithful. All the Old Testament greats were justified by faith. As my friend Christy Joy says, "God's track record is faithfulness." I'm just trying to reciprocate what's long overdue. In a world filled with beauty and brokenness, I'm trying to be thankful for all the little things. I've learned a profound secret in prayer: the greatest response to life is gratefulness.

I like to think that the beginning of eternity will be a sit-down conversation with God, in which He will answer all my questions. But if I'm honest, I think I already know what would happen. I'll sit in beaming silence, just happy to be in the presence of my Father. Knowing all the answers won't give me peace—it's His presence, and His presence alone, that makes everything okay.

To constantly commune with Christ while obeying my calling is the best I can do until that day. This is my humble offering, and it's

---

[3] Except maybe my book editor, Jonathan. He's a pretty mean guy—maybe a frenemy.

all I can give. I'm starting to give up my self-reliance, and I'm beginning to lean hard on Christ in prayer. In a world of turmoil and chaos and upheaval, I'm clinging to the feet of Jesus like never before. I'm resting in His shalom.

I'm hanging out with Dad.

An Invitation

AS I WROTE THIS BOOK, an old Spurgeon quote was rattling around in my brain: "You may make a prayer book, but you cannot put a grain of prayer into a book, for it is too spiritual a matter to be put on pages." It's up to you, the reader, to actually talk to God.

I don't know what motivated you to read *A Year of Living Prayerfully*. Maybe you wanted to know why anyone would walk across a bed of hot coals. Maybe you couldn't believe that people could be raised from the dead. Maybe you were curious about the pope's house, or Mount Athos, or North Korea, or Westboro. Maybe you just needed a good laugh.

Can I offer another possibility?

Maybe God wanted you to read this book. I know it sounds weird and creepy, but maybe some things actually do happen for a reason. Maybe God wants to teach you to pray. Maybe He wants you to share a constant communion with Christ. Maybe He wants to have a relationship with you.

About a decade ago, I discovered that God wanted to have a relationship with me, and His definition of relationship transcends every earthly relationship—combined. The Bible calls Him my Spouse, my Father, my Counselor, my Savior, my Lord, my King, my Master, my Friend who sticks closer than a brother. He's the

Gardener, and I'm His plant. He's the Shepherd, and I'm a whiny lamb. He's the Vine, and I'm a branch. I am His, and He is mine.

As I read through history, Jesus alone stands apart from all mankind. If God is love, and the opposite of love is selfishness, then it makes sense that God's Son is the only *selfless* man to ever live. Selflessness is what makes our world a better place. Selflessness creates shalom. Jesus modeled selflessness, and only a relationship with Jesus can help us to gain Christlikeness. And that relationship with Christ starts with commitment.

I was twenty-two years old when I married Michelle. On that hot July day, it took just two words to seal our relationship: "I do." I was seventeen years old when I started a relationship with God. On that cool September evening, I prayed the most powerful prayer I've ever prayed: "I do."

After reading this book, you know a little bit of my story. I don't know yours. Maybe you grew up in a religious home. Maybe you grew up in an atheist family. Maybe you've been selfishly wasting time and running from God for decades. Maybe there's a war in your soul, like there was in mine. Maybe you've been hurt, or maybe you've hurt others. Maybe you've never prayed in your entire life. Set aside the past for a moment. If you desire a relationship with God, it's time to pray your first true prayer:

"I do."

If you prayed this prayer, welcome, welcome, welcome. You've passed from death to life. You've been spiritually reborn into an incredible family, and I'd love to introduce you to some of them. Send my team an e-mail at newlife@livingprayerfully.com, and we'll point you toward a local faith community that will walk through life with you. They'll help you grow in your relationship with God. They'll encourage you in the dark seasons of your soul. They'll help equip you for your unique calling to be all that you were created to be and to do all that you were created to do. They'll help you discover shalom. They'll teach you to pray.

Seven Ways to Pray

HERE ARE A FEW prayer ideas to get you started. Remember: prayer is about relationship, not routine. It doesn't have to be boring!

1. Shalom
If you watch the news, witness a conflict, or hear of a tough situation, pray for peace. You can also say hello or good-bye or sign your e-mails with this powerful, one-word prayer.

2. Bible verses
If you read a verse that sounds like it could be a prayer for a certain situation, tailor it accordingly and pray it out loud.

3. Silence
As the Rule of Taizé encourages, "maintain inner silence in all things so as to dwell with Christ." Practice stillness in order to commune with Jesus.

4. Move
Attach physicality to spirituality, whether it's through breathing, walking, running, eating, bathing, or driving. Get creative!

5. Hold in the light
Have you run out of words to pray? Picture someone in the light of God's grace. Hold them there, and ask God to do what only He can do.

6. Prevail

Write down a list of everyone you know who is far from God who you'd like to be filled with life in Christ. Speak their names out loud every day. Commit to sixty-three years and eight months!

7. Sing

If a song fits a situation that you've been praying about, use it as a tool to express your thoughts to God.

If you'd like Jared to lead your church or group through these prayers, he has prepared a special talk titled "A Good Old-Fashioned Prayer Meeting." Please visit JaredBrock.com/speaking for details.

Acknowledgments

THIS BOOK WOULD NOT exist without the gracious championing of Mark Buchanan, the most gifted Christian writer alive today. Thanks for saying yes on Skype to that crazy kid in the Costa Rican rainforest.

Ann Spangler, my Christian literary agent. You opened doors that I couldn't have battered down. Thank you, thank you, thank you.

Michelle Brock, my long-suffering wife and best friend. I owe you a million dollars.

Beth Fisher, at Wordplay Editorial, my personnel edittor, who done makes good literarily every paragraph I write more better. Your literary cuts are better than kisses from an enemy. Thanks for "wounding" with love.

The Tyndale team has been pretty fantastic. Jon Farrar, you immediately caught the vision and then put up with a highly demanding first-time author as we chased excellence together. Lisa Jackson, for your support and recognition of this book's potential. Ron Beers, thank you for saying yes. Jonathan Schindler, for improving this book by at least 42 percent. (If, by the time this goes to print, you've edited it to read "72 percent," you'd be correct.) Cheryl Kerwin, for all you do that no one sees, which makes it possible for this book to be seen basically everywhere. Stephen Vosloo, thank you for capturing the essence of this uproarious journey. Jennifer Ghionzoli, you did an absolutely masterful job on the book cover. Kara Leonino, what exactly do you do? Oh, that's right. *Everything.*

Anneli McCulley, for letting me hole up in her attic as I wrote the manuscript, and for not giving me an overly hard time when I fell short of my daily word count goal. Nate Stewart, my favorite "fifth cousin through marriage," for acting as my last-minute tailor and chauffeur on the same day his dog died. Hakjun, without whom I would still be hopelessly lost on the streets of Seoul. Michelle Sigulim, my favorite Messianic Jew, for her travel advice and passion for Israel. Wendy Thompson, the darling of Southall, for her faithful hospitality. John and Cathy, my Chicagoland parents. Rachel Black, along with Dave and Jill Black, to whom a "special credit" is due. Lea Uotila, my caring mother-in-law, who acted as our in-house travel agent and introduced me to Chauncey. Ari Uotila, for letting his daughter marry a writer and all that it entails. Karen Brock, my favorite mother. Gord Brock, the wisest spiritual leader I've ever met.

And so many more: Maya, Isa, Holly, Thierry, Laura, Patricia, PierreYann, Tessa, Gabriel. Jeremy and Laura, for your timely gift when "all was lost." A. J. Jacobs, for modeling a standard of beardliness and for letting me draft off your title. Rhoda, Randy, Jordan, and Kyle, for clothing me when I was (almost) naked. Richard Saunders, my dear friend, theological counselor, and racket sport partner. Cat and Cody Greene, our greatest pleasure is the precious moments we get to spend with you and the boys. Cody, if you're reading this, I'm glad to see that you finally finished reading an entire book.

My small army of mighty prayer partners, the worldwide boiler room that fans the flame in our hearts. Lewis and Ellie, Christy, Cammy, Mark and Cheryl, Jake, Justin, Matt and Andrea, Sarah and Matt, Beth, Aban, Wilma, April and Bill, Chris and Katherine, Kim, Saara, Kat, Lea and Ari, Gord and Karen, Dave and Jill, Danny, Natalie, Katie, Rob, Lauren, Janet, Kristie, Wendy, Diane, Jeff and

Gillian, Matt, Jeff, Heather, Elaine, Doug, Aaron and Emily, Emily, Steph, Chantale, Nicki, Cindy, Rich, Andrea, Jess, Leslie, Niki, Eric and Laura, Chandler and Maria, Matt and Laura, Liz, Sarah, Stephen, Jennifer, James and Karen, Maria, Cathy, Ashley, Charlie and Alison, Dave and Mandy, Cat and Cody, Jay and Freyja, Pete and Sarah, and Bobby.

My mentors from afar. Craig Groeschel, our de facto "pastor on the road." Mark Batterson, who, by the time he dies, will be the most quotable storyteller on the planet. Francis Chan, for living authentically and inspiring us to live in a trailer. Randy Alcorn, for modeling what a writing ministry can become if fully surrendered to God. Shane Claiborne, for his writing advice and inspiring prophetic imagination. Bill Hybels and the investment made in me through the WCA. Andy Stanley and the massive impact that Catalyst has played in my life.

Everyone who gave me their time in the writing of this book: Pope Francis, Father Alfred, Rabbi Aaron, Rabbi Beryl, Don Pierson, Father Philotheos, Gustav, Brother Alois, Brother Artur, Pastor Allen, Dr. Crandall, Charles Hockenbarger, Rachel Phelps-Hockenbarger, Pete Greig, even Dr. David Cho. I'm sorry I missed you, Billy.

The hundreds of prayer warriors throughout history—Francis of Assisi, Brother Lawrence, Nikolaus Zinzendorf, John Brock, Keith Green, and Brennan Manning, to name a few—upon whose shoulders I stand.

To you, the reader, who I don't for a moment take for granted.

Best for last, Jesus Christ. I cling to Your feet.

Notes

CHAPTER 1: HAMILTON, ONTARIO

5 *send out workers into [the] harvest field:* Matthew 9:38.

CHAPTER 2: NEW YORK CITY

16 *We have come to know man as he really is:* Viktor Frankl, *Man's Search for Meaning* (Boston: Beacon Press, 2006), 134.

16 *the pledge of allegiance for Jewish people:* Charlie Harary, "Hear O Israel," Aish .com, http://www.aish.com/sp/pg/Hear_O_Israel.html.

18 *time to become the answer to our own prayers:* See Shane Claiborne, *Becoming the Answer to Our Prayers* (Downers Grove, IL: IVP Books, 2008).

21 *the siddur is our gift to God:* Benjamin Blech, *The Complete Idiot's Guide to Understanding Judaism*, 2nd ed. (New York: Penguin Group, 2003), 293.

CHAPTER 3: ISRAEL

42 *your will be done . . . deliver us from the evil one:* Matthew 6:10, 13.

48 *great drops of blood:* Luke 22:44, ESV.

54 *uncovered his feet:* Ruth 3:7.

CHAPTER 4: MOUNT ATHOS, GREECE

80 *a rubble of stones overrun with rats:* Michael Lewis, *Boomerang: Travels in the New Third World* (New York: W. W. Norton & Company, 2011), 70–71.

81 *Lawsuits are pending:* You can read more about the controversy surrounding Vatopedi in Michael Lewis's book *Boomerang.*

86 *carbuncle on the face:* Jonathan Glancey, "Life after Carbuncles," *The Guardian*, May 17, 2004, http://www.theguardian.com/artanddesign/2004/ may/17/architecture.regeneration.

87 *in his bloodline:* See Helena Smith, "Has Prince Charles Found His True Spiritual Home on a Greek Rock?" *The Guardian*, May 12, 2004, http://www .theguardian.com/uk/2004/may/12/monarchy.helenasmith.

CHAPTER 5: ITALY

105 *sacred lots to determine God's will:* See Acts 1:23-26; Numbers 27:21.

115 *work as if everything depended on you:* Though it is sometimes attributed to John Wesley as well, the Vatican, in the Catechism of the Catholic church, attributes the quote to St. Ignatius. See "Give Us This Day Our Daily Bread" in part four, section two, article three of the Catechism.

117 *almost 200,000 soldiers were killed or wounded:* Peter Caddick-Adams, *Monte Cassino: Ten Armies in Hell* (New York: Oxford University Press, 2013), 8.

119 *I must live my life with others:* David Gibson, "Five Things We Learned about Pope Francis from His Blockbuster Interview," Religion News Service, September 20, 2013, http://www.religionnews.com/2013/09/20/5-things -learned-pope-francis-blockbuster-interview/.

129–130 *the Five-Finger Prayer:* Omar Gutierrez, "A Simple Prayer Method from a Simple Pontiff," CatholicVote, http://www.catholicvote.org/a-simple -prayer-method-from-a-simple-pontiff/.

CHAPTER 6: SPAIN

144 *You have the words of eternal life:* John 6:68.

147 *the Prayer of Quiet:* St. Teresa, *The Life of Teresa of Jesus: The Autobiography of St. Teresa of Ávila* (New York: Doubleday, 2004), 61.

148 *a band with iron points turning inwards:* Frances Calderón de la Barca, *Life in Mexico*, repr. (1843; University of California Press, 1982), 286.

CHAPTER 7: FRANCE

162 *how to become wholly God's:* Brother Lawrence, *The Practice of the Presence of God*, first letter.

162 *to impress deeply upon his heart, the Divine existence:* Brother Lawrence, *Practice*, fourth conversation.

163 *I found no small pain in this exercise:* Brother Lawrence, *Practice*, first letter.

163 *I possess God in as great tranquility:* Brother Lawrence, *Practice*, fourth conversation.

163–164 *I am prevailed on by your importunities:* Brother Lawrence, *Practice*, first letter.

164 *Let us pray for one another:* Brother Lawrence, *Practice*, fifteenth letter.

164 *Men invent means and methods:* Brother Lawrence, *The Spiritual Maxims of Brother Lawrence*.

164–165 *this exercise of the presence of God:* Brother Lawrence, *Practice*, sixth letter.

165 *a holy habit:* Brother Lawrence, *Practice*, ninth letter.

165 *the best and easiest method I know:* Brother Lawrence, *Practice*, ninth letter.

165 *the end of all his actions:* Brother Lawrence, *Practice*, second conversation.

165 *mend what is amiss:* Brother Lawrence, *Practice*, second conversation.

165 *re-collect the mind easily:* Brother Lawrence, *Practice*, eighth letter, emphasis mine.

165 *a sense of the presence of God:* Brother Lawrence, *Practice*, fourth conversation.

165 *conversation of the soul:* Brother Lawrence, *Practice*, second letter.

170 *he was no more:* Genesis 5:24.

CHAPTER 8: EASTERN USA

190 *the Quaker definition of "brief":* Faith and Practice, as adopted in 1988, Baltimore Yearly Meeting of the Religious Society of Friends, http://www .bym-rsf.org/publications/fandp/1988approved/88section2.html.

191 *rightly dividing the word of truth:* 2 Timothy 2:15, KJV.

192 *sit quietly and let God love me:* Dick Eastman, *The Hour That Changes the World: A Practical Plan for Personal Prayer* (Grand Rapids, MI: Baker, 2002), 37–38.

192 *a voice of gentle silence:* 1 Kings 19:12, KJV. See *The Pulpit Commentary* on 1 Kings 19:12, StudyLight.org, http://www.studylight.org/commentaries/tpc /view.cgi?bk=10&ch=19.

193 *The Old Testament prophets:* See Hosea 1:2; Ezekiel 4:4-17; Isaiah 20:1-6.

194 *a small white building:* "Nude Church in Virginia, White Tail Chapel, Invites You to Bare More than Your Naked Soul," *Huffington Post Religion*, February 10, 2014, http://www.huffingtonpost.com/2014/02/10/nude-church-white -tail-virginia_n_4765199.html.

199 *become all things to all people . . . follow my example:* 1 Corinthians 9:22; 11:1.

207 *the soaking fleece:* See Judges 6–7.

210 *Let this cup pass from me:* Matthew 26:39, KJV.

210 *every unanswered prayer:* A. E. Richardson, *The Kneeling Christian* (Grand Rapids, MI: Zondervan, 1986), 38.

211 *five malpractice lawsuits:* Eben Alexander has faced scrutiny following the publication of *Proof of Heaven*, including a look at his malpractice suits. See, for example, "'Proof of Heaven' Doctor Faced a $3 Million Malpractice Lawsuit When He Fell into a Coma," *Daily Mail Online*, December 24, 2013, http://www.dailymail.co.uk/news/article-2529048/Proof-Heaven -doctor-faced-3million-malpractice-lawsuit-fell-coma.html.

218 *the prayers that go unanswered:* Mark Batterson, *Be a Circle Maker: The Solution to 10,000 Problems* (Grand Rapids, MI: Zondervan, 2011), 28.

218 *100 percent of the prayers we don't pray:* Mark Batterson, *Praying Circles around Your Children* (Grand Rapids, MI: Zondervan, 2012), 93.

CHAPTER 9: THE OUTER LIMITS

225 *a private jet named "Dove One":* "Dove One," on Benny Hinn's official website, accessed October 2, 2014, http://www.bennyhinn.org/articles/ articledesc.cfm?id=1000.

225 *the circles in which Hinn rolls:* See the following sources: Clifford Pugh, "After Move to $10.5 Million River Oaks Mansion, Joel Osteen Offers Tanglewood Land for $1.1 Million," *CultureMap Houston*, July 9, 2010, http://houston .culturemap.com/news/real-estate/07-04-10-after-move-to-river-oaks-joel -osteen-wants-to-sell-tanglewood-land-for-11-million/; John Burgdorf,

"Kenneth Copeland's 18,000+ Sq. Foot Lake House on Eagle Mountain Lake—Includes Airport!" *North Texas Luxury* (blog), July 4, 2011, http://northtexasluxury.blogspot.ca/2011/07/kenneth-copelands-18000-sq-foot-lake.html; Mfonobong Nsehe, "The Five Richest Pastors in Nigeria," *Forbes*, June 7, 2011, http://www.forbes.com/sites/mfonobongnsehe/2011/06/07/the-five-richest-pastors-in-nigeria/; Nina Golgowski, "Private Jets, 13 Mansions and a $100,000 Mobile Home Just for the Dogs: Televangelists 'Defrauded Tens of Million [sic] of Dollars from Christian Network,'" *Daily Mail Online*, March 23, 2012, http://www.dailymail.co.uk/news/article-2119493/Private-jets-13-mansions-100-000-mobile-home-just-dogs-Televangelists-defrauded-tens-million-dollars-Christian-network.html; "List of the Richest Pastors Worldwide," Nehanda Radio, January 7, 2014, http://nehandaradio.com/2014/01/07/list-of-the-richest-pastors-worldwide/; Marlow Stern, "'Mission Congo' Alleges Pat Robertson Exploited Post-Genocide Rwandans for Diamonds," *Daily Beast*, September 7, 2013, http://www.thedailybeast.com/articles/2013/09/07/doc-mission-congo-alleges-pat-robertson-exploited-post-genocide-rwandans-for-diamonds.html.

236 *Listen, my son:* Proverbs 4:10-13.

239–240 *Their stats are impressive:* Westboro Baptist Church, http://www.godhatesfags.com/index.html. The stats are updated even as you look at the page.

240 *For more information about WBC:* Westboro Baptist Church, "About WBC," accessed October 5, 2014, http://www.godhatesfags.com/wbcinfo/aboutwbc.html.

240 *The heart of Calvinism:* Nathan Phelps, "The Uncomfortable Grayness of Life," Atheist Nexus (speech, American Atheists Convention, April 11, 2009, Atlanta, GA), http://www.atheistnexus.org/page/nate-phelps-2009-aa-speech.

241 *entitled to "special protection":* Warren Richey, "Supreme Court: 'Hurtful Speech' of Westboro Baptist Church Is Protected," *The Christian Science Monitor*, March 2, 2011, http://www.csmonitor.com/USA/Justice/2011/0302/Supreme-Court-hurtful-speech-of-Westboro-Baptist-Church-is-protected.

242 *Fred Sr. shared choice words for Billy Graham:* "Billy Graham Hell-Bound False Prophet Says Fred Phelps," YouTube video, 7:12, posted by Westboro Baptist Church, December 18, 2012, https://www.youtube.com/watch?v=UhSOi0Cg1MA.

244 *Phelps had reportedly been excommunicated:* Caitlin Dickson, "This Man Is the Future of Westboro Baptist Church," *The Daily Beast*, March 24, 2014, http://www.thedailybeast.com/articles/2014/03/24/this-man-is-the-future-of-westboro-baptist-church.html.

251 *the first to throw a stone:* John 8:7.

252 *children are the victims:* Louis Theroux, "The Most Hated Family in America," YouTube video, 58:35, from a documentary originally aired on BBC Two

on April 1, 2007, posted by "Lotte patat," January 7, 2014, https://www
.youtube.com/watch?v=3pxE6_VY8aM.

252 *rightly [divide] the word of truth:* 2 Timothy 2:15, KJV.

CHAPTER 10: KOREA

253 *Kim Il-sung, a hardy fellow:* This quote about Kim Il-sung is prevalent
around the Internet. See, for example, "Kim Il-sung: Biography and Picture,"
iBiography, accessed September 29, 2014, http://www.ibiography.info/facts
/kim-il-sung.html.

254 *over half . . . require food aid:* Rick Newman, "Here's How Lousy Life Is in
North Korea," *U.S. News,* Rick Newman (blog), April 12, 2013, http://www
.usnews.com/news/blogs/rick-newman/2013/04/12/heres-how-lousy-life
-is-in-north-korea.

254 *Millions of people have starved to death:* Joshua Stanton and Sung-Yoon Lee,
"Pyongyang's Hunger Games," *New York Times,* March 7, 2014, http://www
.nytimes.com/2014/03/08/opinion/pyongyangs-hunger-games.html?_r=0.

254 *over two hundred thousand prisoners:* Mark McDonald, "North Korean Prison
Camps Massive and Growing," *New York Times,* May 4, 2011, http://www
.nytimes.com/2011/05/05/world/asia/05korea.html.

254 *listening to a South Korean song:* "North Korea FAQs," Liberty in North
Korea, accessed September 29, 2014, http://www.libertyinnorthkorea.org
/learn-faqs/.

254 *the hardest place in the world to be a Christian:* Katherine Burgess, "Aiming
for 'Effective Anger': The Top 50 Countries Where It's Hardest to Be a
Christian," *Christianity Today,* January 8, 2014, http://www.christianitytoday
.com/gleanings/2014/january/50-countries-where-hardest-to-be-christian
-world-watch-list.html.

254 *at least fifty thousand Christians in work camps:* Morgan Feddes, "North Korea
Announces Death of Kim Jong-Il," *Christianity Today,* December 19, 2011,
http://www.christianitytoday.com/gleanings/2011/december/north-korea
-announces-death-of-kim-jong-il.html.

259 *one in three of its citizens were church-attending Christians:* Andrei Lankov,
"North Korea's Missionary Position," *Asia Times,* March 16, 2005, http://
www.atimes.com/atimes/Korea/GC16Dg03.html.

259 *Christians simply disappeared:* Elizabeth Kendal, "Remembering North Korea,"
ChristianNewsToday.com, accessed September 30, 2014, http://www
.christiannewstoday.com/Christian_News_Report_9005034.html.

264 *A teenage schoolgirl once drowned:* Hélène Hofman, "Girl, 14, Drowns Saving
Kim Jong Il Portrait in North Korea," GlobalPost, June 27, 2012, http://
www.globalpost.com/dispatches/globalpost-blogs/weird-wide-web/girl-14
-drowns-saving-kim-jong-il-portrait-north-korea.

271 *Send a 19th-century missionary:* Andrea Palpant Dilley, "The Surprising
Discovery about Those Colonialist, Proselytizing Missionaries," *Christianity*

Today, January 8, 2014, www.christianitytoday.com/ct/2014/january-february/world-missionaries-made.html.

271 *prayer is the greater work:* "The Key of the Greater Work," My Utmost for His Highest Daily Devotionals, RBC Ministries, October 17, 2013, http://utmost.org/the-key-of-the-greater-work/.

280 *reaching out after God:* Andrew Murray, *With Christ in the School of Prayer,* thirteenth lesson.

280 *abstain from whatever hinders:* Andrew A. Bonar, *Sheaves after Harvest: A Group of Addresses* (Glasgow: Pickering and Inglis, 1936), 39.

280 *pray in right earnest:* Andrew A. Bonar, *Diaries and Letters,* ed. Marjory Bonar (London: Hodder and Stoughton, 1894), 129.

281 *fasting reduces the power of self:* Bill Bright, *Preparing for the Coming Revival: How to Lead a Successful Fasting and Prayer Gathering* (Wayne, NJ: New Life Publications, 1995), 18.

CHAPTER 11: ENGLAND

284 *the man who most influenced:* "Stephen F. Olford Memorial Page - Biography - 1983," Billy Graham Center Archives, January 5, 2005, http://www2.wheaton.edu/bgc/archives/memorial/sfolford/bio2.htm.

285 *to move man:* Dr. and Mrs. Howard Taylor, *Hudson Taylor's Spiritual Secret* (Chicago: Moody, 2009), 33.

292 *the only genuine Christocentric:* Karl Barth, The Doctrine of Reconciliation, vol 4.1 of *Church Dogmatics,* trans. G. W. Bromiley (New York: T&T Clark, 2010), 171.

294 *great books on prayer:* J. E. Hurtgen, Jr., "An Interview with Philip Yancey," RELEVANT magazine, November 1, 2006, http://www.relevantmagazine.com/god/deeper-walk/features/1171-an-interview-with-philip-yancey.

296 *The more we receive . . . , the more we can give:* Dorothy S. Hunt, ed., *Love: A Fruit Always in Season: Daily Meditations by Mother Teresa* (San Francisco: Ignatius Press, 1987), 83.

301 *We must never let our profit interfere:* Charles Spurgeon, "Order and Argument in Prayer" (Sermon #700).

301 *omnipotent in all things that glorify God:* Spurgeon, "Pleading" (Sermon #1018).

301 *the slender nerve:* Spurgeon, "The Raven's Cry" (Sermon #672).

301 *Our prayers are in the predestination:* Spurgeon, "Prayer Certified of Success" (Sermon #1091).

301 *the giver of all prayer:* Spurgeon, "Order and Argument in Prayer."

301 *a secret work of the Spirit:* Spurgeon, "The Raven's Cry."

301 *prayer has a corresponding blessing:* Spurgeon, "Prayer Certified of Success."

302 *trading of the heart:* Spurgeon, "The Raven's Cry."

302 *the soul has unburdened itself . . . We are powerless:* Spurgeon, "Pleading."

302 *"He that hath made his refuge God":* Spurgeon, "Order and Argument in Prayer."

302 *keep to present need:* Spurgeon, "Order and Argument in Prayer."

302 *concentrated all my prayers into one:* Spurgeon, "The Exaltation of Christ" (Sermon #101).

302 *a higher place in the esteem of Christians:* Spurgeon, "The Kind of Revival We Need," The Spurgeon Archive, accessed October 6, 2014, http://www .spurgeon.org/revival.htm.

302 *a thousand to twelve hundred attendants:* Spurgeon, "Prayer-Meetings;—As They Were, and As They Should Be," *Only a Prayer Meeting.*

303–304 *Five young college students:* Taken from *Our Daily Bread,* April 24, 1983.

CHAPTER 12: HAMILTON, ONTARIO

307 *died of overwork:* J. Edwin Orr, "Prayer and Revival," on J. Edwin Orr's website, accessed November 9, 2014, http://www.jedwinorr .com/resources/articles/prayandrevival.pdf.

309 *baptized them in the cold water:* Orr, "Prayer and Revival."

312 *preach the gospel . . . and be forgotten:* Quoted in Colt McCoy and Matt Carter, *The Real Win: Pursuing God's Plan for Authentic Success* (Colorado Springs, CO: Multnomah, 2013), 158.

314 *every need is a call to prayer.* Watchman Nee, *Journeying towards the Spiritual: A Digest of the Spiritual Man in 42 Lessons* (New York: Christian Fellowship Publishers, 2006), 129.

AN INVITATION

317 *it is too spiritual a matter:* Charles Spurgeon, "The Raven's Cry" (Sermon #1018).

See Jared LIVE

Mixing humor, creativity, audience interaction, and biblical teaching, Jared Brock is a great keynote choice for any audience:

- CONFERENCES
- FESTIVALS
- CHURCH SERVICES
- GUIDED PRAYER RETREATS
- WRITER'S CONFERENCES
- BUSINESS MEETINGS
- COLLEGE EVENTS
- WORKSHOPS
- SEMINARS

Drawing from a deep well of incredible stories and practical insights, consider Jared for your next event on:

- PRAYER
- CHRISTIAN LIVING
- SOCIAL JUSTICE
- SIMPLE LIVING
- PREVENTING HUMAN TRAFFICKING
- CHARITIES AND NONPROFITS
- WRITING
- LEADERSHIP
- CREATIVITY
- REDEMPTIVE BUSINESS

Please visit JaredBrock.com/speaking for details and availability, and learn how Jared Brock could help lead your audience closer to Jesus.

Explore Jared's abolitionist charity at HopefortheSold.com. Watch Jay and Michelle's documentary at RedLightGreenLightFilm.com. If you'd like to join Jay's monthly reading list and receive a free digital bundle of prayer books ($100+ value), visit JaredBrock.com/bookclub.

CP0859